Sentencing reform

Sentencing reform
Guidance or guidelines?

Edited by
Martin Wasik *and* Ken Pease

Manchester University Press

Copyright © Manchester University Press 1987

Whilst copyright in the volume as a whole is vested in Manchester University Press, copyright in individual chapters belongs to the respective authors and no part of this book may be reproduced without express permission in writing of both author and publishers.

Published by Manchester University Press
Oxford Road, Manchester, M13 9PL, UK
Wolfeboro, NH 03894–2069, USA

British Library cataloguing in publication data
Sentencing reform: guidance or guidelines?
   1. Sentences (Criminal procedure) – Great
      Britain   2. Sentences (Criminal procedure)
      – United States
   I. Wasik, Martin   II. Pease, Ken
     344.105'772   KD8406

Library of Congress cataloguing in publication data
Sentencing reform.
   1. Sentences (Criminal procedure) – Great Britain.
   I. Wasik, Martin.   II. Pease, K. (Kenneth)
     KD8406.S46   1986   345.42'0772   86-18256
     344.205772

ISBN 0 7190 1890 0 *hardback*

Typeset in Great Britain
by Williams Graphics, Abergele, Clwyd

Printed in Great Britain
by Biddles Ltd, Guildford

Contents

Notes on contributors   *Page* vii

1 Discretion and sentencing reform: the alternatives
  Martin Wasik and Ken Pease   1

2 Disparity in dispositions: the early ideas and applications
  of guidelines *Leslie T. Wilkins*   7

3 Sentencing guidelines and sentencing commissions:
  the second generation *Michael H. Tonry*   22

4 Guidance by numbers or words? Numerical versus
  narrative guidelines for sentencing
  Andrew von Hirsch   46

5 Sentencing guidance in the Magistrates' Court
  Brian Harris   70

6 Devising sentencing guidance for England
  Andrew Ashworth   81

7 Guidance, guidelines and criminal record
  Martin Wasik   105

8 Sentencing and measurement: some analogies from
  psychology *Ken Pease*   126

9 Sentencing reform and the structuring of pre-trial
  discretion *A. Keith Bottomley*   139

10 Sentencing reform and the Probation Service
  Nigel Stone   163

Appendix: Minnesota Sentencing Guidelines and
  Commentary (extracts)   183

Index   206

Notes on contributors

Andrew Ashworth
Fellow and Tutor in Law, Worcester College, Oxford. Associate, Centre for Criminological Research, University of Oxford. Editor of the *Criminal Law Review*, member of the Criminal Law Revision Committee, and author of much published work, notably, *Sentencing and Penal Policy* (1983).

A. Keith Bottomley
Reader in Criminology, Department of Social Policy and Professional Studies, University of Hull, and Director of that University's Centre for Criminology and Criminal Justice. Joint Editor of the *Howard Journal of Criminal Justice* (1979–85), and former member of the Parole Board for England and Wales. Author of several books, including *Decisions in the Penal Process* (1973), *Criminology in Focus* (1979), *Understanding Crime Rates* (with Clive Coleman, 1981), and *Crime and Punishment: Interpreting the Data* (with Ken Pease, 1986).

Brian Harris QC
A former President of the Justices' Clerks Society and Editor of the *Justice of the Peace Review*. Author of *Criminal Jurisdiction of Magistrates* (tenth edition in preparation) and senior co-editor of Clarke Hall and Morison on Children. Now Director of Professional Conduct at the Institute of Chartered Accountants.

Ken Pease
A Psychologist and Reader in Criminology at Manchester University. Has published extensively, notably *The Psychology of Judicial Sentencing* (with Catherine Fitzmaurice, 1986). He is Joint Editor

of the *Howard Journal of Criminal Justice* and a former Principal Research Officer in the Home Office Research Unit.

Nigel Stone
Lecturer in Social Work, University of East Anglia, and part-time probation officer in Norfolk. Editor of *Probation Journal*.

Michael H. Tonry
President, Castine Research Corporation. Editor, *Crime and Justice: An Annual Review of Research*. Sometime Professor of Law in the University of Maryland.

Andrew von Hirsch
Professor, School of Criminal Justice, Rutgers University, Newark, New Jersey, USA. Former Visiting Professor of Law, Uppsala University, Sweden. Author of *Doing Justice: The Choice of Punishments* (1976); *Past or Future Crimes: Deservedness or Dangerousness in the Sentencing of Criminals* (1986), and numerous articles on sentencing theory and policy.

Martin Wasik
Barrister, and Lecturer in the Faculty of Law at Manchester University. He has written numerous articles in legal journals on topics in criminal law and sentencing. He is a member of the Council of the Howard League for Penal Reform and Vice-Chairman of the Local Review Committee at Manchester Prison.

Leslie T. Wilkins
Research Professor (Emeritus), Rockefeller College of Public Affairs and Policy, State University of New York. Formerly Dean of the School of Criminology, University of California at Berkeley. Author of many books and articles. From its inception until 1964 he served in the Home Office Research Unit. Among other honours he was awarded the Francis Wood Prize of the Royal Statistical Society in 1949 and the Sutherland Award of the American Criminological Society in 1972.

1 Martin Wasik *and* Ken Pease

Discretion and sentencing reform: the alternatives

Unfettered judicial discretion in sentencing exists nowhere in the modern world. The means by which that discretion is fettered, however, varies widely. Each method has its advantages and drawbacks, sometimes recognised but often not. Reasoned choice among known alternatives is an object to which to aspire. We hope that this book moves us towards meeting this aspiration.

In the United Kingdom there has been very little legislative guidance on sentencing. The twentieth century has witnessed a major trend towards the broadening of criminal offence definitions, one effect of which has been to render maximum sentences almost entirely unhelpful in providing guidance in day-to-day sentencing practice. The irrelevance of maxima to the control of judicial sentencing is now generally recognised (Advisory Council on the Penal System, 1978). What statutory guidance there has been has generally taken the form of requiring sentencers, for example, only to impose a custodial sentence where 'no other method is appropriate', or to impose a non-custodial sentence where 'having regard to the circumstances, including the nature and character of the offender, it is expedient to do so' (Powers of Criminal Courts Act 1973, s. 20 and s. 2 respectively). A number of new sentences have been made available to the courts (fully suspended and partly suspended sentences, community service) often with very little guidance on their appropriate use. The giving of reasons for sentence selection is still generally not required. The orderly and fair exercise of discretion in sentencing in the United Kingdom therefore rests to a large degree upon sentence review on appeal to a higher court. The Court of Appeal (Criminal Division) is in effect the ultimate appellate body on sentencing in England and Wales. At least since 1909 that Court has accepted as part of its legitimate function 'the revision of sentences ... to harmonise the views of those who pass them, and so ensure that varying punishments are not awarded for the same amount of guiltiness' (*Woodman*, 1909). In fact, for a range of reasons, the Court of Appeal is not particularly well placed to provide such guidance. There is no prosecution appeal against lenient sentencing in England, so the court's pronouncements are generally confined to prison sentencing in the upper reaches of the tariff. Such authorities are of little help to magistrates' courts, where the vast bulk of sentencing is carried out. There is a great diversity in the penal philosophies underlying the available sentencing options and in the assumptions and approaches of individual sentencers. If, however, the Court of Appeal handed down consistent judgments and if the lower courts came to be aware of and constrained by those judgments, a more uniform and fair sentencing practice could be attained. Yet even those sympathetic to the appellate approach to sentence review are critical of the English system. It is argued that the decisions of the Court of Appeal are increasingly inconsistent (Thomas, 1983) and that they are in any event out of step with (and probably for the most part made in ignorance of) levels of sentence typically imposed in the lower courts (McLean, 1980). The English sentencing process is described by a leading English writer as 'a disgrace to the common law tradition' (Ashworth 1983, p. 450).

Whether in response to such criticisms or for other reasons, there is more recently evident a movement to strengthen the consistency and persuasive force of appellate guidance. The Court of Appeal has gradually come to accept the value of consideration of its own previous decisions when determining sentencing matters on appeal. Lord Lane, the Lord Chief Justice, has increased the scope of so-called 'guideline judgments', where the Court of Appeal, often considering several appeals together, has been prepared to travel beyond the specific facts in issue towards the setting out of broader principles of sentencing, whether this be on the appropriate sentencing bands for a species of lawbreaking (e.g. serious drug offences in *Aramah* (1982) or rape as in *Roberts* (1982) and *Billam* (1986), or in the provision of guidance on the proper use of a penal measure (e.g. the partly suspended sentence in *Clarke* (1982) and deferment of sentence in *George* (1984). On the other hand the judges have set their faces firmly against the first attempt to extend the Attorney-General's reference procedure to sentencing cases, whereby supposedly lenient sentencing decisions could be referred to the Court of Appeal for a ruling, and Lord Lane has vetoed the academic investigation of sentencing practices of Crown Court judges on the basis that it 'would not be worth the expenditure of judicial time and public money' (Ashworth et. al., 1984). But concern is growing and the pressure for change is increasing. In early 1986 the Conservative Government produced a White Paper foreshadowing a Criminal Justice Bill aimed in part at improving the consistency and persuasive force of appellate guidelines by 'stiffening the power of the appeal court to make and enforce guideline judgments' (Sunday Times, 9 Feb 1986). It is envisaged that over a period of time a standard set of such judgments would be drawn up for all crimes and built into a written code. The Lord Chief Justice would consult with the Home Secretary and the Lord Chancellor in the drawing up of such judgments and subsequent legislation would be designed to ensure that the lower courts would observe them.

Guidance and guidelines

In the context of this book, the word 'guideline' as used to refer to appellate guidance on sentencing is rather misleading. In discussions of sentencing reform, 'guidelines' are best reserved for reference to a different, and relatively recent, tradition in the control of judicial discretion. What is clearly envisaged by *guidance* is the use of judgments made in respect of individual appellants which are used as vehicles to enunciate principles of more general application. With *guidelines*, each offence/offender combination is classified. This is done in advance, the product of research effort, and not in reference to the adjudication of any particular case. The criteria according to which the combination is arrived at stems from a close analysis of earlier sentencing practice ('descriptive' guidelines) or from some value-judgment of what should be considered, or from the first modified by the second ('prescriptive' guidelines). The classification yields, for any possible offender, a presumptive sentence. In the case before him the sentencer may decide not to impose the presumptive sentence, but if he does not do so he is obliged to justify his decision. This justification may well be the subject of appeal to a higher court. The guidelines themselves are subject to regular review to take account of changing circumstances.

Both writers of this short Chapter have come to regard the

implementation of sentencing guidelines as an approach with much to commend it. We have taken the view that the possibilities for sentencing reform which it offers should not be understated in the British context. At the very least, discussion of sentencing reform should not take place uninformed by the mistakes made and the lessons learned so far by the 'guidelines movement', particularly in the United States, where the movement has swept the board in the last decade. Fearing the premature dismissal of guidelines as a direct option in Britain, and sensing the lack of general appreciation of the movement's achievements, we decided to organise a conference whose title was eponymous with this book. It took place at the University of Manchester in April 1985. To it we invited distinguished speakers who discussed the alternative approaches to sentence review, and whose expertise ensured that the most recent developments in these approaches were considered. This proved particularly helpful in respect of guidelines systems, where application and diversification has proceeded apace.

The support which the Economic and Social Research Council and Manchester University Press provided for the conference is gratefully acknowledged. The modified proceedings of that conference form the basis of the current volume.

Overview of contents

It is fitting that the first Chapter is the work of Leslie Wilkins, whose pioneering research on parole guidelines set the scene for the mushrooming growth in sentencing guidelines since that time. He stresses in his statement of desirable features of guidelines their evolutionary aspect, in which decision-makers must be centrally involved for survival and development of the system to be assured. The involvement of British judges and lay sentencers which would be necessary is an aspect which is called into question elsewhere in the book. In his Chapter, Michael Tonry assesses the work of the Minnesota Sentencing Guidelines Commission as being 'probably the most significant development in sentencing policy and practice in the English-speaking world since the establishment of parole boards half a century ago'. Despite this accolade, Tonry's account of the successes and failures of reform in a variety of US states makes clear the many pitfalls of guidelines design and implementation and indicates some of the ways of avoiding them. Andrew von Hirsch sets out the alternatives of numerical guidelines (the Minnesota approach) and explicit sentencing principles, which he describes as being under development in Sweden. He suggests that on balance the Swedish approach might be the more suited of the alternatives to the British context. If he is right, the influence of guidelines on British sentencing reform will be indirect, via some form of Swedish refinement. If the description 'American' leads British policymakers into scepticism, von Hirsch may be proved correct by the intrinsic merits of the Swedish approach, or because it is European. Brian Harris describes the 'state of the art' concerning sentencing guidance in magistrates' courts in England, in ways which reveal the scope for the kind of local sentencing disparity which was documented by Tarling (1979). Andrew Ashworth's Chapter takes on the task of outlining a system of sentencing guidelines which would 'codify' English sentencing practice and might thereby prove more acceptable to judges and politicians. He warns, though, that this cannot simply be a task of restatement since 'there is divergence (i.e. confusion) on so many issues' in sentencing. He suggests a scheme which has more in common with the Swedish one described by von Hirsch, with guidance to courts incorporating detailed offence tabulations associated with recommended sentences. In his Chapter, Martin Wasik discusses the issue of the relevance of the defendant's previous criminal record to the sentencing decision. This is a matter which has caused great difficulty to both English and American theorists but is one which requires resolution prior to the adoption of any system of guidelines. Ken Pease, drawing upon his work in the psychology of sentence decision-making, argues that the role of numerical guidelines in laying bare extant principles of sentencing should not be understated. Keith Bottomley discusses the important issue of the relocation of discretionary power within the criminal justice system which tends to follow the introduction of constraints upon the sentencer. He links the discussion to the recent development in England of guidelines for formal cautioning and on the decision to prosecute. Finally, Nigel Stone addresses the role of the probation service in the presentation of information to the courts in relation to the kinds of reform postulated in this book.

It is perhaps fair to say that none of the British participants at the Manchester conference was complacent about sentence review as currently carried out in England. Acceptance of the need for change was more general than agreement about the proper direction for change. This book will become available at a time when the debate is lively and policy change is imminent. We hope that the work collected here will serve to inform the debate and that some of the ideas promulgated by those who now benefit from experience elsewhere may be taken up in the change of policy. For our part, we would wish to thank all those concerned in the production of this book for contributing so much to our understanding of the options which are now available.

References

Advisory Council on the Penal System (1978), *Sentences of Imprisonment: A Review of Maximum Penalties*, London, HMSO.

Ashworth, A. J. (1983), *Sentencing and Penal Policy*, London, Weidenfeld and Nicolson.

Ashworth, A. J., Genders, E., Mansfield, G., Peay, J., and Player, E. (1984), *Sentencing in the Crown Court*, Centre for Criminological Research Occasional Paper No. 10, University of Oxford.

McLean, I. (1980), *Crown Court: Patterns of Sentencing*, Chichester, Barry Rose.

Sunday Times (1985), 'Sweeping changes proposed for courts', 9 February.

Tarling, R. (1979), *Sentencing in Magistrates' Courts*, Home Office Research Study 56, London, HMSO.

Thomas, D. A. (1983), 'Sentencing discretion and appellate review', in Shapland, J. (ed.), *Decision-making in the Legal System*, British Psychological Society, Issues in Criminological and Legal Psychology, Occasional Paper No. 5, 61.

Cases

Aramah (1982) 4 Cr. App. R. (S), 407.

Billam (1986) I W.L.R. 349.

Clarke (1982) 4 Cr. App. R. (S), 197.

George (1984) 6 Cr. App. R. (S), 211.

Roberts (1982) 2 Cr. App. R. (S), 8.

Woodman (1909) 2 Cr. App. R. 67.

Disparity in dispositions: the early ideas and applications of guidelines

Like many other terms in the social sciences, if not in law, the term 'guidelines' or 'sentencing guidelines' is used to refer to many forms of intervention in the disposition decision. It may be that there are the proverbial '57 Varieties' of guideline system. Most are concerned with the time, if any, to be spent in a penal institution; few provide for constraints upon decisions which do not involve some form of incarceration (see Wilkins, 1980).

Much of the discussion in this book is concentrated on the system of sentencing guidelines enacted by the Minnesota Legislature and the application of the system in the courts of that state (see in particular the chapter by Tonry in this volume). It is probably true that in so far as the use of legislative constraints upon dispositions of courts has been based upon strict modelling and consistent theoretical underpinnings, the Minnesota system is, at the present time, the most highly developed and effective. The Minnesota system, however, was not the first application of the mathematical-model guideline idea, nor is it the only variety of guidelines control currently in use in the United States.

Sentencing guidelines (in theory) in Britain in 1895

Over a hundred years ago, Parliament came near to setting up a Sentencing Commission – a century before the United States actually did so. Sir Henry Hawkins in the *News Review* in 1893 (cited in Thorpe 1900) wrote: '... the inequities of punishment, now so frequent, would be materially lessened by the adoption of fixed principles to be determined by a Commission of competent persons having knowledge and aptitude for dealing with the subject.'

In the 1894–5 parliament a Sentencing Commission linked with the idea of guidelines possessed, according to Thorpe (1900), many merits. He wrote:

... a large discretion would still be left to the judge who has to try the case. The standard units would, in fact, be only so many starting points from which the judge would make his reckoning. The scale of sentences would have to be justified by him in open court, if only out of respect for the 'table' ... and it would be subject to periodical revision as the necessity for checking a growing evil or other like occasion might require.

The 'table' was to be constructed by using the averages of sentences awarded to simulated cases. The method of averaging of averages from hypothetical cases which was then proposed would be challenged today when there are more sophisticated statistical methods available. There is, however, nothing against the idea of using simulation which is now commonplace and extensively used in business, and in the form of war-gaming, though it remains undeveloped in relation to judicial thought and decision-making.

Thorpe proved to be a prophet as well as a historian, for he noted: '... the project fell through from one cause or another, and having regard to the conflict of theories ... it is not likely to be renewed.'

Thorpe's prediction has held good. The idea of sentencing guidelines with the use of statistical information embedded in their construction, was not to be revived in Britain until recently when, in 1978, the Advisory Council on the Penal System published its report *Sentences of Imprisonment* (1978) in which they again rejected the idea with the comment: 'Sentencing guidelines would have, of course, a more direct impact upon sentencing than our proposals, and we doubt that such a sophisticated formulation of the tariff would be acceptable in the English context. Nonetheless we consider that the progress of this new concept (sic) in sentencing should continue to be watched.'

It seems that in this extract the report was incorrect in at least one respect, namely, in regarding sentencing guidelines as a 'new concept', and, perhaps worse, as an American idea! They were probably correct as to the more 'direct impact'.

It does not appear that the discussion of sentencing guidelines and a Sentencing Commission in Britain almost a century earlier, was related in any way to the development of the Act setting up a Sentencing Commission for the United States, nor to any other of the guideline developments in penal policy control over the last decade in the United States, including of course the Minnesota system. The earlier British ideas were related to a concentration upon prior decisions by courts in respect of similar cases and were stimulated by concern for disparity. The developments in the United States emerged from the experience with parole.

In many states, and in the Federal penal system, the time served by a committed offender was determined in major degree by the parole authority. In some states the judges did no more than commit the offender to the Youth Authority or to the Adult Authority which would then decide the time of release as well as organise supervision after release. The rationale for this was that it was permissible for offenders to serve 'the remaining portion of their sentences in the community', supervised by agents who had the power to invoke the recall provisions whereby the parolee could be returned to serve the residue of his term in incarceration without a further trial.

Impact of utilitarian philosophy in United States

Parole authorities (or bureaucracies carrying out similar functions) in the United States seem from their early days to have been more open in style than have courts or similar bodies in Britain. Though courts talk of the concept of the visibility of justice, any challenge to their authority is minimal. What is done in court may be seen, but it is often difficult to see the reasons behind what is done. Perhaps the lack of criticism of the courts is partly due to the fact that in so far as they incarcerate they 'put away' the offender; it is the parole authority which releases. Some released offenders will commit further crimes and a few of these will be sufficiently dramatic to attract the attention of the mass media, and a 'public demand' for the paroling authority to be more cautious. (For a general background to parole in the United States, see Carter and Wilkins 1976).

It may have been such sensitivity to public criticism which led some parole authorities to take very seriously their assessment of the likelihood of recidivism of the offenders. It seemed obvious that for those offenders who were likely to commit further crimes, release should be deferred, perhaps until the sentence originally awarded had gone its full course. Then, at least, the parole authority could not be blamed for releasing a 'dangerous person' to the community. For whatever reason, the state of Massachusetts early in the 1920s invited Professor S.B. Warner (see Warner, 1923) to examine the parole decision process. He took a sample of 680 prisoners, 300 of whom were regarded as parole successes, and 300 parole failures, with the remaining 80 not having been given parole. By comparing the groups he was able to show that many of the beliefs which determined the decisions were unfounded. His published findings were challenged by Hornell Hart (1923), who suggested that Warner's failure to show results was due to his lack of statistical sophistication. From this time on there has been argument as to the appropriateness of forms of statistical analysis and some even who seek to question its morality. Among the latter are retributionists and those of the 'just deserts' school' (see, for example, von Hirsch 1976) who claim that the only matter of concern in the disposal of offenders is the nature of the act committed (with perhaps, in some cases, some features of the offender and/or the victim). The just deserts school looks only to the past and regards any estimation of what is likely to happen as an irrelevant or immoral consideration.

Quite soon after the initial studies of the 1920s the focus upon the decision process of the parole authorities was diverted to what were then regarded as 'more scientific' matters relating to the 'causes of crime'. Influential among those who fostered this unfortunate diversion were Sheldon and Eleanor Glueck (1940).

It was not until the early 1970s that attention was once again specifically directed towards decision-making. Operational research during the 1939–45 war had influenced and enriched statistical methods. Decision Theory had developed and techniques which required fewer assumptions to be made as to the nature of the underlying distributions had become available. Of more impact than the increase in the available methods was the hardware of the computer. There was, however, an interlink between the prediction methods of the 1950s and the origin of the current format of guidelines. This was the discovery (see Mannheim and Wilkins 1955, 120, Table 7), that the equations which could be found to provide discrimination between the relatively good and the relatively bad risks of recidivism, could also provide a new method for assessing the value of different forms of 'treatment' of offenders.

It had long been obvious that the apparent good results of some dispositions, such as probation, were largely accountable to the fact that only the better risks were awarded probation by the judges. Indeed, in some states, there were statutory limitations to the award of probation in relation to the prior record of the offender. Even where few or no restrictions were in statute (as in Britain), probation was largely reserved for the good risks.

Evaluation and probability

The evaluation of different treatment modalities required an answer to the question as to whether the 'better' or 'worse' *output* of the dispositions involved were due only to the differences in the *input*. The prediction devices could classify offenders so that expected levels of recidivism could be calculated. Departures of the observed from the expected rate (in the light of the kind of 'material input' to the treatment) could be compared and some indication of the value of different dispositions became possible.

Many regretted that these more powerful methods served only to demonstrate that very large differences in dispositions had no systematic impact upon the rates of recidivism. Thus it became clear that the problem of crime could not be simplified to the problem of the offender. Whatever was done to offenders, little if any impact could be expected upon the amount of crime in society. There were, then, two kinds of problems of equal concern: what to do with those offenders who were identified and proven guilty, and what to do about crime.

Decision makers v. those decided about

The study of individual offenders had, by the early 1970s reached its peak. It was crime research boom time. But for some of the research community the study of individual offenders had begun to seem unrewarding. Newcomers to the field were making big promises as to the outcome of projects, which, though based upon humanitarian principles, had little else to commend them. The larger the promises, the more likely it seemed that money would be made available; the more dramatic the promises of successful outcome, the lower was the quality of the research, and the more dramatic the failure.

At this time also the increasing availability of computers in government agencies meant that greater quantities of information could be obtained and processed. But the mere increase in the amount of information, or even its improved quality, was no guarantee of improved decision-making. It seems likely that the application of research methods directly to the decision processes in the criminal justice field might offer an area where sound research could be carried out without the requirement to promise in advance the precise nature of the results to be achieved. Administrators accepted that the computer was new and that it presented problems. Furthermore, research workers who were unwilling to make promises provided an antidote for the enthusiastic hardware salesmen who were at that time seen as a 'bit of a plague' by many administrators. The caution of this section of the research community matched the caution of the administrator; collaboration became attractive.

It was a series of chance events, luck, and personalities which led to the first operational guidelines system. This was the system which in only a slightly modified form is still in operation in the Federal Parole Commission (formerly the Parole Board) of the United States. It was this system which led, in turn, to the sentencing provisions of the Act which also set up the Sentencing Commission which is currently being implemented.

The parole guidelines were the final outcome of a research collaboration between members of the Research Center of the State University of New York at Albany and the United States Parole Board. The projects concerned began with an 'open-ended' approach which was reflected in the title given, namely, the *Parole Decision-making Project*. There was no thought of inventing guidelines. (For discussion of several of these issues, see Gottfredson et al., 1978.) Much of the first half-year was spent in working through an information retrieval system which it was thought might be developed to become an on-line interactive system, based on the information storage and search software known as 'Dialog' and owned by Lockheed. Indeed it was a demonstration of an adaptation of 'Dialog' which provided the first contact with the chairman of the Parole Board and the funding of the project. However, it soon became evident that members of the Parole Board did not wish to 'talk to the machine', and it was not long before they became quite unwilling to do so. The next idea was to have a research staff member who would 'talk to the machine' for them.

At that time we knew no better than to attempt to provide a human personal interface between the computerised data base and the decision-makers of the Board. This approach also crashed. The system soon became no more than a gimmick, and although it might have provided some symbolic defence against criticism of the Board, it was not having any impact upon the decision processes.

The origin of the current idea of statistically based 'guidelines' (though the word came later, and may not be the most appropriate term) can be traced to a specific time and place: a most unusual feature in any social research. The first record was on a paper table napkin in the Patroon Room (the dining room of the University of New York at Albany). Later an improved record (but still in extremely crude notes and sketches) was made on a 'flip chart'. Those present at the time, in addition to myself, were Dr Peter Hoffman (who was at that time acting as the human interface between the computer and the Board) and Dr Huy Jo Shin, a Korean post doctoral student who has since returned to Korea. These facts might have been forgotten had not the 'flip chart' been used as packaging of some books for storage. The flip chart, rediscovered some six years later, still survives as a reminder of the occasion and of the elements of the 'matrix' which has characterised 'guidelines' in almost all of the 57 varieties ever since.

It is impossible to allocate credit to any of the three individuals present, (the chart preserves input by the three of us), nor can we claim that primacy should be accorded to us collectively. There were others who had been involved from the beginning of the project, though few remained until its completion, and the 'matrix' was, of course, a mere simplification of a more complex equation.

The next step was critical. How were we to move from an idea evolved at an academic lunch to applications by the United States Parole Commissioners? We liked the idea, of course, but the Board had continuously stressed that each of their decisions was made on an individual basis. There was only one policy, to treat each case on its merits. Our approach would involve the determination of the release date mainly upon two dimensions (the 'matrix'), namely, the seriousness of the instant crime, and the probability of recidivism (almost entirely determined by reference to prior record). If this basis for decision were adopted, the Board would have a policy which was made explicit in the general rules which were in the form of a 'chart'. It was also proposed that any departure from the rules (the indicated time to be served in the chart) would require to be explained by the decision-makers concerned. Furthermore, every six months a review of departures from the general rules would be made by the whole Board sitting *in banc*.[1]

It may be that our inefficiency was the clue to our success in selling the concepts to the Board! It had taken us a very long time to get to the idea of the 'matrix'. We had worked with the Board for almost a year, meeting all members regularly and working with them. The parole decision-making problem was a shared problem, not one which had been *referred to research workers*. We were not doing research *for* the Board but *with* the Board. The Chairman of the Board took responsibility (and probably paid a political price) for instigating the system. Chairman Reed and his successor Chairman Zigler were full partners in the research enterprise.

There are many persons and many serendipitous events to which an accurate history would draw attention (if they could all now be identified). In addition to the administrative support the research team received, it would be absurd not to recognise the importance of the support of many academic colleagues at the State University of New York at Albany. Certainly there was some strong criticism from academicians in other universities, and the encouragement of the Dean of the Graduate School was most significant. Not all academic criticism has ceased, but it is certainly muted, and the simple, original idea of logical, principled structuring of individual judicial discretion has become a widespread movement in the United States.

By the end of the 1970s most paroling authorities had developed some form of guidelines system as a method of policy control. The transition to sentencing guidelines was a natural development. The methods could not remain solely in the field of parole decision-making. For one thing, the courts became involved through challenges to the provisions of the parole guidelines, mainly based on constitutional issues and brought in the higher courts.[2] Some judges began, unofficially, using the Federal Parole Guidelines to guide their sentencing. Probation officers became accustomed to making the necessary calculations as did some prosecutors and defence counsel.

Corruption of original model

The first guidelines were designed as a *management tool* for the United States Parole Board. They were designed in collaborative effort with the Board members and took into direct consideration the previous decisions of the Board. Somehow, gradually the idea of guidelines, as it moved from parole to the courts, became a legal instrument involving legislatures. Originally it was expected that the requirement to show that decisions were principled and in accord with an explicit policy would itself be sufficient to ensure the adoption of a system of guidelines. In the same way as the Parole Board had itself dealt with disparity engendered by individual discretion and had itself 'cleaned up its own house', so, it was hoped the judiciary collectively would defend its independence from legislative (political) intervention. To do this, they might need to show that there was not much disparity in their dispositions. A guidelines system would be a most effective tool of policy control whereby this might be done, overseen perhaps by a body such as a judicial conference.

This has not happened. Judges have rather defended the right of each individual member to independence from each other individual member. This, it seems, is what most members of the legal profession understood by the independence of the judicial arm of government. It would seem to a non-lawyer that the independence of a profession might be better and more effectively achieved by co-operation among those involved in the defence of independence. Though each judge is answerable to his own conscience, how is it that this is regarded as incompatible with the idea of accountability to the society in which the judicial role is carried out?

Varieties of guidelines

Any form of advice or directive can be called a 'guideline'; even expressions of pious hope are sometimes called 'guidelines'. It has, however, become practice to refer the term sentencing guidelines to fairly specific suggestions to judges as to the disposition of persons found guilty. The methods whereby the sets of tables or other formats are arrived at fall into three classes. These may be simply designated:

(a) Those based upon what is.
(b) Those based upon what 'ought' to be.
(c) Those based upon a *belief* as to 'what is'.

The first group start by empirical research into recent past practice in the belief that precedent should be followed unless there is good reason to do otherwise.

The second group begins by establishing a group of persons who are expected to know that which ought to be done. In this class are the various 'model penal codes' as well as the suggestion of Sir Henry Hawkins in 1893 noted earlier.

The third group is derived from evidence based on introspection, i.e. on what decision-makers believe they are doing when they make decisions.

The Advisory Council report (1978) quoted earlier commended the original guidelines form for the fact that it 'adopted a penalty structure based on the existing practice of the courts'. While this method is different from that categorised as the 'ought' basis, it does not avoid value choice. If this approach is used, then it is believed to be the method which 'ought' to be used. Furthermore, there must be some belief that the collective 'is' of present practice has greater merit than merely seeking to think through what ought to be done, or to seek to derive procedures from philosophies and logical principles alone.

Election to use an empirical basis in current practice raises a number of subsidiary questions as to how to collect information regarding current practice and how those data are best summarised. A major consideration is whether to use simulated case materials so that the stimulus for each decision can be standardised, or to collect, classify and analyse field data.

A difficult problem with any method which takes information from the existing system is to discriminate the observed variation from the concept of disparity. Thomas (1979) goes so far as to suggest that no disparity was involved in two cases where one offender received probation and the other a sentence of five years, although each had committed a precisely similar crime and had an almost identical prior record and personal history. No disparity was involved because two distinct principles were used in the decisions. In the former case the judge had in mind rehabilitation, whereas in the latter the concern was with prevention. Disparity between principles in his opinion, which he claims is shared by the Court of Appeal, is not 'disparity' in disposition. The question would seem to arise as to how many different sets of principles might be identified. Perhaps there could be one for each offender? Thus the principles upon which decisions are based might be 'individualised' as well as any and all dispositions!

Another issue is that of local conditions. To what extent, where dispositions would otherwise be considered to be similar, would the local environment be a factor in modification of the decisions? Should there be one set of rules in one county and a different set in the adjoining county? Should the town areas be distinguished from the rural areas within a jurisdiction? If the influence of local geography, cultural values and local public opinion are relevant, then perhaps time is also of significance? Are times of day important? Can these features be dealt with as aggravating or mitigating circumstances, or do we require a different set of principles? Exemplary sentences take into account the prevailing crime pattern, both in terms of time and place. Is this to be an accepted principle? If so, how is it to be regulated? What superior principles can be stated as to when such determinations are morally acceptable? Is precedent in the form of data as to past decisions sufficient to sort out these and all other related issues?

It would seem that the mere reference to past decisions does not resolve all questions of procedure and principle.

If empirical data are not collected but a committee, commission or other body is set up to work through to a model code which would specify the right decisions for each case, they would seem to have an impossible task. Can any group of persons imagine the variety of acts, circumstances of offenders and victims, times and places which will be the material evidence upon which future decisions will have to be made? *Doing Justice* (1976) sets forth some principles of commensurate punishment and some might take the view that a system of guidelines could be built from (first) principles. But why reject all the experience of those who have made decisions in the past? Perhaps as one person has said, 'if we know one thing about present sentencing practice it is that it is wrong'. Is that not somewhat arrogant?

The 'believed to be' method may seem to have little to commend it. Data derived from introspection is not usually of high quality. However, it is possible to partition elements and to use Bayesian methods of analysis of subjective probability. Though no attempt has been made to put this method to practical use, a doctoral dissertation has demonstrated (Burnham 1969), that it might be worth further exploration.

Essential elements of guidelines

In the course of working with parole boards and, later, judges and producing systems of guidelines, some of which have survived and others of which have fallen prey to political intervention, many value choices have had to be made.

The social scientist cannot avoid becoming involved in policy decisions, and it may be well to make the position obvious rather than to claim scientific objectivity. The original guidelines forms were worked out within a small team of research workers in collaboration with those who might use them. As the number of sites grew and the research team personnel increased and diversified, different options came to be favoured by different persons. This writer's idea of the separation of management from legislative functions was soon to be questioned. To the lawyer-members of the research team it seemed that guidelines would be ignored unless they had the force of law. The only way that the system would become effective, they considered, was through legislative guidelines. A framed illuminated script was distributed (by an anonymous author) which read: 'God does not favour voluntary guidelines!! If voluntary guidelines would have worked, Moses would not have come down with his tablets of stone.'

For my part I still would take the view that managerial functions should not be confused with legislative functions, and that there is no reason why the one should work and the other not. It is essential that the original approach is not ossified. However it seems to me that it might be useful if I were to state my position on the desirable features of sentencing guidelines. In brief these are:

(a) The method of construction should recognise the distinction between 'policy' and 'case' elements in the decisions and accommodate these by providing *Decision Rules* (vehicles for policy functions) and *Procedures*. The latter are to be applied in cases where a decision-maker considers that policy constraints should be set aside (or precedent departed from). There should always remain a significant proportion of cases of reasoned departure from the indicated guideline decision. This is because these cases provide information which is the raw material for an evolutionary system. As a rule of thumb, a departure of about ten per cent is proposed.

(b) The method must be an evolutionary system. Engineered into the structure of the system must be an information feed-back component to provide an incentive for change or a continuing challenge to the accepted policy. As Radzinowicz and Hood (1978) pointed out, 'a danger lies in freezing current practice rather than giving scope for sentencing policies to respond to the changing social values and penal considerations of a plural society'. This danger was guarded against in the original form in that the Parole Commissioners were to meet every six months and review the reasons given for and the statistics of departures from the indicated disposition. If the reasons seemed appealing, the system might be adjusted so that future similar decisions would not require individual justification, because they would now fall within the up-dated policy.

(c) It is my view that experience of the decision-makers concerned (at all levels) should be explored and utilised in setting the base position. Guidelines should not be derived from pure thought, or the exercise of power by those who know what is right or have the power to so arrange it.

In addition to these three items, essential if any version is claimed to be of the same genre as the original model, there are some personal preferences of style which do not form essential elements of a guideline system.

(d) The persons (parole boards, judges or others) who are responsible for putting the policy into effect should have a direct input to, and responsibility for policy maintenance, modification and initially its formulation as noted in (c) above.

(e) It is preferable that any system is not tied closely to any current theory of crime and its control.

(f) Systems of accountability should be designed at a high level of generality. That is to say, the level of accountability should not be related to detailed operational procedures but to principles and objectives.

(g) The design and organisation of a guideline system should be such that it stimulates research and can incorporate research findings.

The original problem

Perhaps too much stress has been laid upon the original model. The original problem still remains, but the environment in which that problem is to be faced has changed. Its solution will, perhaps, always evade us. Discretion may be an essential element of any decision system which involves the high variety of human behaviour. If discretion is squeezed out of one part of the system it will appear in another. We may seek to control where it appears, but not to destroy it. It is better that discretion is structured and that it is exercised where it is highly visible and by persons who are fully accountable to all sectors of a democratic society. One thing is clear, some means must be found to ration the expensive commodity of penal punishment.

If constraint in expenditure is acceptable in the health services, some constraint must also be acceptable in the disposition of offenders. We may be morally indignant about criminals, but that does not justify bankrupting the social system by the means we choose to deal with those we identify. We may be indignant also that we cannot afford enough kidney machines to provide them for all persons who need them to survive. The time has come for the criminal justice system to accommodate to the financial constraints of a well-managed society. There is not an infinite source of funds available for punishment even though many judges may wish to demonstrate their morality by behaving as though this were so. Criminal justice should develop as a sector of social management.

Paraphrasing Churchill's much quoted statement, the criminal justice system cannot manifest a brand of morality which is out of keeping with that of the total society.

Notes

1   The United States Parole Commission continues to review and update its guidelines system based upon a continuing programme of research. Reports are published as occasional papers.
2   An early case of this kind is that of Luppo v. Norton, and Zagarino v. Attorney-General of the United States, Federal Distict 2d Connecticut, 1970 (430).

References

Advisory Council on the Penal System (1978) *Sentences of Imprisonment*, London, HMSO.
Burnham, R. W. B. (1969) *A theoretical basis for a rational case decision system in corrections*, unpub. D.Crim. Dissertation, School of Criminology, University of California, Berkeley.
Carter, R. and Wilkins, L. T. (1976) *Probation and Parole* (2nd ed.), New York, John Wiley.
Glueck, S. and Glueck, E. (1940) *Juvenile Delinquents Grown Up*, New York, The Commonwealth Fund.
Gottfredson, D., Wilkins, L. T. and Hoffman, P. B. (1978) *Guidelines for Parole and Sentencing*, Lexington, Lexington Books.
Hart, H. (1923) 'Predicting parole success', *Journal of Criminal Law and Criminology*, 14, 405.
Mannheim, H. and Wilkins, L. T. (1955) *Prediction Methods in Relation to Borstal Training*, Studies in the Causes of Delinquency and the Treatment of Offenders I, London, HMSO.

Radzinowicz, L. and Hood, R. (1978) 'A dangerous direction for sentencing reform', *Criminal Law Review*, 713.
Thomas, D. A. (1979) *Principles of Sentencing* (2nd ed.), London, Heinemann.
Thorpe, M. G. (1900) 'Can sentences be standardised?' *The Nineteenth Century*, January, 112.
von Hirsch, A. (1976) *Doing Justice*, New York, Hill and Wang.
Warner, S. B. (1923) 'Factors determining parole from the Massachussetts Reformatory', *Journal of Criminal Law and Criminology*, 14, 172.
Wilkins, L. T. (1980) *The Principles of Sentencing Guidelines*, Department of Justice Monograph, Washington DC, Government Printing Office.

3 Michael H. Tonry

Sentencing guidelines and sentencing commissions – the second generation

American sentencing reform initiatives since 1975 have taken a variety of forms – sentencing commissions, sentencing guidelines, parole guidelines, parole abolition, mandatory sentencing laws, statutory determinate sentencing, plea-bargaining bans and rules, and appellate sentence review (for comprehensive summaries see Shane Dubow, 1985; Blumstein, 1983). Sentencing commissions and guidelines have attracted the greatest attention outside the United States. In 1980, the Australian Law Reform Commission proposed that Australia establish a federal sentencing commission (Law Reform Commission, 1980). At the time of writing, Canadian and Australian commissions are considering recommendation of a sentencing commission for those countries, and a similar Victorian deliberative body is at work in that Australian state. This Chapter is intended to discuss 'second generation' issues and problems that have arisen in jurisdictions adopting the sentencing commission approach.

A considerable number of states now have, or have had, sentencing commissions. Sentencing commissions have promulgated guidelines in Minnesota, Pennsylvania and Washington. Commissions in New York, South Carolina, Maine, and Connecticut have tried but failed; others are at work. In late 1984, the US Congress enacted the Sentencing Reform Act 1984 which established a federal sentencing commission;[1] the seven commissioners were confirmed by the United States Senate in October 1985 and must present proposed guidelines to the Congress early in 1987.

Section I describes the background to the sentencing commission and sentencing guidelines ideas. Section 2 introduces the sentencing commission and summarises the experience of the Minnesota Sentencing Guidelines Commission, the first, and most celebrated, sentencing commission. Section 3 reviews the experience with sentencing commissions in other states. Section 4 discusses the strengths and weaknesses of the sentencing commission approach to sentencing reform.

Background of reform

For readers who are not familiar with American sentencing laws and practices, a brief general introduction may make this essay more intelligible. Until 1975, all fifty American states, the District of Columbia, and the overlapping Federal jurisdiction had indeterminate sentencing systems. Statutes always specified maximum lawful sentences and occasionally specified mandatory minimum sentences. The prosecutor had unreviewable discretion over the charges to be filed and over plea bargaining. The judge, more or less influenced by prosecutorial recommendations or constrained by plea bargains, determined the nature of the sentence and, if incarceration was ordered, the minimum or maximum sentence or both. The parole board decided when the offender would be released. Prisoners became eligible for release, depending on the jurisdiction, after serving one year, or the minimum sentence set by the judge, or – at most – one-third of the maximum sentence. Finally, the prison authorities had power to alter the minimum sentence, the maximum sentence, the date for parole eligibility, or all three, by awarding or denying 'good time' (remission of sentence for good behaviour) which could reduce the nominal sentence by a third or more. No two jurisdictions' systems were exactly alike, but the broad outlines were the same everywhere. (Rothman, 1980).

These indeterminate systems, it is now generally agreed among policy-makers, reformers, and academics, had a number of serious deficiencies. First, on principle, many objected to the hypocrisy of 'bark and bite' sentencing in which the judge's bark bore little relation to prison's bite; a nominal twenty-year sentence might result in parole release after fifteen months. While the preceding example is extreme, release after serving twenty-four to thirty-six months of a ten-year sentence was common.

This resulted, second, in sentence inflation. Trial judges, who are generally elected, could pander to popular and media sentiment by announcing severe sentences that they expected the parole board to mitigate. Conversely, judges who wished to assure a long sentence could try to anticipate parole decisions. A judge who wanted an offender to serve five years in prison might impose a fifteen-year sentence because eligibility for parole release ripened after service of a third of the imposed sentence. If the parole board released the prisoner when he first became eligible, the judge's aim would be realised. If the parole board elected not to release the offender, he might serve many more years in prison than the judge intended or foresaw.

Third, the inflation of nominal sentences and the wide and essentially unreviewable discretions of judges, parole boards, and prison officials combined to make sentencing disparities inevitable and often substantial. It may be helpful to note salient differences between the American and English sentencing systems. While most English prison sentences are of not more than a few years' duration, sentences of five, ten, or twenty-five years are not uncommon in the United States. Parole release was not established in England until 1968, and generally serves to shorten sentences by a few months; parole release was ubiquitous after 1930 in the United States and often reduced nominal prison terms by sixty to eighty per cent. Finally, appellate sentence review has existed in England since 1907; in the United States even today it exists in any meaningful sense only in Minnesota.

About the intensity of reform activity after 1975, there can be no doubt. A mere six years later, in 1981, a federally supported sentencing project reported that sentencing guidelines projects had by that date been established in twenty-three states, (Criminal Courts Technical Assistance Project, 1980); the number is now in excess of forty states (most of these were at local, not state, levels, and many have since been abandoned). By 1985, forty-nine of the fifty states had enacted mandatory sentencing laws for selected offences (Shane DuBow, 1985). At least nine states have abolished parole release since 1975 and most of those have enacted statutory determinate sentencing laws in which presumptive sentencing ranges are set out in legislation. At least fifteen states have developed parole guidelines (several of these later abolished parole). Sentencing commissions in three states have developed and promulgated presumptive sentencing guidelines; sentencing commissions are at work in several jurisdictions and have tried but failed to produce guidelines in three states. In other states, the organized judiciary has promulgated statewide sentencing guidelines; at least five jurisdictions have received considerable attention – Massachusetts, Michigan, New Jersey, Maryland, Florida – but there are others (See Cohen and Tonry, 1983).

There is an emerging consensus that the sentencing commission is the most promising of the four major approaches to sentencing reform. Parole guidelines systems have the fundamental drawback that, however intelligently they are developed and however consistently they are applied, they affect only the twenty-five to thirty-five per cent of cases that result in prison sentences. Disparities as to who goes to prison are beyond their reach. Statutory determinate sentencing laws also are silent on the In/Out question of who receives prison sentences, and, while they have sometimes reduced sentencing disparities somewhat among those imprisoned, they are less effective at that than parole guidelines. Judicially developed and promulgated sentencing guidelines tend to be ignored. This is partly because the vast majority of prosecutions are resolved by plea bargains and partly because the guidelines lack the authority of legislation.

The sentencing commission approach, however, does seem to 'work.' In both Minnesota and Washington State, sentencing practices radically changed after guidelines took effect. Sentencing disparities have been reduced both as to who goes to prison and for how long, (Knapp, 1984; Sentencing Guidelines Commission, 1985).

The sentencing commission model

To many observers, the story of modern American sentencing reform is the Minnesota story. The Minnesota guidelines were principled; they incorporated ideals of racial, social, and sexual neutrality; they seriously attacked sentencing disparities, and they were intended to alter Minnesota sentencing practices substantially. To the surprise of sceptics, trial judges adhered to the guidelines most of the time and Minnesota sentencing patterns shifted in the intended ways. Sentencing disparities were reduced. And, for the first time in the United States, a meaningful system of appellate sentence review developed (Knapp, 1985).

Notwithstanding Minnesota's successes, it is misleading to focus only on the Sentencing Commission. More sentencing commissions have failed than have succeeded in their efforts to promulgate guidelines embodying meaningful sentencing policies. A combination of institutional arrangements − together constituting what this essay calls the 'sentencing commission model' − were central to the Minnesota experience.

The 'sentencing commission model' incorporates three main

elements – the sentencing commission, presumptive sentencing guidelines, and appellate sentence review. Each is an inseparable part of the
Minnesota story. The *sentencing commission* (see Frankel, 1972) was
indispensable because it possessed the institutional capacity to develop
fine-tuned sentencing standards of much greater subtlety and specificity than any legislature could. *Presumptive sentencing guidelines*[2]
provided a mechanism for expressing sentencing standards in a form
that has more legal authority than voluntary guidelines, is less rigid
than mandatory sentencing laws, and is much more specific than the
maximum and minimum sentences set out in the criminal codes.
Appellate sentence review provided a mechanism for assuring that
trial judges either imposed sentences that were consistent with the
applicable guidelines or, if not, that acceptable and convincing reasons
justified a different sentence.

Appellate sentence review has been available in various American
jurisdictions from time to time throughout this century and probably
earlier. However, it has seldom amounted to much, primarily because
there has been no substantive sentencing law. Most criminal statutes
simply authorised maximum lawful sentences. If the maximum for
robbery was twenty-five years, there were no standards to guide a
judge in deciding whether probation, five years, ten years, or twenty-
years was the appropriate sentence.

Even in jurisdictions having appellate sentence review, the scrutiny
given to appealed sentences has been slight and doctrines of extreme
deference to the trial judge have developed. It is hard to see what else
could have happened. The long maximum sentences in indeterminate
sentencing systems were intended to permit judges to individualise
sentences. For an appellate judge to have reversed a sentence, in the
absence of established standards for evaluating the appropriateness
of sentences, would have seemed, and been, *ad hoc* and arbitrary.

Minnesota was the first jurisdiction to establish a sentencing
commission (Knapp, 1985). Minnesota's nine-member part-time
Commission was created in 1978 and was directed to submit guidelines
to the legislature on 1 January 1980. The Commission met regularly,
conducted frequent public meetings, took its task seriously, and
invested substantial energies and resources in training practitioners in
use of the guidelines. After implementation, an elaborate monitoring
system was established in order to determine rates and patterns of
compliance with the guidelines.

The Minnesota Commission made a number of bold policy

decisions. First, it decided to be 'prescriptive', and explicitly to establish its own sentencing priorities and policies; every other sentencing guidelines system to that date had purported to be 'descriptive,' to attempt to replicate existing sentencing patterns. Second, the Commission decided to alter existing sentencing patterns by de-emphasising imprisonment for property offenders and emphasising imprisonment for violent offenders; research showed that repetitive property offenders tended to go to prison and that first-time violent offenders tended not to. Third, in order to attack sentencing disparities, the Commission established very narrow sentencing ranges, generally plus or minus five to eight per cent from a mid-point (for example thirty to thirty-four months or fifty to fifty-eight months), and to discourage departures from guideline ranges, authorised them only in the presence of 'substantial and compelling' reasons. Fourth, the Commission elected to adopt 'Just Deserts' as the overriding consideration in determining which offenders should be imprisoned. Fifth, the Commission chose to interpret an ambiguous statutory injunction that it take correctional resources into 'substantial consideration' as a mandate that its guidelines not increase prison population beyond existing capacity constraints. Sixth, the Commission forbade consideration at sentencing of many personal factors – such as education, employment, marital status, living arrangements – that many judges believed to be legitimate. This decision resulted from a policy that sentencing decisions not be based on factors that directly or indirectly discriminated against minorities, women, or low-income groups.

The Minnesota Commission divided all offences into ten categories and categorised offenders into seven groups on the basis of 'criminal history scores' (calculated mostly on the number of prior felony convictions). The resulting offence and criminal history rankings were arrayed on a seventy-cell grid which thus shows for every combination of offence severity and criminal history the applicable presumptive sentence. The grid in use at the time of writing is reproduced in the Appendix to this volume. Persons whose offence and prior record place them in a cell above the bold black line are presumptively *not* to receive a state prison sentence (the number in each such cell is the prison sentence that should be imposed on failure of probation or similar conditions). State prison is the presumptive sentence for persons whose cases fall within a cell below the bold line. The single number is *the* presumptive sentence in months but the judge may impose any sentence from within the narrow range shown at the bottom of each cell.

The sentence indicated by the grid is *not* mandatory; it is rebuttably presumed to be appropriate. The judge may however impose any lawful sentence if he indicates the circumstances that overcome the presumption. Only 'substantial and compelling circumstances' can overcome the presumption and either the defendant or the prosecution can appeal the trial judge's decision to 'depart'.

The Minnesota Commission has published a series of detailed reports on the guidelines' impact. A summary report of the first three years' experience is available and has recently been summarised for English readers (Knapp, 1984; Wasik, 1985). Here I summarize some key findings to demonstrate why many people believe the sentencing commission model can serve as a useful mechanism for development and implementation of sentencing policy.

First, as a deliberate policy matter, the Commission decided that persons convicted of serious offences should be imprisoned, even if they have no prior record. In 1978, before guidelines were promulgated, only forty-five per cent of persons convicted of the four most serious levels of offence, but having no, or a scant, prior record went to prison; in the guidelines' first year, seventy-eight per cent of these offenders were imprisoned − as the guidelines directed.

Second, conversely, a decision was made to de-emphasise imprisonment for nuisance property offences, with comparable results. In 1978, fifty-four per cent of offenders convicted of the two least serious levels of offence, but having criminal history scores of three, four, or five, were imprisoned; in 1981, only fifteen per cent of offenders fitting that description were imprisoned.

Third, the vast majority of sentences imposed under the guidelines comply with them: if sentences imposed in 1978 are viewed relative to the guidelines, 19.4% of sentences would have been dispositional departures (that is, sentences to prison when the guidelines direct non-imprisonment or vice versa); the actual departure rate in 1981 was 6.2%, clearly indicating increased uniformity in state imprisonment policies.

Fourth, notwithstanding that the guidelines represented substantial alterations in prior sentencing patterns, other aspects of the criminal justice system were not disrupted:

(a) during the first year of guidelines' experience, prison populations remained within projected levels;

(b) trial rates in 1981, 1982, and 1983 were slightly lower than in 1978 (some hypothesized that trial rates would increase substantially because the guidelines made sentences more predictable and thereby reduced defendants' risks of receiving especially harsh sentences after conviction at trial);

(c) case processing time did not increase;

(d) only one per cent of persons sentenced under the guidelines appealed their sentences (some hypothesized that appeals would flood the courts).

In the interest of balance, it should be noted that there were criticisms both of the Minnesota approach and of its operations. Some critics rejected Minnesota's fundamental premise that individualised sentencing was undesirable or objected in principle to creation of meaningful constraints on trial judges' discretion. The principal criticisms of the guidelines in operation were that they were too rigid, that they shifted too much power to the prosecutor, and that their failure to set standards for non-prison sentences exacerbated pre-existing disparities in imposition of jail sentences. Since approximately eighty per cent of Minnesota felony convictions do not result in prison sentences, Minnesota's failure to develop non-prison guidelines permitted unrestrained discretion to continue in respect of most convictions.

On balance, however, Minnesota's guidelines system undertook and largely achieved major changes in sentencing policy and did so without precipitating hypothesised negative effects. It should be stressed here, lest an English reader not be aware of it, that many sentencing innovations in America have been nullified in practice by judges and lawyers who chose to ignore or circumvent them (see Cohen and Tonry, 1983). Minnesota avoided that.

It was not coincidence that the Minnesota system 'worked.' The Commission had a number of things going for it. First, it was blessed with an unusually talented staff – a former director, Kay Knapp, was appointed director of the US Sentencing Commission. Second, its first chairman, Jan Smaby, was able to devote a large proportion of her time to the Commission's work and, because she was politically knowledgeable and effective, was able to anticipate and avoid political problems that later overwhelmed commissions in other states. Third, key members were able both to represent the interests of their constituencies, notably the judiciary and the prosecutors, and, later, to persuade their constituencies to support the Commission and its product. Fourth, the Commission early decided that its work would be an 'open political process' in which the views, opinions, and concerns of affected groups would be solicited. Thus, when the Commission elected to take principled positions or to undertake bold policy initiatives, it was able to test those decisions on the affected constituencies, to modify those decisions when opposition appeared intractable or insurmountable, and, once those constituencies were won over, to be relatively confident that the Commission's policies would not be seriously opposed before the legislature.

Although the Minnesota story and the sentencing commission model are difficult to separate, they are separate. The sentencing commission model offers promise to other jurisdictions only if it is transferrable. The experience to date is mixed. The next section reviews the sentencing commission's experience in jurisdictions other than Minnesota.

The experience in other jurisdictions

The experience with sentencing commissions in jurisdictions other than Minnesota teaches that creation of the sentencing commission by itself is not enough. Minnesota's successes depended on political acumen, effective leadership, and a bit of luck. Of six other jurisdictions in which sentencing commissions have completed their work, four were complete failures, one was largely a failure, and one was successful.

Maine

In June 1983 the Maine legislature created the Maine Sentencing Guidelines Commission and charged it to 'make recommendations of sentencing guidelines' to the legislature. The Commission's primary recommendation in a five-page report in November 1984 was 'that a new commission be created to continue the responsibilities of this commission' (Phillips, 1984). The Commission did not give a detailed explanation of why it had failed to develop guidelines.

The Maine Sentencing Guidelines Commission suffered from a number of limitations. A sizable number of its members apparently decided early on that Maine did not need sentencing guidelines; as a consequence, institutional momentum never developed. Most of the Maine Commission's nine part-time members had no prior knowledge of sentencing reform developments elsewhere, and, partly because no full-time professional staff were appointed, that knowledge was never acquired. State funding was insubstantial and outside funding was neither sought nor obtained. At the time of writing, it is unclear whether the Commission's existence will be renewed and, if it is, whether its prospects of success will be any greater the second time around.

Connecticut
The Connecticut legislature created a sentencing commission in 1979. The Commission undertook research on past sentencing practices and developed a 'descriptive' sentencing grid based on that research. Rules were developed for departures and for the role of aggravating and mitigating circumstances. However, 'after developing this sentencing guidelines system, the Sentencing Commission went on record stating that it was strongly *opposed* to the adoption of the sentencing guidelines system, but rather *recommended the replacement of the indeterminate sentencing system in Connecticut with a determinate sentencing scheme* (emphasis in original) (Shane-DuBow, 1985, p. 48). The legislature heeded that advice and, effective 1 July 1981, abolished parole and established a statutory determinate sentencing system.

South Carolina
The South Carolina Sentencing Guidelines Commission was appointed by the Governor of South Carolina in 1982, and somewhat later separate enabling legislation was passed. The Commission was chaired by a supreme court justice and its members included judges, legislators, and prosecutors. Sentencing guidelines were proposed to the legislature for adoption in 1985 but were rejected. To a considerable extent, this resulted from the Commission's inability to gain support from the judiciary. The guidelines were opposed in the legislature by both the Chief Justice of the South Carolina Supreme Court and by the trial judges who had served on the Commission.

New York
Appointed in 1983, the New York State Committee on Sentencing Guidelines had a number of things going for it, including both

a sizable budget and a staff larger than that of any other sentencing commission. The Committee's members were sophisticated and many of them were aware of developments in other jurisdictions. The staff director had directed a major statewide sentencing guidelines project in an urban industrial state and the staff counsel was a veteran of political wars in New York. The New York Committee met regularly, and occasionally lengthily, and generated a substantial volume of proposals, staff papers, working drafts, and impact projections. A report setting out recommendations, including proposed guidelines, was presented to the New York legislature in April 1985; the report met with considerable hostility and was not approved.

The Committee's work had suffered throughout from political posturing and interest group politics. No consensus was reached about the goals or premises of the Committee's recommendations and the resulting *ad hoc* compromises pleased virtually no one. One especially influential Committee member dissented from the Committee's report, thereby undermining its credibility and shattering any illusions that the Committee had reached consensus positions. A *Newsday* feature on the New York experience captured the result: '[The Committee's] final report, in April, also drew contradictory complaints. It reduces mandatory minimums. It is too tough. It is too soft. It will lead to an explosion in prison populations. It won't do enough to reduce sentencing disparity.' (Keeler, 1985).

At the time of writing, the New York Sentencing Committee continues to exist and a few members continue to attend meetings. The staff director resigned long ago as did the general counsel, who had succeeded him as director. What comes next remains to be seen.

Pennsylvania
The Pennsylvania Commission on Sentencing was established in 1978 and began work in April 1979 (Martin, 1983). The Commission proposed guidelines to the legislature in January 1981. They were rejected in March 1981 and the Commission was directed to revise and resubmit the guidelines, to make the sentencing standards more severe (in a variety of specified ways), and to increase the scope of judicial discretion under the guidelines. The Commission complied and the resulting guidelines were submitted to the legislature in January 1982 and took effect on 22 July 1982.

The guidelines promulgated in July 1982 are set out as Table 1. Parole release has been retained in Pennsylvania and the guidelines

Table 1 *The courts*

Offence gravity score	Prior record score	Minimum range[a]	Aggravated minimum range[a]	Mitigated minimum range[a]
5	0	0–12	12–18	non-confinement
For example: Criminal	1	3–12	12–18	1½–3
Mischief (Felony III); Theft	2	5–12	12–18	2½–5
by Unlawful Taking (Felony	3	8–12	12–18	4–8
III); Theft by Receiving Stolen	4	18–27	27–34	14–18
Property (Felony III);	5	21–30	30–38	16–21
Bribery[b]	6	24–36	36–45	18–24
4	0	0–12	12–18	non-confinement
For example: Theft by	1	0–12	12–18	non-confinement
receiving stolen property, less	2	0–12	12–18	non-confinement
than $2,000, by force or threat	3	5–12	12–18	2½–5
of force, or in breach of	4	8–12	12–18	4–8
fiduciary obligation[b]	5	18–27	27–34	14–18
	6	21–30	30–38	16–21
3	0	0–12	12–18	non-confinement
	1	0–12	12–18	non-confinement
	2	0–12	12–18	non-confinement
Most Misdemeanour I's[b]	3	0–12	12–18	non-confinement
	4	3–12	12–18	1½–3
	5	5–12	12–18	2½–5
	6	8–12	12–18	4–8
2	0	0–12	Statutory limit[c]	non-confinement
	1	0–12	Statutory limit[c]	non-confinement
	2	0–12	Statutory limit[c]	non-confinement
Most Misdemeanour II's[b]	3	0–12	Statutory limit[c]	non-confinement
	4	0–12	Statutory limit[c]	non-confinement
	5	2–12	Statutory limit[c]	1–2
	6	5–12	Statutory limit[c]	2½–5
1	0	0–6	Statutory limit[c]	non-confinement
	1	0–6	Statutory limit[c]	non-confinement
	2	0–6	Statutory limit[c]	non-confinement
Most Misdemeanour III's[b]	3	0–6	Statutory limit[c]	non-confinement
	4	0–6	Statutory limit[c]	non-confinement
	5	0–6	Statutory limit[c]	non-confinement
	6	0–6	Statutory limit[c]	non-confinement

Notes (a) Weapon enhancement: At least 12 months and up to 24 months confinement must be added to the above lengths when a deadly weapon was used in the crime.

(b) These offences are listed here for illustrative purposes only. Offence scores are given in S. 303.7.

(c) Statutory limit is defined as the longest minimum sentence permitted by law.
[Pa. B. Doc. No. 82–121. Filed 22 January 1982, 9.00 a.m.]

Source Pennsylvania Bulletin, 12, 4, 23 January 1982.

accordingly prescribe ranges for minimum sentences; the judges retain full discretion over the maximum.

For every offence, including misdemeanours, the guidelines specify three 'ranges' — a normal range, an aggravated range, and a mitigated range. The judge may impose a sentence from within any of the three ranges and may do so for any reason, so long as a reason is given. The guidelines set no general criteria for imposition of aggravated or mitigated sentences, or for 'deviations' from the guidelines and no special findings of fact need be made.

Pennsylvania annually publishes statistical analyses of the guidelines' impact. 'Compliance rates' are very high, but are essentially meaningless, because the guidelines are so broad that substantial disparities can occur even within the guidelines, because judges can use the aggravating/mitigating guidelines at will, and because no efforts have been made to account for the role of plea bargaining in sentencing.

Pennsylvania only vaguely represents the sentencing commission model. Because the guidelines concern only minimum sentences, there is no structural reason for appellate judges to take appellate sentence review seriously — the parole board makes release decisions and, if it chooses, can disregard idiosyncratic maximum sentences. More importantly, because the guideline ranges are broad, and because there are no rules governing when judges may depart from them, Pennsylvania appellate courts will have difficulty knowing the basis by which a sentence appeal can or should be evaluated.

In summary, of the three elements of the sentencing commission model, Pennsylvania has a sentencing commission, barely has presumptive sentencing guidelines, and lacks a realistic potential for meaningful appellate sentence review.

The Pennsylvania Commission on Sentencing seems never to have gelled or have developed a sense of collective mission. Several Commission members took little interest in the Commission's work and seldom appeared at meetings. The initial chairman, a judge, played a passive role, unlike Minnesota's energetic and involved chairman. Finally, little effort was made, and no success achieved, at winning over the affected interests and constituencies. As a result, when the initial guidelines reached the legislature, the Commission had few allies or supporters and, in a law and order climate, did well to remain in existence.

Washington

The one success story, other than in Minnesota, occurred in Washington State (Boerner, 1985). Most of the Minnesota ingredients were present: a capable staff, an effective chairman, an adequate budget, achievement of a sense of joint mission among the Commission's members, a comprehensive and principled approach to policy problems, and an acknowledgment of the need to make tactical political compromises. When the Washington guidelines were submitted to the legislature, they passed amidst relatively little controversy and have been in effect since 1 July 1984.

The Washington guidelines, which are shown as Table 2, resemble Minnesota's. Sentencing ranges are much narrower than those in Pennsylvania but somewhat broader than those in Minnesota. The guidelines set out illustrative aggravating and mitigating circumstances and permit departures only, as in Minnesota, for 'substantial and compelling' reasons. Parole release has been abolished. As in Minnesota, the Commission decided to shift sentencing policy toward more use of incarceration for violent offenders.

Finally, the Washington legislature had learned a number of lessons from the Minnesota experience and built these into the Washington legislation. The Commission was directed to be sensitive to prison population capacity constraints and to promulgate state-wide prosecutorial charging and bargaining guidelines. This last feature is a Washington original and resulted in part from the frequent observation that determinate sentencing and narrow guidelines increase the power of prosecutors. The Washington solution was to try to structure the discretion of the prosecutor. Finally, the Washington guidelines apply to all felonies and misdemeanours (unlike Minnesota's that applied only to felonies).

The preliminary evaluation of Washington's first year under guidelines suggests considerable accomplishments: the shift toward imprisonment for violent offenders and away from prison for property offenders is happening; compliance with the guidelines has been high (3.4% overall departure rates) and trial rates have not increased.

Other jurisdictions

Many other states have established bodies that have been called 'sentencing commissions'. Sometimes they have been fact-finding or advisory bodies charged to formulate policy recommendations for

Table 2 *Washington sentencing guidelines*

Seriousness level	Offender score									
	0	1	2	3	4	5	6	7	8	9 or more
XIV	Life sentence without parole/death penalty									
XIII	23y 4m **240–320**	24y 4m **250–333**	25y 4m **261–347**	26y 4m **271–361**	27y 4m **281–374**	28y 4m **291–388**	30y 4m **312–416**	32y 10m **338–450**	36y **370–493**	40y **411–548**
XII	12y **123–164**	13y **134–178**	14y **144–192**	15y **154–205**	16y **165–219**	17y **175–233**	19y **195–260**	21y **216–288**	25y **257–342**	29y **298–397**
XI	6y **62–82**	6y 9m **69–92**	7y 6m **77–102**	8y 3m **85–113**	9y **93–123**	9y 9m **100–133**	12y 6m **129–171**	13y 6m **139–185**	15y 6m **159–212**	17y 6m **180–240**
X	5y **51–68**	5y 6m **57–75**	6y **62–82**	6y 6m **67–89**	7y **72–96**	7y 6m **77–102**	9y 6m **98–130**	10y 6m **108–144**	12y 6m **129–171**	14y 6m **149–198**
IX	3y **31–41**	3y 6m **36–48**	4y **41–54**	4y 6m **46–61**	5y **51–68**	5y 6m **57–75**	7y 6m **77–102**	8y 6m **87–116**	10y 6m **108–144**	12y 6m **129–171**
VIII	2y **21–27**	2y 6m **26–34**	3y **31–41**	3y 6m **36–48**	4y **41–54**	4y 6m **46–61**	6y **67–89**	7y **77–102**	8y 6m **87–116**	10y 6m **108–144**
VII	18m **15–20**	2y **21–27**	2y 6m **26–34**	3y **31–41**	3y 6m **36–48**	4y **41–54**	5y **57–75**	6y **67–89**	7y 6m **77–102**	8y 6m **87–116**
VI	13m **12+–14**	18m **15–20**	2y **21–27**	2y 6m **26–34**	3y **31–41**	3y 6m **36–48**	4y 6m **46–61**	5y 6m **57–75**	6y 6m **67–89**	7y 6m **77–102**
V	9m **6–12**	13m **12+–14**	15m **13–17**	18m **15–20**	2y 2m **22–29**	3y 2m **33–43**	4y **41–54**	5y **51–68**	6y **62–82**	7y **72–96**
IV	6m **3–9**	9m **6–12**	13m **12+–14**	15m **13–17**	18m **15–20**	2y 2m **22–29**	3y 2m **33–43**	4y 2m **43–57**	5y 2m **53–70**	6y 2m **63–84**
III	2m **1–3**	5m **3–8**	8m **4–12**	11m **9–12**	14m **12+–16**	20m **17–22**	2y 2m **22–29**	3y 2m **33–43**	4y 2m **43–57**	5y **51–68**
II	0–90 **Days**	4m **2–6**	6m **3–9**	8m **4–12**	13m **12+–14**	16m **14–18**	20m **17–22**	2y 2m **22–29**	3y 2m **33–43**	4t 2m **43–57**
I	0–60 **Days**	0–90 **Days**	3m **2–5**	4m **2–6**	5m **3–8**	8m **4–12**	13m **12+–14**	16m **14–18**	20m **17–22**	2y 2m **22–29**

Note Bold type presents presumptive sentence ranges in months. Midpoints are included as a reference point (y = years, m = months). 12+ equals one year and one day. For a few crimes, the presumptive sentences in the high offender score columns exceed the statutory maximums. In these cases, the statutory maximum applies.

Additional time added to the presumptive sentence if the offender or an accomplice was armed with a deadly weapon: 24 months (Rape 1, Robbery 1, Kidnapping 1) 18 months (Burglary 1) 12 months (Assault 2, Escape 1, Kidnapping 2, Burglary 2 of a building other than a dwelling, Delivery or Possession of a controlled substance with intent to deliver) a governor, a legislature, or a state Supreme Court. Sometimes these have been appointed by governors, sometimes by a state's judiciary, sometimes by the legislature. In this essay, I have written almost exclusively of the experience of bodies created by a legislature and given a mandate to develop sentencing guidelines. Some mention should be made of other jurisdictions in which there has been significant sentencing commission activity. A sentencing commission acting under legislative authority began work in Wisconsin early in 1985. In the District of Columbia, a sentencing commission began work in 1983 and is expected to issue its proposed guidelines in 1986; this commission was created by the Chief Judge of the Superior Court of the District of Columbia but it includes, besides judges, legislators, the District of Columbia prosecutor and public defender, and several citizen members. Finally, Florida and Maryland have passed legislation to create sentencing commissions. In both cases, however, the newly created sentencing commissions were actually existing 'steering committees' for voluntary sentencing guidelines systems in those states. A major evaluation of Maryland's and Florida's voluntary systems concluded that they, like most voluntary systems, had had little demonstrable impact on sentencing practice. (Carrow and Feins, 1983).

Although the sentencing commission model is the most promising sentencing reform development in America, and the one that has received much the greatest attention in other lands, its success is by no means easy of accomplishment. Whether the Federal Sentencing Commission, which is just beginning its work, repeats the Minnesota-Washington story, or that of Connecticut, Maine, New York, Pennsylvania, and South Carolina, remains to be seen.

Problems and prospects

As a governmental institution, the sentencing commission is in its early days. There have been successes and failures and future efforts, in the US and elsewhere, may be guided by both. This section discusses both the limitations of Minnesota's experience and lessons that can be drawn from other states.

Limitations of the Minnesota approach
The initial dramatic impacts of Minnesota's guidelines have weakened. The details can be read in a recent article by Martin Wasik (1985), but in brief outline, here are the major points.

Reduced compliance
One of the Commission's major successes was in achieving its goal
of shifting sentencing practice towards more incarceration of violent
offenders with no or minor criminal records, and less incarceration
of repetitive property offenders; in both cases, by the third year of
guidelines experience, practices were reverting to those that preceded
the guidelines: for low record, violent offenders, 1983 imprisonment
rates exceeded pre-guideline rates but declined significantly from the
levels achieved in 1981 and 1982; for long record, property offenders,
the '1983 imprisonment rate ... was almost at the same level as the
pre-guidelines imprisonment rate'. (Knapp, 1984, p.31)

Disparities in non-incarcerative sentences
One major weakness of the Minnesota guidelines is that they deal only
with felony sentencing and then primarily with state prison sentences.
Although the enabling legislation provided 'the commission may also
establish appropriate sanctions for offenders for whom imprisonment
is not proper ...', the Commission elected not to do so. As a consequence, the guidelines created presumptions as to who goes to prison,
but provide no guidelines concerning sentencing of persons not
receiving *state prison* sentences. Inasmuch as up to one year's *jail
incarceration* may be imposed as a condition of probation, the absence
of guidance could well have produced considerable disparity. Moreover, for those repetitive property offenders who the Commission
preferred not receive prison sentences, gaol remains an available
option. The foreseeable confusion resulted: the Commission's three-
year evaluation concluded: 'nonconformity of (jail) use is found for
every racial and gender group, and there has been very little improvement in uniformity of jail use from 1978 to jail use in 1981, 1982,
and 1983'. (Knapp, 1984, p.48)

Plea bargaining
Critics of Minnesota's guidelines have consistently hypothesised that
guidelines would reduce judicial discretion and increase the significance of prosecutorial discretion. Because there are few constitutional
constraints on prosecutors' charging and plea bargaining decisions,
prosecutors have the ability to control the charges of which offenders
are convicted and, assuming judges comply with the guidelines,
can thereby nearly determine the narrow range from within which
sentences must be imposed. In addition, since in the United States

most convictions result from plea negotiations, in Minnesota and elsewhere, there is little reason for judges vigorously to oppose negotiating practices which theretofore had been common in their courts. The Commission's three-year evaluation concluded 'there was an increase in charge negotiations after the Guidelines and a substantial decrease in sentence negotiations'. (Knapp, 1984, p. 72)

Prosecutors have deliberately manipulated the guidelines. Because prosecutors tended to oppose the Commission's policy judgment that repetitive property offenders should not be imprisoned until they had accumulated extensive prior criminal records, prosecutors began to insist that property offenders plead guilty to multiple charges. This had the effect, compared with prior practice, of causing offenders to accumulate prior convictions rapidly. For example, an offender who in 1978 might have been permitted to plead guilty to one of four charged counts of larceny, might in 1982 be required to plead guilty to all four. The next time he appeared in court, under the guidelines he would have four prior convictions and therefore be eligible for prison. The Commission changed its rules on counting prior convictions in an effort to offset this prosecutorial manipulation, with some success. Nonetheless, the experience demonstrates that even in Minnesota prosecutors will willfully attempt to undermine policies with which they disagree.

Finally, and perhaps most surprisingly, while the extent of explicit sentence negotiations diminished under the guidelines compared with prior years, sentence negotiations did not disappear and in 1981 and 1982, one quarter of all convictions in eight counties studied resulted from sentence negotiations. Furthermore, although the Minnesota Supreme Court, in a sentence appeal, held that a sentence negotiation was not adequate justification for imposing a sentence other than as specified in the guidelines, both Kay Knapp and Debra Dailey, the former and the current directors of the Minnesota Sentencing Guidelines Commission, inform me that 'pursuant to sentence negotiation' is the single reason most commonly given by judges for departing from guidelines. Although these decisions on their face defy the policy set by the Minnesota Supreme Court, as a practical matter, defendants who have agreed to a departure pursuant to a sentence negotiation, which will almost always be a departure downward, are unlikely to lodge a sentence appeal.

Charge reductions
Consistent with the plea bargaining changes described in the preceding subsection, after the guidelines took effect there was a substantial increase in the percentage of convictions in which charge
reductions reduced the severity of the offence of conviction. A similar
pattern was apparent in the first year of experience for the Washington
State guidelines and extensive charge reductions also appeared in
Pennsylvania.

Prison crowding
Although prison populations in Minnesota did not increase during
the first year of experience with guidelines, in 1982 and 1983 the
population increased substantially. This was partly because of legislative and Commission policy decisions to increase sentencing severity
for certain offences, and partly because 'fears expressed by determinate sentencing critics concerned with prison population levels
materialised in 1982 sentencing practices. The increased power of the
prosecutors was used to effect harsher sentences.' (Knapp 1984, p. 90).
   Perhaps surprisingly, this problem has abated. The Minnesota
Commission made several changes to the guidelines with the intent
to reduce average sentence lengths and the Minnesota Legislature
made a number of statutory changes directed at the same end.

Failures in process
Of the seven sentencing commissions described in some detail in this
essay, four came to nought. Pennsylvania's commission failed to gain
legislative approval of its first proposed guidelines and eventually
produced weak and vague guidelines. Only in Washington and
Minnesota did commissions promulgate meaningful guidelines. There
is no simple or single explanation for why most of the commissions
failed. Money clearly isn't the explanation, for the richest commission,
in New York, was also one of the most ineffective. Minnesota was
blessed with an especially talented staff. Minnesota and Washington
both had strong, politically sensitive and effective chairmen. Several
of the commissions never developed a strong sense of joint enterprise
and shared goals. The reasons for success and failure vary from place
to place. Future commissions would be well advised to examine closely
the experiences of their predecessors to determine what lessons can
be gleaned about process.

What of the future?

The question naturally arises, have the accomplishments of the Minnesota experiment been worth the effort and, even if they have been, should efforts to implement the sentencing commission model continue?

I continue to believe that the sentencing commission model is the most encompassing of modern American sentencing innovations and that both the limitations of the Minnesota experience and the successes and failures elsewhere are opportunities for the future. However, the experience in Minnesota and elsewhere has clearly identified a formidable array of problems facing any jurisdiction considering creation of a sentencing commission.

A political process

The Minnesota staff and Commission have consistently claimed that one of their most important decisions was that their work should constitute an 'open political process' (Knapp, 1984, pp. 15–16). Washington State followed Minnesota's lead and has little difficulty in obtaining legislative approval for the guidelines that resulted from the process of extensive consultation with affected constituencies during the policy-making process. By contrast, the commissions in Maine, Pennsylvania, and South Carolina were much less successful at this. The New York State Commission was a battleground for conflicts between the affected constituency groups and, whether or not it tried to operate as 'an open political process', it foundered on the shoals of political opposition.

The moral of this experience is that jurisdictions establishing sentencing commissions in the future must give serious consideration both to the raw talents and the political acumen of the chairman particularly, but also other commissioners and the staff. A commission that lacks the ability to convert or co-opt foreseeable sources of opposition is unlikely to succeed.

Plea bargaining

Minnesota's was the first sentencing commission and its members and staff were not unaware of the vulnerability of guidelines to prosecutorial manipulation. A conscious policy decision was made, however, that, being the first jurisdiction to promulgate presumptive sentencing guidelines, it was premature to try to constrain prosecutorial discretion. While there is clear evidence of prosecutorial manipulation of Minnesota's guidelines, there has not been radical subversion. Moreover, mechanisms are available for addressing prosecutorial discretion. The Washington State legislature, for example, recognized this problem and directed its sentencing commission to promulgate statewide guidelines for prosecutorial charging and plea bargaining. Although the prosecutorial guidelines are relatively general, they are not meaningless, and subsequent jurisdictions can build on Washington State's effort. The US Sentencing Commission, for example, has expressly been given authority to promulgate guidelines governing judicial acceptance of plea bargains.

Guidelines for non-incarcerative sentences
There is no inherent reason why sentencing guidelines cannot bring greater principle and consistency to the use of sanctions other than imprisonment. The Washington State guidelines, for example, apply to both misdemeanour and felony sentencing and provide guidance on the use of incarcerative sentences in both state prison and local jails. In principle, there is no reason why guidelines eventually cannot create presumptions concerning various alternative sanctions, including fines, probation, and community service. The greater problem with such guidelines is that the United States has relatively little experience with the use of sanctions other than incarceration or nominal probation. Fines, community service, and other alternatives are as yet undeveloped in most American jurisdictions. The draughtsmen of the legislation creating the United States Sentencing Commission recognized the need for sentencing guidelines in respect of alternative sanctions and have authorised their development.

Conclusion

Most of the limitations to the Minnesota accomplishments that are clear on hindsight are soluble and have been, or will be, attacked by the Washington State or Federal Sentencing Commission.

Insofar as one believes, as I do, that the state should be as even-handed in dispensing suffering as it should be in dispensing benefits, there is much to be said for a sentencing system that appears capable of increasing the consistency of punishments suffered by offenders. Surely in England, as in America, values, attitudes, and opinions concerning crime and punishment vary between judges and inevitably the identity of the judge must often play a decisive role in determining sentences. One way to constrain the influence of judicial idiosyncrasy is through the mechanism of system-wide policies and standards to govern all sentences imposed. At least in the American context, the sentencing commission model is the most effective approach yet devised for establishment and enforcement of principled system-wide standards for sentence.

The Minnesota and Washington experiences show that sentencing commissions can develop meaningful jurisdiction-wide sentencing policies. Such policies have never heretofore existed in the United States. Such policies can be set and substantial compliance with them can be obtained, even when those policies substantially depart from prior practice and are likely to be resisted by practitioners and judges. From this perspective, the resistance from some prosecutors in Minnesota is a relatively minor set-back and should be seen as no more than an incentive for devising ways to overcome resistance.

A second major accomplishment of Minnesota's and Washington's guideline systems has been that they have, for the first time in the United States, made a reality of appellate sentence review. Informed only by the exiguous guidance of statutory provisions concerning minimum and maximum sentences, appellate judges in most states have lacked criteria for determining when sentences are inappropriate and have instead developed doctrines of extreme deference to the trial judge. Minnesota's and Washington's narrow guidelines, however, afford concrete norms which thereby make identification of suspect sentences especially easy. Minnesota's policy statements concerning approved and disapproved reasons for parting from guidelines provided a set of standards that appellate judges could interpret. As a consequence, the Minnesota Supreme Court, which decided more than 300 sentence appeals during the first four years of its use of guidelines (see Knapp, 1985), has taken a stance protective of the concept of guidelines, and has restated as binding case law several Commission policy decisions with which many trial judges disagreed (for example, that predictions of dangerousness should not serve as the basis for increased sentences; that sentence bargains should not serve as the basis of departures), and, finally, has created a set of case law standards governing the extent of increases of sentences for various cases in which the court held that departures were appropriate.

Washington's guidelines system has been in operation only since mid-1984 and insufficient time has elapsed for appellate case law to

develop. Minnesota is, therefore, the only American state that can
be said to have a common law of sentencing and, so long as the
guidelines persist, the sentencing case law can be expected to grow
and become increasingly complete. It is likely that the significance
of the appellate case law concerning the sentences will steadily increase
even if the importance of guidelines declines in future years.

A third major consequence of the Minnesota system has been the
establishment of monitoring and information systems designed to
assure compliance with the guidelines but available to inform both
official and public knowledge of the operations of the criminal justice
system. Because the Commission viewed reliable monitoring as a
crucial part of its work, in order that it be able to discover the extent
to which guidelines were complied with, and in what kinds of cases,
a detailed system was established for obtaining and maintaining
records of every case in which sentences were imposed. That system
is now well institutionalised and means that more is known about the
operations of the Minnesota criminal courts than ever before, thus
affording a sounder basis for informed policy-making in the future.

The work of the Minnesota Sentencing Guidelines Commission is
probably the most significant development in sentencing policy and
practice in the English-speaking world since the establishment of
parole boards half a century ago. It is no wonder that governmental
bodies in other English-speaking countries are seriously considering
the establishment of sentencing commissions in those countries. While
the experience in other American states demonstrates that successful
operation of the sentencing commission model is not easy, it is clear
from the Minnesota and Washington State experiences that it is not
impossible and that, when successful, the sentencing commission
model offers enormous promise for enhancing the quality and
consistency of justice delivered by the criminal courts.

Notes

1   Sentencing Reform Act 1984, The Comprehensive Crime Control Act
1984, S. 217, Public Law 98–473.
2   The United States has been experimenting with guidelines since the
pioneering work on parole guidelines was undertaken in the late 1960s by
Don M. Gottfredson and Leslie Wilkins. After Federal parole guidelines were
established in the early 1970s, experiments were conducted on 'voluntary
sentencing guidelines'. These were conspicuously ineffective (see Rich et al.,
1981), but their failure was perhaps a necessary first step toward recognition
of the promise of presumptive sentencing guidelines. Many experiments have
also been conducted with bail guidelines.

References

Blumstein, A., Cohen, J., Martin, S. E. and Tonry, M. (eds.) 1983) *Research on Sentencing: The Search for Reform*, Washington DC., National Academy Press.

Boerner, D. (1985) *Sentencing in Washington: A Legal Analysis of the Sentencing Reform Act of 1981*, Seattle, Butterworth.

Carrow, D. M. and Feins, J. D. (1983) *Evaluation of the Multijurisdictional Sentencing Guidelines Field Test: Volume 1*, Cambridge Mass., Abt Associates Inc.

Cohen, J. and Tonry, M. (1983) Sentencing Reforms and their Impacts. In Blumstein, A. *et al.*, *op. cit.*

Criminal Courts Technical Assistance Project (1980) *Overview of State and Local Sentencing Guidelines and Sentencing Research Activity*, Washington DC, American University Law Institute.

Frankel, M. (1972) *Criminal Sentences: Law Without Order*, New York, Hill and Wang.

Keeler, B. (1985) 'The debate over sentencing', *Newsday*, 16 June, Long Island, New York.

Knapp, K. (1984) *The Impact of the Minnesota Sentencing Guidelines Commission*, St Paul, Minnesota.

Knapp, K. (1985) *Minnesota Sentencing Guidelines and Commentary Annotated*, St Paul, Minnesota, Minnesota CLE Press.

Law Reform Commission (1980) *Sentencing of Federal Offenders*, Interim Report 15, Canberra, Australian Government Publishing Service.

Martin, S. E. (1983) 'The politics of sentencing reform: sentencing guidelines in Pennsylvania and Minnesota', in Blumstein, A. *et al.*, *op. cit.*

Phillips, H. J. (1984) *Final Report of the Maine Sentencing Guidelines Commission*. Submitted to the 111th Maine Legislature, Augusta, Maine.

Rich, W. D., Sutton, L. P., Cleer, T. R. and Saks, H. J. (1981) *Sentencing Guidelines: Their Operation and Impact on the Courts*, Williamsburg, National Centre for State Courts.

Rothman, D. J. (1980) *Conscience and Convenience: The Asylum and its Alternatives in Progressive America*, Boston, Little Brown.

Sentencing Guidelines Commission (1985) *Sentencing Practices under the Sentencing Reform Act: A Preliminary Report*, Olympia, Washington, Sentencing Guidelines Commission.

Shane-DuBow, S., Brown, A. P. and Olsen, E. (1985) *Sentencing Reform in the United States: History, Content and Effect*, Washington DC, National Institute of Justice, US Department of Justice, US Government Printing Office.

Wasik, M. (1985) 'Sentencing guidelines in America − are they working?' *Justice of the Peace*, 149, 584.

Guidance by numbers or words? Numerical versus narrative guidelines for sentencing[1]

How can the exercise of judicial sentencing discretion be guided and structured? In the last decade, a number of US states have been experimenting with control methods. Of these, the most discussed have been numerical sentencing guidelines, which prescribe definite quanta or ranges of punishments as the normally-indicated sanctions for various criminal acts. Minnesota, Washington, and Pennsylvania already have such guidelines.[2] The Federal judicial system is in process of developing them.[3] New York State has tried, and seemingly failed, to establish them.[4]

To most American scholars, numerical guidelines have been the technique *par excellence* for structuring a jurisdiction's sentencing policy. Particular guidelines in particular jurisdictions have been criticised, and some observers doubt the value of restricting sentencing discretion at all (e.g. Zimring, 1983). But *if* control of discretion is desired, and *if* the politics of the jurisdiction permit the writing of reasonable standards, it is seldom doubted that numerical guidelines are the preferred technique.

Is this necessarily so? Can guidance best be provided through detailed, numerical standards? The United States for years had enormous sentencing discretion with vast ranges of permitted punishment, no requirement that the judge give reasons for the sentence, and, usually, no appellate review. From such unregulated sanctioning, is it necessary to go to the other extreme of adopting numerical guidelines saying, e.g. that a convicted armed robber with two prior felony convictions should receive between say, thirty-eight and forty-four months confinement, except in specified circumstances? Are there not stopping points between unfettered discretion and such narrow constraints?

Certainly, there could be such stopping points, and they are being tried in some European countries. England relies upon appellate review: upon a case-law jurisprudence of sentencing, developed by one of its appellate courts. Finland and Sweden have been developing statutory statements of sentencing purpose, designed to shape and guide a sentencing jurisprudence. Perhaps it is worth comparing these different methods: to examine the relative merits of numerical and narrative forms of guidance. This is the topic of my essay.

Numerical sentencing guidelines

Let me begin with numerical sentencing guidelines. In the United States, a variety of different methods of controlling sentencing discretion have been tried. These include mandatory minimum sentences, extensively used in New York and several other states; legislatively prescribed presumptive-sentence schemes, such as California's; and paroling guidelines, such as Oregon's and that of the US Parole Commission (von Hirsch and Hanranan, 1981). What is commonly termed sentencing guidelines is yet another species of guidance, but one that has received more attention and favourable comment in the United States.

Numerical guidelines' main features
Numerical guidelines, typically, are prescribed by a rule-making body, known as a sentencing commission (first proposed by Frankel, 1972). The commission is authorised by statute to prescribe detailed norms that judges must follow unless they can give satisfactory reasons not to do so. Under the statute, the commission's guidelines become law either automatically after promulgation (in the absence of a legislative resolution of disapproval) or, alternatively, upon submission to and approval by the legislature. In either case, the commission has the responsibility for writing the standards, and is supposed to have enough leisure and insulation from political pressures to draft them with care, and to monitor their use in sentencing practice.

The commission establishes a sentencing grid: a two-dimensional table of prescribed sanctions. The vertical axis of the grid, or offence score, grades the seriousness of various species of criminal conduct. The horizontal axis, or offender score, typically grades the extent of the offender's prior criminal record. Across the grid is drawn a so-called dispositional line. Above the line are prescribed prison sanctions of varying duration, and below it are lesser sanctions. In each grid cell above the line, a narrow numerical range of imprisonment is prescribed: the grid cell applicable to convicted armed robbers having two prior felony convictions might, as I mentioned, have a cell range of thirty-eight to forty-four months in prison. The guidelines thus are both numerical and definite.

The range for any particular cell constitutes, however, only the *normally* applicable sentence. A sentencing court is authorised to deviate from the cell range on account of aggravating and mitigating circumstances. However, such deviations are to be invoked only in unusual situations, and the guidelines themselves may contain a suggested list of factors that qualify as extenuating or aggravating.

Once established, the guidelines system is enforced through appellate review. The higher courts hear sentence appeals, to determine compliance with the guidelines. In so doing, those courts develop a supplementary jurisprudence – on, for example, the interpretation of what constitutes aggravation or mitigation. The sentencing commission remains in existence to study patterns of implementation of the guidelines, and to note areas of difficulty. Frequent departures from the cell ranges for a particular type of case, for example, may suggest that the ranges themselves may need amendment. Through such 'feedback', the commission can alter and try to improve the guidelines over time.

Guidelines and the 'disparity' issue
It is often said that guidelines' primary purpose is to help cure 'disparity'. This leads to heated discussions about whether disparity is or is not endemic in a particular jurisdiction. The presence or absence of discernible patterns of sentences – of 'going rates' for various kinds of crime or criminals – is treated as indicative of how much 'disparity' there is. All this breeds confusion.

Disparity cannot be determined in a vacuum. It consists of differences in sentence that cannot be accounted for on the basis of the purpose one is seeking. Does it constitute disparity when unemployed offenders receive more severe sentences than employed ones? That depends upon the rationale. If the aim is to punish offenders as they deserve, an offender's employment status is not germane to the reprehensibleness of his conduct and therefore it *is* disparity. If, on the other hand, the aim is to sentence offenders according to their risk of recidivism, it is not necessarily disparity, because available studies suggest a link between joblessness and recidivism (see, e.g. Greenwood, 1982). In order to combat or even identify disparity, the first needed step is the specification of a rationale. Yet that is precisely what is missing in a discretionary sentencing system.

The existence of discernible sentencing patterns ('going rates') is, moreover, no guarantee of consistency. Without significant constraints on discretion, such patterns will merely be statistical norms. Individual decision-makers remain free to deviate from the 'going rate' without explanation. Most offenders may get the norm for that kind of crime or criminal, but some will be unlucky and get more, and others perhaps be too lucky and get considerably less. A consistent patterns requires control of deviating decisions.

Consistency is, also, no guarantee of the rationality or fairness of a system. Sentencing offenders invariably according to their height or weight would be consistent, but nevertheless irrational. What is needed is a *considered* judgment of what the basis of the sentence should be. After the prevailing sentencing patterns in a jurisdiction are examined, it needs to be determined whether those patterns should be continued, or whether the direction of sentencing policy should be changed. The critical tasks are to decide the direction of sentencing policy, and establish norms for sentences on the basis of that policy. Only then does a standard exist against which 'disparity' can be measured and judged.

What, then, are the functions of numerical guidelines? There are three: selecting a rationale, establishing a tariff, and controlling growth of prison populations. Let me examine each.

Choosing the rationale

The sentencing commission, in fashioning its guidelines, must choose a rationale. Should the system aim primarily at punishing offenders proportionately to the gravity of their offences? Or should it base sentences, instead, on the degree of risk offenders pose? Or should some other purpose predominate? This choice of rationale is critical, because it will determine what features of the offence or offender should be relied upon in determining the punishment. On a rationale emphasising proportionality and desert, the factor primarily to be relied upon is the seriousness of the offender's present crime (von Hirsch, 1986, Chs 7 & 11). On a predictive rationale, however, the primacy would shift to risk factors − chiefly the offender's previous record and his social and employment history (von Hirsch, 1986,

Chs 9 & 11). The commission does not have to choose one rationale to the exclusion of all others, but where a hybrid rationale is used, it is still necessary to decide which aim should receive most emphasis.

A sentencing commission is well situated to make this choice. Given its task of establishing a comprehensive sentencing policy, it can consider the rationale for the whole system. Because the commission has a professional research staff and has sentencing policy as its primary function, it can make the choice of aim in an *informed* fashion. When considering treatment or deterrence, the commission can inform itself of the limitations of present knowledge of treatment and deterrent effects. When considering incapacitation, it can examine prediction research to see how well we can forecast criminality, and where the empirical and ethical problems lie. When considering deserts, it can examine the recent literature on the subject, in order to understand this conception and see how it could be implemented (von Hirsch, 1986, Chs 3−12).

With the rationale selected, the commission is in a position to identify the factors chiefly to be relied upon, and the comparative emphasis these factors should receive. Choosing between deserts and prediction, for example, enables the commission to decide the relative weight to be given the current offence, as compared with the prior record and other information about the offender (von Hirsch, 1986, Ch. 11.

A striking illustration of this policy-making process is provided by Minnesota's Sentencing Commission. The Minnesota Commission studied judges' decisions about whether or not to impose a prison sentence. It found that, under previous judicial practice, the main determinant of an offender's going to prison was the length of his criminal record. An offender with a string of lesser felonies would be imprisoned, whereas a first offender with a considerably more serious offence would not. In other words, the dispositional line on the grid − the line separating prison from non-prison dispositions − would be steep (emphasising the criminal record), were past practice to be made the basis of the guidelines. The Commission then proceeded to decide whether or not this practice was desirable.

To make that decision, the Commission developed models comparing the slope of the dispositional line on two rationales: a deserts rationale, and an incapacitative one relying on prediction of risk. After consulting the literature on deserts and prediction, the Commission determined that a deserts rationale would have a relatively flat line, giving primary weight to the seriousness of the offence. A predictive rationale would (because of the link between previous record and recidivism) have a much steeper line, emphasising the prior record – as did the state's previous practice. With this in mind, the commission was able to debate the rationale. It decided that a more desert-oriented rationale was preferable, for a variety of reasons both of fairness and practicability. The Commission thereupon chose as its dispositional line one which, it asserted, reflected a 'modified' deserts conception; the line was flat for most cases, albeit steep for offenders with lengthy criminal histories. The result of this decision was a substantial change from prior policy. According to the grid, the seriousness of the offence is to be given considerably more importance than it had under the state's past practice, and the extent of the criminal history is to be given much less.

Having done so elsewhere, (von Hirsch, 1982) I shall not discuss here my judgment of the merits of the Minnesota Commission's particular solution for the slope of its dispositional line. What is of interest is the Commission's technique: of selecting the primary rationale for the sentencing system, and then using it to determine the structure of the guidelines.

Constructing the tariff
Once the system's rationale is chosen, and the offence or offender factors to be relied upon are identified, the laborious work begins, namely constructing the sentencing tariff. Different species of criminal conduct need to be graded according to their seriousness. Offenders' criminal records also need to be graded. Above all, the penalty scale needs to be fashioned: it must be decided how much punishment offenders typically should receive, given the seriousness of their crimes and the extent of their records. This is time-consuming work. Grading crimes' seriousness involves assessing the harm and culpability involved in a wide variety of criminal acts. Assigning penalties, or penalty ranges, to offences involves complex comparative judgments. The setting of sentencing policy is only as good as its resulting tariff. However sophisticated the rationale, the sentencing system becomes incoherent if it is not established how much various crimes typically are 'worth' or if the scaling is not done with the rationale seriously in mind. In numerical guidelines, the sentencing commission constructs the tariff, and it is embodied in the sentencing grid.

Controlling growth of prison populations

Many jurisdictions, both in North America and in Europe, have been experiencing sharp rises in prison populations. The result has been prison overcrowding, with its attendant evils of deteriorating living conditions and increased frictions among prisoners and between prisoners and guards. If crowding is serious and endemic to the system, the conventional palliatives offer little hope: emergency release, accelerated parole and similar stopgap measures are only short-term solutions and soon generate opposition, as involving the 'premature' release of undeserving or dangerous felons. New prison construction is costly, time-consuming and (if prison commitments continue unabated) creates space that itself soon will be filled. Crowding can be effectively prevented only by controlling the inflow into the prisons, and length of stay there.

How can inflow and length of stay be influenced? One way is through sentencing guidelines. Numerical guidelines can be written so as to achieve a stated aggregate level of imprisonment. Minnesota, again, provides the model. The Minnesota Sentencing Commission devised its guidelines so that, given constant conviction rates, the aggregate prison population would not exceed the capacity of the state's prisons. The Commission accomplished this by projecting the impact of its tentatively proposed guidelines on prison populations, comparing those projections with the rated capacity of the state's prison system and then making the appropriate adjustments to yield the final guidelines. (Minnesota's approach involves 'freezing' prison populations at existing levels. A variant of the technique might involve setting a population target that was either somewhat higher or some-what lower than existing institutional capacity. Then, as long as any authorised increase in commitments were not to take effect until the necessary space had been built, the guidelines still would perform the function of holding prison populations to a stated target level.)

The effectiveness of the Minnesota projection technique depends upon cell ranges that are fairly narrow, and departure rules that are fairly stringent. With wide ranges, it will be difficult or impossible to project actual sentence levels and hence the impact. Eventually, the Minnesota Commission's projections proved reasonably successful. Prison commitments have remained within available space, following a transition period where some adjustments had to be made (Knapp, 1984a), and the state is no longer experiencing the problem of uncontrolled prison-population increases it once had.

What, however, of the propriety of considering prison-space availability in the setting of sentencing policy? The question seems hardest to answer on a deserts rationale, since prison space seems not to have much bearing on the reprehensibleness of an offender's criminal deeds.

A deserts rationale is most stringent in the determination of *comparative* punishments (von Hirsch, 1986, Ch. 4). Equally reprehensible conduct merits equal punishment, and penalties should be scaled to reflect the gravity of crimes. These requirements would be infringed if prison space were used as a basis for imprisoning some armed robbers for shorter periods than others. Deserts, however, imposes less stringent requirements on the determination of the *overall* severity levels of a system. If one had a scheme of scaled punishments, and were to make modest *pro rata* increases or decreases in all penalties, while holding constant the internal proportions between the penalties, this still would leave one with a scheme of punishments commensurate with the gravity of crimes. Since a scale's aggregate severity levels are thus not determined wholly by deserts, it might well be proper to consider a jurisdiction's penal traditions and penal resources in deciding those levels (von Hirsch, 1986, Ch. 8). That is what Minnesota did. In deciding the aggregate quantum of imprisonment permissible under the guidelines, the Commission looked to the availability of prison resources. But in deciding *comparative* punishments – which crimes get more and which less – prison space is not a factor, and the decision rests chiefly on the seriousness of offenders' crimes (von Hirsch, 1982, pp. 179–81).

The limitations of numerical guidelines

What are the limitations of numerical sentencing guidelines? To answer that question, it might be helpful to examine some of the shortcomings of Minnesota's standards. The Minnesota Commission, as we have seen, did perform its most important functions: it drew the dispositional line on the grid with reference to an explicit rationale; and it did take prison populations into account in fashioning its standards. It is precisely the quality of the Minnesota Commission's efforts that make it worthwhile to see where it ran into difficulty – as that might suggest the limitations even of carefully-crafted guidelines.

The Minnesota guidelines have two significant anomalies. The first of these concerns the slope of the dispositional line in the right-hand portion of the grid, for offenders having lengthy criminal records. On the basis of the Commission's 'modified' desert rationale, the line should have sloped modestly downward, so that most repeat offenders convicted of lesser felonies would not have been imprisoned (von Hirsch, 1982, pp. 189–91). The Commission, however, decided to be quite severe here, and to prescribe imprisonment for most cells in the right-hand portion. The data available to the Commission suggested that there would be few offenders with high criminal history scores, so that the impact of imprisoning such offenders would be small. Taking a tough line with the minority of multiple recidivists seemed also to increase the political acceptability of the guidelines. The other anomaly concerned the scoring of the prior record. The general rule was that each prior felony conviction counted one point on the prior-record score that constitutes the guideline grid's horizontal axis. However, conviction on multiple counts was, under certain circumstances, treated as though each count was a separate felony with the result that the offender could, in a single sentencing proceeding, run up a considerable score through accumulation of counts.

Both these deficiencies have come back to haunt the Commission. Prosecutors in Minnesota have been 'building up' certain offenders' records by obtaining multiple convictions, thus pushing such cases more quickly toward the right-hand portion of the grid where imprisonment is prescribed for most cells. As a result, an increasing number of persons convicted of routine property crimes are being sent to prison, contrary to the Commission's original intent of reserving imprisonment chiefly for the more serious offences, i.e. those against the person (Knapp, 1984b).

These anomalies are remediable. By reducing the steepness of the dispositional line in the right-hand portion of the grid, and by changing the method of scoring multiple-count convictions, the Commission could reduce the rate of prison commitments for lesser felons. That, however, would require the commission to undertake the effort and political risks of making substantial changes in the guidelines and this it has so far been unwilling to do.

Numerical guidelines, as we saw in the previous discussion, require a commission to undertake *two* major tasks. The first of these is selecting and elaborating a rationale: establishing the system's primary aim to be, say, deserts or incapacitation, and then identifying the features of the offence or the offender that must principally be relied upon. The second is constructing the tariff: selecting the penalties normally to be imposed in various types of case. The danger in this process and one illustrated by Minnesota's just-mentioned difficulties is that construction of the tariff can, so to speak, overshadow the rationale. Filling in the numbers on the grid takes on a life of its own, and produces results inconsistent with the principles of sentencing supposedly chosen. The inconsistency can happen through inadvertence as was probably true of Minnesota's scoring scheme for multiple-count felonies. Or it can happen through efforts to make the grid seem politically more attractive, as was true with the slope of Minnesota's dispositional line in the grid's right-hand portion.

A sentencing commission writing numerical guidelines must produce, under considerable exposure to public and legislative scrutiny, a complete table of sentences. This puts the commission under pressure to produce an acceptable-looking set of numbers, and to treat this as its main task. Once the numbers have been selected and the guidelines have gone into effect, moreover, there are disincentives to making substantial changes in the absence of pressing practical problems, as amendments risk reopening debate over the guidelines as a whole. It is thus not surprising that the Minnesota Commission has changed its grid mainly where that has been necessary to prevent prison populations from rising above capacity.

Narrative sentencing guidelines

Principles instead of numbers

Might it not be better to separate the two functions? Perhaps the rule-maker should concentrate its efforts on its first mission, of determining the general direction of sentencing policy. Its standards would comprise a statement of sentencing principles. These principles would specify the primary rationale for sentencing, identify the features of the offender or offence chiefly to be relied upon in deciding sentence, and perhaps, provide broad policy guidance about when imprisonment is and is not a suitable sanction. The courts would then be called upon to evolve the details of the sentencing tariff, over time.

Let us imagine how a rule-maker might describe, in sentencing principles, the main policies purportedly embodied in the Minnesota guidelines. Instead of a grid, the standards would be in words. They might begin with a statement of purpose, to the general effect that sentences should be based upon and be fairly proportionate to, the seriousness of offenders' criminal conduct. Then might come an identification of primary factors. This might consist of a statement that the principal factor in sentencing should be the seriousness of the offender's current crime of conviction; and that previous convictions may be considered but must be given less weight than the current crime (von Hirsch, 1986, Chs 6–7). Finally might come general policy directives concerning use of imprisonment. These might say that imprisonment should ordinarily be imposed upon offenders convicted of serious crimes; that offenders with intermediate-level crimes should be imprisoned only if their criminal records are substantial; and that offenders with low-seriousness crimes should generally receive the more modest, non-prison sentences, irrespective of their records. A system of appellate review of sentences would be instituted, if not in existence already. The appellate court would be directed to decide appeals in accordance with these principles, and to develop over time a case-law jurisprudence to implement these principles further.

This approach might, conceivably, make it easier to avoid the difficulties Minnesota encountered. Because no table of numbers is presented, the politics might be less contentious. It should be easier to gain assent to the general proposition that lesser felons (even with long records) ought ordinarily not be imprisoned, than to defend a grid in which the car thief convicted for the thirtieth time never receives a prison sentence. In addition unintended consequences are more easily avoided. If prosecutors start obtaining multiple-count convictions to 'build up' offenders' records, these would not automatically turn into high criminal-history ratings. It would be easy enough for the appellate courts to decide according to the underlying principle: to insist that a long record means a record of truly repeated convictions, not merely an artefact of multiple-count counting.

Let us, then, examine whether existing or proposed law outside the United States provides any models for developing such sentencing principles.

The English 'principles' and their deficiencies

In a well-known book by that title, David Thomas asserts that the Court of Appeal, Criminal Division, has been developing principles of sentencing for use by English sentencing judges (Thomas, 1979). These 'principles' are developed by the Court of Appeal alone, with little or no outside policy guidance. Sentences are appealable by the defendant, and the Court of Appeal from time to time issues 'guideline' sentences that specify how a particular type of case should be sentenced.

The English sentence-review mechanism has some readily-apparent weaknesses. The Court of Appeal's opinions on sentencing were not in the past readily available to litigants, except as summarized in Mr Thomas' writings. One-sided appeal, by the defendant only, means that unwarrantedly lenient sentences cannot be appealed, and impedes the development of a case-law jurisprudence. It is not known to what extent trial courts and magistrates actually follow the Court of Appeal's opinions in unappealed cases, and the extent of such compliance or non-compliance has not been systematically measured (see Ashworth, 1984).

My objections to the English approach are more fundamental, however. The technique might help develop some kind of tariff with, say, imprisonment ordinarily recommended for this kind of case, probation for that kind. What is likely to be lacking, however, is any *principled* resolution of sentencing policy issues. Let me give an example. Martin Wasik has collected and examined all Court of Appeal cases concerning perjury (Wasik, 1986). The cases, considered together, furnish a kind of rule: it is that perjurers almost invariably should be imprisoned. What remains opaque, however, is the rationale. The Court's stated rationale is deterrence, but this brings a number of questions immediately to mind. Do we know enough about the magnitude of deterrent effects to say that routine imposition of imprisonment will deter perjury better than a more selective imprisonment policy would? Even a cursory examination of today's deterrence research suggests how limited is our ability to gauge the magnitude of deterrent effects (National Academy of Science report on deterrence research in Blumstein *et al.*, 1978), but the Court seemed unaware of such limitations in our knowledge. Perjury, moreover, is not the only crime we might wish to deter. Don't we also want to stop burglary and car theft and insurance fraud? Should those crimes also have their penalties decided on the basis of deterrence, and should they also routinely be punishable by imprisonment? Without serious inquiry into such issues, merely seizing upon deterrence (or, for that matter, dangerousness or treatment) tells us very little indeed.

My thoughts about perjury extend more broadly to the present English scheme. The Court of Appeal, according to Thomas (Thomas, 1979, pp. 14–15), has evolved an informal scale of penalties for various crimes, based on deterrence and allied notions; it then permits deviations from this 'tariff' on special-preventive grounds. Perhaps the English cases do reveal this pattern. My doubts concern whether the pattern was the result of any sustained critical analysis of what the direction of sentencing policy ought to be; and whether, however evolved, the pattern and its purported array of purposes are ones that readily could be defended in principle.

Could another jurisdiction do better with the English technique? Could an appellate court, that is, succeed in developing a tariff based on a carefully developed rationale? Conceivably, but there are impediments. The court is not likely to possess the requisite information. Sentencing is a somewhat arcane subject. Common-sense beliefs about deterrence or treatment or dangerousness are not necessarily correct; questions about fair distribution of penalties do not necessarily resolve themselves easily. This makes it essential for the policy-maker to be familiar both with the sentencing literature and with sentencing regulation in other jurisdictions. A sentencing commission is in a position to obtain this information: even if the members initially are not expert, they can obtain the assistance of a specialised staff and consultants. Appellate court judges, given the press of court business, are not likely to be or become particularly knowledgeable about the intricacies of sentencing theory and policy. The litigants, absorbed as they are in their particular case rather than in wider policy ramifications, are not likely to provide judges with much assistance.

More troublesome still is the question of perspective. Setting sentencing policy requires the taking of a comprehensive view: deciding what rationale should predominate, and comparing different types of crimes and of sanctions. A sentencing commission can take such a view because of the systematic nature of its task. An appellate court, however, deals serially with particular cases, arising in no predictable order. The incentive is to decide the particular case or type of case, rather than to examine the wider reasons underlying a comprehensive sentencing policy.

The reply sometimes heard to these objections is that case-by-case decision-making is, after all, the tried and tested way of the common law. This begs the question, however. No developed legal system, not even that of England, relies entirely on the common law. Some issues, such as income taxation, are dealt with by comprehensive legislation. Others, such as tort liability, remain primarily matters for the common law. Still others begin as common-law dominated, and then become an area of more systematic regulation, as has become true of commercial law in most US states since the Uniform Commercial Code. Such a mixture makes it appropriate to ask whether, for a particular field, policy can best be made by appellate courts alone, or by appellate courts interpreting more systematically devised rules or standards. I suggest that the latter approach is more appropriate to sentencing policy.

Where does that leave the appellate courts? On a true sentencing-principles approach, they would have a crucial role in developing the tariff. But they would do so pursuant to aims and general policy directives fashioned by explicit rule. To see examples of this, we need to turn to the Scandinavian countries.

Statutory statements of purpose: the Finnish model

Statutory statements of purpose have had a deservedly bad reputation. Customarily, they list several, potentially conflicting aims, thereby providing the appellate courts with little guidance. An example is section 46 of the German Penal Code. It is the product of two competing drafts, one of which emphasised proportionality and deserts, and the other special prevention. The two conflicting versions were combined to yield the following language:[5] 'The guilt of the offender shall be the basis of the measurement of sentence. However, the expected effect of the sentence on the future life and conduct of the actor is to be taken into account.'

The problem should be apparent. The first sentence appears to reflect a deserts philosophy, and focuses on the seriousness of the offender's criminal acts. The second is predictive and rehabilitative in emphasis. There is, notoriously, a tension between these concepts: the sentence that would be fairly commensurate with the gravity of the offender's criminal conduct is not necessarily the same as the sentence that optimally would forestall future offending on his part. The paragraph does not clearly indicate the relative priority that should be given these conflicting ideas. The German case law and doctrine on sentencing has suffered from these ambiguities.

Statutory statements of purpose are potentially useful, only if the stated principles are coherent and are not in potential conflict with one another. One aim must be chosen as primary, in order to give the appellate courts guidance in choosing between the conflicting aims of deserts, deterrence, incapacitation, or treatment.

One European country has adopted a reasonably coherent statement of sentencing purpose: Finland. In 1976 the Finnish Criminal Code was amended to add a new chapter 6, dealing with the choice of sentence. The most important provision of the chapter reads as follows:[6] 'The punishment shall be measured so that it is in just proportion to the damage and danger caused by the offence and to the guilt of the offender manifested in the offence.'

This provision does constitute a clear choice. The sentence is to be proportionate to the gravity of the crime. It also specifies the main factors that should be relied upon in deciding sentence: the harmfulness of the conduct and the culpability of the actor. Risk should be considered only in so far as it relates to the potential injuriousness of the conduct for which the offender is being sentenced. Risk of *future* misconduct by the defendant – the positivist's preferred criterion and the one mentioned in the German law – is, quite intentionally, omitted. If I am convicted of driving dangerously, the risk of injury I created through my act of bad driving is part of the harmfulness of the conduct that may properly be taken into account. Not included, however, would be the risk of recidivism: the danger that I might *again* decide to climb into my car and drive badly.

Other provisions of the Finnish Article 6 deal with aggravating and mitigating circumstances. Several of the listed factors concern special circumstances relating to harm or culpability,[7] and thus square with the general rationale of the law. Somewhat puzzling, however, is the provision relating to recidivism. It makes prior criminal record an aggravating factor if that record suggests that 'the offender is apparently heedless of the prohibitions of law'.[8] While a deserts rationale would permit limited weight to be given to the offender's record (von Hirsch, 1986, Ch. 7), it is not clear how much importance this provision permits the prior record to be given, or how the elusive quality of 'heedlessness' should be judged. The Finnish penologists with whom I have spoken regard this to be a weak point in the law.

How helpful is this Finnish statute? Empirical studies of its impact on sentencing practice are not yet available. On its face, however, it is a considerable improvement over the German law, for it at least suggests a general direction for sentencing policy. Courts, it suggests, should be making their sentencing judgments primarily in terms of the gravity of the criminal conduct, rather than on the basis of offenders' supposed treatability or dangerousness.

Nevertheless, the statute leaves much, perhaps too much, unspecified. The role of the prior criminal record is uncertain, as just mentioned. Little also is said on the crucial issue of the use of imprisonment . Should a large variety of crimes be punished by imprisonment, albeit with appropriately graded durations? Or should imprisonment be a sanction of last resort, reserved only for quite serious felonies? Perhaps narrative guidelines can give the courts guidance on such important matters, while still remaining principles rather than a table of numbers. To see how that might be done, it is worth examining legislation that is being proposed in Sweden.

A fuller statement of principles: The proposed Swedish law
The Swedish provisions, yet to be enacted, have been drafted by the Committee on Prison Sanctions (Fängelsestraffkommitèn), a government-appointed study commission that has been examining sentencing policy for some years. Its proposal is embodied in two proposed new chapters of the Penal Code, dealing with sentences.[9] Those chapters were drafted for the Committee by a consultative working party, which included several of the country's principal authorities on sentencing.

The basic idea is similar to the Finnish, emphasising punishments proportionate to the gravity of the criminal conduct. However, the provisions are more elaborate. The measurement of the punishment is to depend ordinarily on the 'penal value' of the actor's offence. Penal value, in turn, is determined by the harmfulness of the conduct and the 'guilt' (culpability) of the actor manifested in the offence. Imprisonment is to be invoked for crimes having high penal value. Offences of intermediate penal value are to be punished by imprisonment if the offender's previous criminal record is extensive, and otherwise by probation or conditional sentence. Crimes of lower penal value are punishable by fines.[10]

The proposed Swedish provisions give the courts more guidance than the Finnish law does, because the steps for determining the sentence are more clearly spelled out. First, the penal value – i.e., the seriousness – of the crime-category is to be determined, based upon the harmfulness and culpability that is typical for such conduct. Next, the penal value of the offender's particular criminal act is ascertained, by considering the presence and extent of any aggravating and mitigating factors – and these are defined in the statute in considerable detail.[11] Next comes the choice of type of sanction, which depends on whether the penal value thus ascertained is high, medium or low. The role of the prior criminal record is more clearly spelled out: its primary role is to decide between imprisonment and lesser sanctions for offences in the middle range of seriousness, and its effect on duration of confinement is supposed to be smaller. Treatment may be considered in the choice of sanction only under quite limited circumstances, which the statute spells out.[12]

Swedish law provides already for appellate review of sentences.[12] The proposed statute is designed to provide the appeals courts with guidance in their sentence-review decisions. The law would spell out the penal aims to be achieved, and offer a broad framework for deciding when imprisonment would and would not be the appropriate sanction. The tariff would then be evolved by the courts over time. The difference between this approach and the English is that the courts would not be working in a vacuum. They would receive guidance as to aims and the general shape of the sentencing structure, and the steps to be considered when a sentence is imposed. That would put them in a better position to decide how much punishment various kinds of crimes should normally receive.

Suppose, for example, that the issue were the one I touched upon already: the appropriate punishment for perjury. The Swedish courts would not need to select, as the English court had to, the purpose to be achieved: it would not be necessary to decide (on scant penological knowledge) whether one was seeking to deter perjurers, or treat them, or whatever. The statute would already have established the aim: the imposition of deserved, proportionate punishment. It would also supply the principal criterion for deciding the quantum of punishment, namely, the penal value of the offence. The court's job, therefore, would be to assess perjury's penal value. How much harm does perjury do or threaten? How culpable is the conduct? What grounds for mitigation might various kinds of perjurers have? Deciding this is concededly no easy task, but the court and the litigants would at least have the issues framed for them more clearly. There would be an incentive to begin to break down perjury into different types, and distinguish among their penal value. Since not all types of perjury would be likely to be rated high in penal value, not all would routinely receive sentences of imprisonment. The courts would retain their primary responsibility for deciding sentence severity, but now would have assistance in reasoning through such decisions. The drafters of the statute would be doing what rule-makers are well positioned to do: establishing aims and general policy directions for the system as a whole, for the courts then to implement in greater specificity.

Prerequisites for sentencing principles' success

The Swedish legislation is still only a proposal. It is too soon to know whether the government will give it sufficient support to secure enactment, or what its actual impact would be if enacted. Its value for the present discussion is as a model: whether or not it becomes law in Sweden, it represents an alternative to numerical guidelines for policy-makers to consider. The approach, however, is likely to work only where the following prerequisites are satisfied.

1. There needs to be a sufficiently skilled body to draft the standards. Drafting sentencing principles is as exacting work as devising numerical guidelines. True, one need not undertake the time-consuming task of filling in the details of the tariff. But that makes it necessary, all the more, to state the intended policies with care. If deserts is selected as the primary rationale, this cannot be expressed merely by drawing a flat or flattish dispositional line on a grid; one needs to state the principle of proportionate sanctions, and its criteria for application, with reasonable precision.[14] The drafting body thus needs to have time and the expertise comparable to those possessed by a sentencing commission. The proposed Swedish standards are in statutory form, and call for eventual parliamentary enactment. The process of drafting the standards, however, was not unlike a sentencing commission's process. The work was done over a considerable period of time by a study commission specially organised for the purpose, and aided by a working group of penologists who were familiar with the sentencing literature and with sentencing reform in other jurisdictions. The more routine methods of drafting legislation, e.g. a bill written in a ministry, would have yielded much less satisfactory results.

2. The sentencing-principles approach demands more from the appellate courts. With numerical guidelines, the articulation of policy and construction of the tariff is the task of the commission. The appellate courts' primary role is that of making sure that trial courts ordinarily impose the penalties prescribed in the grid. Adoption of sentencing principles, instead of numerical guidelines, increases the courts' responsibility, since the standards merely point the direction of sentencing policy. The tariff-constructing work, of determining the seriousness of various crimes and their resulting punishments, is

left to the courts. The courts need the competence and the willingness
to undertake this work. The proposed Swedish statement of principles
will, it is true, provide the courts with considerable assistance: it
indicates not only the rationale, but the faint outlines of the tariff
(through the recommendations concerning types of dispositions for
crimes with high, medium, and low penal value). This, however, still
leaves the judiciary with much of the labour, and means that the
opportunity for failure – for ignoring the stated rationale or for
simply not developing any real tariff at all – is considerable.

This issue is illustrated by an episode from Minnesota. That state
has numerical standards, and the state Supreme Court has had some
degree of success in enforcing those standards. It has been insistent
on compliance with the numerical guidelines, and has shown no
hesitation in reversing non-complying lower court decisions. There
is, however, one area where the court's function is closer to that of
implementing sentencing principles. This concerns aggravation and
mitigation. The guidelines provide a non-exclusive list of aggravating
and mitigating circumstances,[15] thus leaving it to the court to decide
what other circumstances of extenuation or exacerbation might be
grounds for departing from the grid ranges. The circumstances listed
in the guidelines chiefly are deserts-related, and concern special
situations of increased or reduced harmfulness or culpability (von
Hirsch, 1982, pp. 205–7). Given the character of the listed circumstances, and the guidelines' stated overall purpose, it would be reasonable to expect any unlisted factors to relate also to the offender's
blameworthiness in a broad sense. Nevertheless, the Supreme Court
decided that 'amenability' or 'unamenability' to probation qualifies
as grounds for departure from the grid's prescriptions on whether or
not to imprison (*State* v *Hagen* (1982), *State* v *King* (1983)). Whatever 'amenability to probation' may mean (and I do not understand
its precise meaning), it is plainly rehabilitative or predictive in
character, and has no visible bearing on the offender's degree of
blameworthiness. This factor has since been used by lower courts to
reduce sentences for persons convicted of crimes against the person.
Its use, according to a recent staff report (Knapp, 1984a, Knapp,
1984b) has been making it harder to achieve the guidelines' original
intent of shifting the use of imprisonment to those convicted for
serious crimes. To remedy the problem, the sentencing commission
would probably need to intervene to amend its definition of aggravation and mitigation. What this suggests, however, it how much

more difficult it is to interpret and extend a stated rationale, than to enforce a table of sanctions.

Could the appellate courts, under a sentencing-principles approach, be provided with a source for advice? Although not included in the proposed Swedish law, a system of technical assistance may well be useful. An advisory commission or bureau could be created, with a small permanent staff. This body would provide aid to the appellate courts in the form of advisory guidelines and opinions on selected issues. It could, for example, develop suggested rankings of seriousness of crimes. Interpreting the statutory principles and developing the tariff would remain the courts' responsibility, but they would have somewhere to turn to for expert help.

3. Sentencing principles also require responsive lower courts. The sentencing principles and the case law interpreting those principles will not have sharp edges: instead of saying things like 'thirty-eight to forty-four months', they will state the recommended dispositions in more qualitative terms. While this provides advantages of flexibility, it requires co-operative sentencing judges: ones who are willing to be guided by a light rein. In some jurisdictions, certainly some in the United States, such a tradition of judicial 'legalism' is weak or non-existent. Trial judges are inclined to follow their own practice, and appellate courts are reluctant to reverse save for clear error. Here, numerical guidelines can provide more authoritative guidance. The normal range for a given grid cell is clearly specified as X to Y months; and grounds for permitted deviation can be stated with considerable specificity. The trial judge is given to understand that he *must* sentence within the grid range, or else come forward with permissible reasons for departure, or face reversal.

Sentencing principles, therefore, are not simply a middle way – a compromise between breadth of unregulated discretion and the specificity of numerical sentencing guidelines. It is a mistake to suppose that if there is too much resistance to numerical guidelines to permit their enactment statutory principles will necessarily be a workable alternative. Sentencing principles are potentially useful only in a certain kind of environment: one in which there is considerable judicial support for regulating and guiding sentencing discretion, but a flexible instrument for guidance is being sought. In less propitious environments, the choice may be the more stark one between poorly-regulated sentencing discretion and the more forceful modes of intervention that numerical guidelines represent.

4. Sentencing principles are not as suited as numerical guidelines to addressing the problem of prison overcrowding. The reason should be evident: the greater open-endedness of the sentencing principles approach. The impact on use and duration of confinement will only become apparent over time, as the courts use the principles to develop the tariff. Numerical guidelines, with narrow cell ranges, allow impact on populations to be projected, and are more amenable to being drafted with population targets in mind.

Most jurisdictions with which I am familiar face some over-crowding problems, either now or in the foreseeable future. However, the extent of the problem varies. In some places, population pressures are comparably modest, and/or can be alleviated by identifiable policy changes. In Sweden, for example, some penologists are beginning to advocate changing the practice of imprisoning most drivers who drink, in part because these cases now occupy so large a portion of prison facilities. There, sentencing principles might prove quite helpful, by providing guidance about when drinking-and-driving cases should receive a sentence of confinement and when not.

In other jurisdictions, however, crowding is persistent and virulent. Here, standards that can be devised with definite population targets in mind may become a necessity. Concerns about prison costs, more-over, may be the one available political antidote to the 'lock-em-up' sentiment that motivates high commitment rates (von Hirsch, 1982, pp. 176–80). As crowding thus comes to occupy the more central role in sentencing policy, numerical guidelines may be the necessary response.

Conclusions

In this essay, I have suggested that guiding sentencing discretion requires, above all, a *considered* choice of sentencing aims and policy, and a technique for developing a sentencing tariff which is consistent with those aims and policy. I have suggested two methods by which this might be accomplished – numerical guidelines and narrative sentencing principles – and have compared their advantages and their requirements for success. Which is preferable is not something for which a uniform answer can be given. The sentencing-principles approach might have potential for Sweden; but Minnesota, with its different problems and traditions, perhaps did wisely to opt for numerical guidelines instead. What I hope I have accomplished in this essay is to describe some issues which policy-makers should consider in choosing between these approaches.

I do not think myself sufficiently expert in English sentencing law and practice to make any confident proposals for England. I do remain sceptical of having the Court of Appeal virtually the sole arbiter of sentencing jurisprudence: purely court-developed 'principles' have not yielded and are not likely to yield a thought-through policy. Some form of explicit, systematic policy guidance is needed. Should this take the form of Swedish-style sentencing principles or Minnesota-style numerical guidelines? *Ceteris paribus*, my preference (for reasons explained already) would be for the more flexible proposed Swedish approach: of having the rationale and overall policy direction articulated through explicitly-stated principles, and then allowing the appellate courts to implement that rationale and policy in a case-law jurisprudence. (Naturally, one should not just import the Swedish principles, but fashion a comparable set of principles that are responsive to English requirements.) That approach, however, requires the active co-operation and support of the courts. How likely that co-operation is to be forthcoming I do not know. If it is not, more drastic intrusions into judicial sentencing discretion may become a regrettable necessity.

Notes

1   I am indebted to my colleagues Andrew Ashworth, Kay Knapp, Michael Tonry, Doug Victor and Martin Wasik for their helpful comments on this chapter.

2   Minnesota Sentencing Guidelines and Commentary (1985), Washington Sentencing Guidelines (1982), Pennsylvania Sentencing Guidelines (1982).

3   The Federal Sentencing Commission was established by law in 1984. Its members were appointed in early autumn 1985.

4   New York State Committee on Sentencing Guidelines, *Determinate Sentencing: Report and Recommendations* (1985). The proposed guidelines require legislative approval, which now does not seem likely to be obtained.

5   German Penal code, s.46.

6   Penal Code of Finland, Art.6, s.I.

7   The listed mitigating factors include (1) partial duress or pressure when committing offence, (2) reduced mental capacity or 'exceptional temptation' or 'strong human sympathy leading to the offence', and (3) voluntary attempts to alleviate the effect of the offence. Penal Code of Finland, Art.6, s.3.

8   Penal Code of Finland, Art 6, s. 2(4).

9   The Committee's report embodying these proposals will be published in the spring of 1986.

10   This is a somewhat simplified account of the Swedish proposals. The rationale is embodied in a proposed Chapter 33 of the Swedish Penal Code and governs the choice between Sweden's two traditional sentences – imprisonment and fines. The tri-partite scheme of penalties described in the text is set forth in a proposed Chapter 34, dealing with the circumstances under which conditional sentences or probation may be substituted for imprisonment.

11   Proposed Chapter 33.

12   Proposed Chapter 40.

13   Unlike England, Sweden permits prosecutorial appeals.

14   The drafting body could use grids for heuristic purposes in the course of developing the rationale. The grid would not be part of the final product, however.

15   Minnesota Sentencing Guidelines and Commentary, s. II(D)(2).

References

Ashworth, A. J. (1984) 'Techniques of guidance on sentencing', *Criminal Law Review*, 519.

Blumstein, A., Cohen, J. and Nagin, J. (eds.) (1978) *Deterrence and Incapacitation: Estimating the Effects of Criminal Sanction on Crime Rates*, Washington DC, National Academy of Sciences.

Frankel, M. (1972) *Criminal Sentences: Law without Order*, New York, Hill and Wang.

Greenwood, P. and Abrahams, A. (1982) *Selective Incapacitation*, Santa Monica, Rand.

Knapp, K. (1984a) *The Impact of the Minnesota Sentencing Guidelines: Three Year Evaluation*, St Paul, Minnesota, Minnesota Sentencing Guidelines Commission.

Knapp, K. (1984b) 'What sentencing reform in Minnesota has and has not accomplished', *Judicature*, 68, 181.

Thomas, D. A. (1979) *Principles of Sentencing*, (2nd ed.), London, Heinemann.

Tonry, M. and Zimring, F., (eds.) (1983) *Reform and Punishment: Essays on Criminal Sentencing*, University of Chicago Press.

von Hirsch, A. and Hanrahan, K. (1981) 'Determinate penalty systems in America: an overview', *Crime and Delinquency*, 27, 289.

von Hirsch, A. (1982) 'Constructing guidelines for sentencing: the critical choices for the Minnesota Sentencing Commission', *Hamline Law Review*, 5, 164.

von Hirsch, A. (1986) *Past or Future Crimes: Dangerousness and Deservedness in the Sentencing of Criminals*, Manchester University Press.

Wasik, M. (1986) 'Some aspects of sentencing in perjury cases in England', *Anglo-American Law Review*, forthcoming.

Zimring, F. (1983) 'Sentencing Reform in the States: Lessons from the 1970s', in Tonry, M. and Zimring, F. *op. cit.*

Cases

State v *Hagen*, 317. N.W. 2d. 701 (Minn. 1982).
State v *King*, 337. N.W. 2d. 674 (Minn. 1983).

5 Brian Harris

Sentencing guidance in the magistrates' courts

In the early days of any judicial system the sentencing of offenders is, within only the crudest of limitations, a matter solely at the discretion, or even whim, of the individual sentencer. It is only as a system matures that machinery comes into being to correct the excesses of idiosyncracy. In this country the machinery came late with the setting up in 1907 of the Court of Criminal Appeal. No similar reform was undertaken in the United States which has in consequence been driven in recent years to various schemes designed to restrict the discretion of sentencers. Criticisms of judicial inconsistency have not been nearly so prevalent this side of the Atlantic, except possibly in relation to magistrates' courts which are the subject of this paper.

In a survey of magistrates' sentencing practice nearly six years ago, Roger Tarling concluded that, while they were internally self-consistent, 'differences between [magistrates'] courts in their use of the various disposals available cannot be accounted for wholly in terms of differences in intake and other external factors and that courts do have very different ways of dealing with similar types of offender' (Tarling, 1979).

The overwhelming majority of indictable offences are triable in the magistrates' courts or the Crown Court according to a complex mode of trial procedure involving decisions on the part of the prosecution, the defence and the magistrates. There is no reason in theory why a convicted person should be treated differently (otherwise than in costs) according to whether he is tried by the Crown Court or the magistrates' court. And yet one informal survey suggests that when dealing with offences of similar severity the Crown Court passes a prison sentence five times more frequently than magistrates' courts and for three times as long (Justices' Clerks Society, 1982). Support for this view can be found almost daily in the decisions of the Court of Appeal. Take for example the leading case of *Upton* (1980) which laid down the need for shorter sentences in the Crown Court. If conscientiously followed by magistrates this decision would lead to a greatly increased use of imprisonment for petty theft.

I am not concerned here with whether the Crown Court or the magistrates' courts' practice is to be preferred, merely to point out that both cannot be right. Before embarking on a discussion of the forms of sentencing guidance therefore we should remember that there is always the antecedent problem of deciding what guidance should be given.

I would like to begin by drawing a distinction between sources of guidance on the one hand and channels, or media, of guidance on the other. The main sources of guidance are statute and decisions of the Court of Appeal, although the views of judges out of court, government ministers, criminologists and others are also treated with respect. According to this terminology a probation officer may be a source of guidance, not of course as to the law, but concerning the likely reaction of the offender to different forms of sentence.

The *sources* of law are the same therefore in the Crown Court and the magistrates' courts. The *channels* of guidance however are different. The judge in the Crown Court learns his law from statute or the law reports. The lay justice receives it through the mediation of his clerk. How the system works in theory can be discovered from any text book. My intention here is to examine, first, the limitations of the theory and, secondly, the extent to which practice falls short of theory. I begin with statute.

For a long time now courts have been forbidden to use custodial sentences on first offenders and young offenders unless, in the words of the rubric, 'no other method is appropriate' (Powers of Criminal Courts Act 1973, s.20(1), Criminal Justice Act 1982, s.1(4)). This phrase is pregnant with ambiguity: are the alternatives to be inappropriate to the offender or to his offence? Magistrates are required to give their reasons why 'no other method is appropriate'. In practice they deal with this requirement (if they remember it at all) by some formula such as 'the gravity of the offence'. The Court of Appeal collude in this downgrading of statutory provisions by regarding these restrictions as no more than a duty to think twice before passing a custodial sentence (*Vassal* v *Harris* (1964), *Morris* v *Crown Office* (1970)). Certainly, they seldom figure prominently in speeches in mitigation and their effectiveness as an influence on decision making must be questioned.

Parliament sometimes prescribes more positive criteria for the use of sentences. Thus, it has long been the rule that a probation order may only be made where the court 'is of opinion that having regard to the circumstances, including the nature of the offence and the character of the offender, it is expedient to do so' (Powers of Criminal Courts Act 1973, s. 2(1)). Whether that offers the sentencer any useful guidance at all may be doubted. I have never heard it argued in court and I cannot trace any decided cases on this formula. There is a similar invocation in regard to the use of absolute and conditional discharge, but with the rather more particular injunction that it must be 'inexpedient to inflict punishment', a phrase which fell for judicial consideration (for the first time to my knowledge) only recently when it was held to prevent the combination of a deprivation of property order and a discharge (*Savage* (1984)).

By far the most ambitious venture in this area was the enactment at short notice and with no real discussion of section 1(4) of the Criminal Justice Act 1982. Before passing a custodial sentence on a young offender the court must be of opinion that no other method of dealing with him is appropriate because it appears that one or other of three circumstances obtains. Two of these criteria are unexceptionable (although their scope is far from clear). The third, which allows the use of a custodial sentence when the offender is 'unable or unwilling to respond to non-custodial penalties', could easily be understood as confirming the widely held misapprehension that an offender may be sentenced 'on his record'. If it is being operated in that way then the effect of the legislation could be the exact opposite of what was intended. Most worrying however is the impression that subsection (4) has very little impact on court decisions. This cannot be the fault of the statute: its terms are mandatory. Yet it is seldom referred to in court by the defence advocate. Where a magistrates' court (but not the Crown Court) passes a youth custody sentence or makes a detention centre order it must not only identify in open court the relevant exception but also (according to my reading of this provision) give the reason for its opinion that the exception applies. My impression of this, as of most other reason-giving provisions, is that magistrates, who take the utmost care before deciding on a custodial sentence, consult the statutory criteria only after they have taken the decision. Reminded by their clerk about the Act, they select the exception which they consider least incompatible with their view. I would make an honourable exception of the criteria for refusing bail which are set out in some detail in the Schedule to the Bail Act. They were devised with care by a working party and, whatever their demerits, are at least the subject of conscientious court room deliberation.

Another example of 'criteria guidance' in sentencing is section 22(2) of the Powers of Criminal Courts Act 1973 which prohibits use of a suspended sentence 'unless the case appears to the court to be one in which a sentence of imprisonment would have been appropriate in the absence of any power to suspend such a sentence'. This did not appear in the original legislation but had to be inserted following the decision in *O'Keefe* (1969). It was a bold attempt to do away with the commonest abuse of the suspended sentence, but although it is widely emphasised in the training of magistrates I am far from convinced that it is always complied with. The wording of the sub-section cannot be faulted: the problem lies in the alluring nature of the suspended sentence (Bottoms, 1981) and I for one am convinced that a restriction on the use of this sentence perhaps by way of a 'guideline' judgment from the Court of Appeal would significantly reduce the prison population.

Deferment of sentence is another power the use of which Parliament sought to define by metes and bounds, but the attempt led to so many difficulties that only recently it had to be the subject of a salvage operation from the Court of Appeal (*George* (1984)).

To summarize, while the practice is well established of erecting statutory barriers against unwise sentencing decisions or statutory criteria for the use of various sentences or orders, we have virtually no knowledge about how courts in general or magistrates in particular respond to these verbal formulae. If legal attitudes are anything to go by however they do not seem to be terribly effective in securing their objectives. This may be because they are badly drafted and do not address themselves to the really critical court room decisions. It may be because of lack of interest in the legal profession towards sentencing law or it may be due to inherent weaknesses in the powers available to the courts or the philosophy for their use. The subject deserves further study.

One of the ornaments of the criminal process this side of the Atlantic is the appellate system. The Court of Appeal has done much, particularly in recent years, to create a coherent approach to the sentencing of offenders in the Crown Court. However, because appeals from the magistrates' courts are by way of rehearing and the case presented on appeal may consist of facts very different from those in the magistrates' court the Crown Court is not in a position, even if its decisions had a binding force which they do not possess, to review the conduct of the magistrates' court or offer it the same sort of principled guidance which the Court of Appeal gives to the Crown Court. It is true that the liaison judge appointed by the Lord Chancellor in each area offers his advice unstintingly to magistrates on a wide variety of matters including sentencing, but, as might be expected, his influence depends very much on his individual character and interests.

The task of reading the criminal appeal judgments with a view to extracting those pieces of advice and interpretation which are of equal application to magistrates' courts as to the Crown Court for which they were conceived is by no means easy. To take only one example, from time to time the Court has to remind sentencers of the prevalence and seriousness of social security frauds and the need for deterrent sentences. That is no doubt true of the typical Crown Court case, but applied literally to the little old lady in the magistrates' court who has succeeded in getting the Ministry to part with a few more pounds than she is entitled to, the results could be disastrous. These criticisms cannot be levelled at the recent 'guideline' judgments reviewing wide areas of sentencing practice in such matters as deferment of sentence (*George* (1984)), partly suspended sentences (*Clarke* (1983)), reckless driving (*Boswell* (1984)), obscene material (*Holloway* (1982); *Cohen* (1982)) and drugs (*Aramah* (1983)) offences. For all the criticism levelled at them the guideline judgments are proving helpful in guiding the decisions of magistrates. The reason for this in my view is that they proceed by way of examples, coupled with statements of broad principle. As a justices' clerk I find that a most helpful way of advising magistrates without trespassing on their proper function in the individual case.

Possibly the piece of sentencing advice most extensively used in the magistrates' courts is the Magistrates' Association's Suggestions for Traffic Offence Penalties, which is 'approved in principle by the Lord Chancellor and the Lord Chief Justice'. The case for such a document is overwhelming, but its success in promoting consistency of approach between benches is only partial (Tarling, 1979) and many of us would criticise magistrates for following it too slavishly.

The Assocation's attempt to promote similar thinking points for compensation for personal injury has been less than a success. They also had a stab at defining the classes of case for which a custodial sentence should be reserved (Magistrates' Association, 1980). It was not a well thought out statement and has happily been lost in oblivion. The excellent Home Office booklet 'The Sentence of the Court' (now in the course of revision) (Home Office, 1978) is given to all new magistrates on appointment, but is far too detailed for this purpose. No new measure is enacted by Parliament without the courts receiving from the Home Office an extensive commentary which frequently deals with its intended purpose and offers advice as to its use.

Once again, these documents are not written in terms suitable for the lay justice. It must be conceded that to write a sentencing treatise in terms suitable for the 20,000 odd magistrates would be a daunting task, but even if it were possible my experience is that literature is not the best medium with which to guide them.

The Home Secretary with his responsibility for sentencing law has not been afraid to urge upon sentencers, particularly magistrates, his department's views on how sentencing measures should be used. This can be very helpful but is not always successful or even well judged. His attempt to limit the use of detention centres to the places available generated a certain amount of resentment. More recently, in its statement 'Priorities for the Probation Service', the Home Office asserts that the provision of social enquiry reports should be concentrated, *inter alia*, where the court may be prepared to 'divert an offender from what would otherwise be a custodial sentence'. It suggests that the first priority in the allocation of resources 'should be to ensure that wherever possible offenders can be dealt with by non-custodial measures ...' It is well known that there is a high degree of congruity between probation officer's recommendations and court disposition, but the ability of probation officers to influence custodial sentencing is far from clear (Thorpe, 1979).

Perhaps the boldest experiment in administrative intervention was the Hampshire project (Smith et. al., 1984). In 1981 a research project was set up by the Home Office 'to ascertain how far alternatives to custody were available, how far they were used and how, if at all, they could be made more useful to sentencers; to consider with participants in the criminal justice process in Hampshire how information about the relevant services might be improved and to what effect, and to explore how far, if at all, there might be other courses available for reducing the extent to which imprisonment might be used'. This interesting piece of action research was geared to the single goal of seeing whether the use made of custody in the county could be reduced in any practicable way. Despite a great deal of work involving the co-operation of local judges, magistrates, justices' clerks, probation officers and police, there was found at the end of the project to be very little change in the sentencing practices of magistrates' courts. There was a measurable reduction of custody use in the Crown Court which the researchers were pleased to assume might be attributable to their efforts. They were forced to concede however that it was unlikely to be capable of replication throughout the country.

In court the magistrate is entitled to call upon the assistance of the probation service (and to a lesser extent the social services department of the local authority) for 'investigations and reports into the character and background of an offender' (Powers of Criminal Courts Act 1973, sch. 3, para. 8.1). I hope that I need not remind any reader of this Chapter of the crucial role of the social inquiry report in the criminal courts of this country. As a result, the obtaining of a report before sentence has recently been required increasingly by statute (Powers of Criminal Courts Act 1973, s. 14(2) and 20A(1); Criminal Justice Act 1982, s. 2(2)). A few years ago the Secretary of State and the then Lord Chief Justice, Lord Widgery, agreed that if an experienced probation officer feels able to make a specific recommendation in favour of (or against) any particular form of decision being reached he should state it clearly in his report (Home Office 1974; and see Home Office, 1983). The probation officer is no more competent than the magistrates to evaluate certain aspects of the sentencing decision, such as the need for punishment or deterrence, yet the official qualification, that recommendations should be confined to the offender's 'treatment needs' is often overlooked by all concerned. This sometimes results in recommendations which are untenable and in criticisms of the probation service which are unjustified (Harris, 1979). To give merely one example: I have frequently seen recommendations in probation reports that an offender should be given a suspended sentence 'because he could benefit from having something hanging over his head'.

More serious criticism came a few years ago from Home Office Research Study No. 48 which concluded that probation reports are not objective documents but rather statements of selected facts which tend to put the defendant in the best possible light (Thorpe, 1979). Information was found to be suppressed because it was thought to be 'too negative' or 'too damaging' to the recommendations. As Philip Bean (1975) wrote, 'the increasing use of probation officers and social inquiry reports has never been linked to any evidence proving that the reports they present are of value — defined in whatever terms one could want'.

Until recently a valued feature of the probation officer — which marked him off from the local authority social services officer — was the fact that he gave the court his own unaided opinion of the offender and not a departmental view or the result of a case conference. More latterly however it has been alleged that some chief probation officers have put pressure on their probation officers never to recommend a custodial sentence in any form. Such an attitude may just be defensible if one takes the view that a custodial sentence can never be relevant to an offender's 'treatment needs', but there is a lurking suspicion that it derives from the existence of a bureaucratic structure which allows the possibility of a single viewpoint being imposed on the professional judgment of a diverse group of professional people.

A concerted pressure from the probation service seems to have had at least one other tangible result. Despite the fact that the Wootton Committee (A.C.P.S., 1970) specifically rejected the notion that community service should be confined to cases where the offender would otherwise have gone to prison (a notion nowhere to be found in the legislation) government ministers enthusiastically promoted this view in Parliament and outside. In many areas of the country probation committees (which run the community service scheme) have been hijacked by the local probation service into adopting this quite erroneous view of the law which has in turn been pressed on local magistrates. The problem is a practical one because upon default in performance of a community serivce order an offender appearing before a bench advocating this view can normally expect to be committed to prison despite the fact that the bench which sentenced him would not have passed a prison sentence had community service not been available.

We must not of course criticise probation officers for not being trained in legal matters. A similar excuse is not available to lawyers.

Despite the fact that most of the statutory restrictions on the unnecessary use of custodial sentences can work to the advantage of the defence it is rare to hear them mentioned, let alone argued in court.

Sometimes this may be due to a natural reluctance to mention limitations on a sanction which the bench might not until that moment have considered. (Lay justices do not have the same facility as a stipendiary to indicate to the advocate the direction in which their minds are going.) Experience suggests however that professional unconcern with sentencing law may be due as much to ignorance as to tactics.

Effectively, therefore, the magistrates' sole mediator of law and guidance on sentencing is his clerk. In each county there is a training officer, usually a justices' clerk, responsible to the magistrates' courts committee for the compulsory and voluntary training of magistrates. Each clerk to the justices is responsible for ensuring that his bench is alive to the current state of the law. In court each bench is clerked by a member of the justices' clerk's staff who is either a lawyer or otherwise qualified under rules of court. The clerk may, in the words of the Practice Direction, 'advise the justices generally on the range of penalties which the law allows them to impose and on any guidance relevant to the choice of penalty provided by the law, the decisions of the superior courts or other authorities'. Some of the credit and most of the blame for the sentencing practice of magistrates' courts may therefore be laid at the feet of this single individual. It would be a fair criticism to say that until relatively recent times there were many justices' clerks who took the view that 'there is no law in sentencing', even that it was no part of their function. That view is no longer tenable and I would like to think that it is no longer held.

Parliament, and even the judges, still maintain the fiction that magistrates know the statutory provisions, read the judgments and consult the official literature. The reality is very different. A few interested magistrates may be aware of the existence of such matters but the detailed understanding and application of sentencing principles is available to them in practice only through their clerk. It cannot be emphasised too strongly that without the clerk the whole corpus of sentencing law and practice might just as well not exist so far as the magistracy is concerned. While literature and training have a place[1] it is in court where advice and guidance are really needed. But in carrying out his duties in this area the clerk is under a substantial disability. The Practice Direction now allows the clerk in court to advise on all aspects of sentencing except of course what sentence should be imposed in the actual case. His scope for taking the initiative in offering advice and the circumstances in which he has to act however are not conducive to good advice giving.

The problem is that in this area the clerk is not required to give his advice in open court unless the magistrates take the initiative in seeking it. Now, there is a lot to be said for the clerk giving advice in open court, but the problem with sentencing is that at the stage when this can be done he does not know how seriously the bench view the offence or what weight they are disposed to give to the mitigation: in other words to offer any useful advice without imposing his own view of the case the clerk may have to span the whole range of penalties, a daunting and pointless task. The difficulty with relying on the magistrates to take the initiative is that, with the best will in the world, they do not know when they do not know something. Furthermore, most sentencing advice is, in the jargon phrase, a question of mixed law and fact in which the clerk needs to take the bench's instructions as to their detailed wishes, remind them of the appropriate guidance, and offer solutions designed to achieve what it is they wish. Perhaps one answer where 'reasons' are involved at least might be to adopt the system used in certain key family proceedings (Magistrates' Courts Rules 1981, r.36), where the magistrates are required before announcing their decision to draw up their reasons in consultation with their clerk. This ensures that proper and sufficient advice is available at the point where it is needed most and in circumstances where it can be used to best advantage.

What I suggest therefore is:

(a) We examine more closely the operation and effectiveness of statutory formulae and criteria as a means of guiding sentencing decisions.

(b) The practice of the Court of Appeal in issuing guideline judgments should be continued with attention being paid to the sentencing problems faced by the magistrates' courts as well as the Crown Court.

(c) The Magistrates' Association thinking points for compensation in personal injury cases should be revised.

(d) The inclusion of recommendations in social inquiry reports should be abandoned in favour of the practice of offering opinions in the manner recommended by the Streatfeild Report (Streatfeild Report, 1961).

(e) Fresh thought should be given to the contents of social inquiry reports and to the need to retain the independence of judgment of probation officers.

(f) More attention should be paid to sentencing law and practice in the training of justices' clerks and advocates.

(g) The Practice Direction of 1981 should be revised to allow the clerk in court properly to advise his magistrates in sentencing matters.

Note

1   Particularly for those justices who can read.

I used to work in a London court where a characterful chairman had the engaging habit of throwing the probation report to the junior member of the bench and saying, 'You read that first and let me have your views.' It was only after he retired that it was discovered how cleverly he had concealed his life-long illiteracy.

References

Advisory Council on the Penal System (1970) *Non-Custodial and Semi-Custodial Penalties*, London, HMSO.

Bean, P. (1975) 'Social inquiry reports – a recommendation for disposal', *Justice of the Peace*, 139, 658.

Bottoms, A.E. (1981) 'The suspended sentence in England 1967–1978', *British Journal of Criminology*, 21, 1.

Harris, B. (1979) 'Recommendations in social enquiry reports', *Criminal Law Review*, 73.

Home Office (1974) Circular 195/1974.

Home Office (1978) *The Sentence of the Court*, (2nd ed.), London, HMSO.

Home Office (1983) Circular 18/1983.

Justices' Clerks Society (1982) *A Case for Summary Trial*, B.H. Forster, Magistrates' Courts, Cwmbran, Gwent.

Smith, D.E. *et al.* (1984) *Reducing the Prison Population*, Home Office Research and Planning Unit Paper 23, London, Home Office.

Tarling, R. (1979) *Sentencing Practice in Magistrates' Courts*, Home Office Research Study 56, London, HMSO.

Thorpe, J. (1979) *Social Inquiry Reports: A Survey*, Home Office Research Study 48, London, HMSO.

Cases

Aramah (1982) 4 Cr. App. R.(s) 407.

Boswell [1984] 1 W. L. R. 1047.

Clarke [1982] 1 W. L. R. 1090.

Cowan [1982] Crim. L. R. 766.

George (1984) 79 Cr. App. R. 26.

Holloway (1982) 4 Cr. App. R.(S) 128.

O'Keefe [1969] 2 Q. B. 29.

Savage (1984) 5 Cr. App. R. (S) 216.

Upton (1980) 71 Cr. App. R. 102.

Devising sentencing guidance for England

The topic is sufficiently wide-ranging for a book in itself, and this Chapter can only deal in outline with some of the problems which have to be overcome in devising sentencing guidance suitable for the English sentencing system. The true test of whether sentencing guidance can be devised lies in the attempt to do so: the task would take a considerable investment of time and resources, beyond the capacity of an individual. What I shall seek to do in this Chapter is to discuss the shape and structure of sentencing guidance in a general way, so as to indicate how I think the substantive task could best be approached. In failing to deal with all the difficulties and all the major decisions which would have to be taken I should not be taken to make light of the problems: even the sternest critic would surely not censure me for failing to be comprehensive within the limitations of so short a study.

One feature of the Chapter which may be found particularly irritating both by academics and by penal reformers is that its chief concern is to devise guidance which would be acceptable and workable in England. A detailed comparative survey of the various American systems of guidance might appear to be a fruitful starting point, but I have chosen to abjure this approach because the English situation is so very different — we have an established system of appellate review which has led to the enunciation of some sentencing principles, and an extraordinarily wide range of penal measures. There are, however, frequent references to the key decisions made in drawing up the Minnesota guidelines, as discussed in a stimulating article by Andrew von Hirsch (von Hirsch, 1982). I have also abjured the aim of reducing the prison population by means of sentencing guidance, which may seem particularly strange in view of my previous

pronouncements (Ashworth, 1982). I have not changed my view on
what is desirable, but I am seeking here to suppress that personal view
in the hope of putting forward a scheme whose acceptance would not
depend upon one's views on the prison population. In a sense, the
enterprise is one of codifying the practice and principles of English
sentencing, although the term 'codifying' needs to be interpreted with
care. It cannot simply be a matter of restating the English approach
to sentencing, because there is divergence (i.e. confusion) on so many
issues. To some extent it would inevitably be a normative enterprise,
which would involve the creation of new principles, but my aim would
be to keep to the spirit of the existing system so far as possible. This
leads to a third source of disappointment for some: I have also abjured
any discussion and ranking of penal aims and penal goals. Despite
the persuasive argument that this must form part of any well-founded
sentencing system which leaves an element of discretion to individual
sentencers (Galligan, 1981), I have adopted the pragmatic view that
the first step is to take proper stock of the existing system. One part
of that exercise would be to lay bare the principles and policies which
underlie sentencing practices, so that they might be evaluated in their
operational context. That would be a more fruitful starting point than
to attempt an *a priori* listing and ordering of penal goals.

The exercise which I have in mind is therefore a rather limited one.
I am heartened that some benches of magistrates have begun to draw
up guidance and guidelines for their own use, which at least suggests
that the exercise is not entirely alien to the mind of the English
sentencer. But who should undertake the formulation of the guidance
which I have in mind? My own preference remains strongly in favour
of some such body as a sentencing council – a body which includes
sentencers from all the different levels of courts, together with others
experienced in the carrying out of sentences, and which has a small
staff at its disposal to undertake the necessary researches. David
Thomas' proposal that the Lord Chief Justice should be given a
personal staff to assist him in preparing guidance may be more likely
to win acceptance from those in power (Thomas, 1983), but I am
troubled by the limitations of such an approach to the formulation
of guidance. Unless circuit judges, recorders and magistrates are to
be brought into the decision-making process, any guidance might not
even be based on an accurate appreciation of existing practices.

The grading of offences

In their decisions every day, sentencers grade crimes according to their relative gravity. There are, in effect, gradings of two kinds – relative gravity within a particular category of offence and the relative gravity of different categories of offence – and the first is generally more straightforward than the second. Nonetheless, sentencers have to consider issues of both kinds, and some steps have been taken to provide guidance, 'starting points' or 'pointers' in relation to these decisions. Perhaps the best known is the Magistrates' Association's list of *Suggestions for Traffic Offence Penalties*, now in its eighth edition. This tackles the problem of the relative gravity of different motoring offences, and gives a list of suggested starting points for average offences committed by first offenders of average means. Some local benches of magistrates have gone further, drawing up lists of suggested penalties which include non-motoring offences. The approaches vary. Court Y, a rural and suburban bench, adds ten varieties of 'criminal' offence to its own list for motoring offences (adapted from the Magistrates' Association's list). For each offence there is a 'thinking point', i.e. 'a starting point recommended for the average defendant in the usual type of case'. Examples are: simple stealing or receiving: three times the value of property stolen or re- ceived – minimum £75; shoplifting: four times the value of property stolen – minimum £100; dishonesty involving breach of trust or other aggravated circumstances: five times the value of property stolen or received minimum £150. Court Z, an urban bench in the same part of England, has prepared a lengthy dossier of starting points for over 200 non-motoring offences (and over 200 motoring offences too). The guidance – expressed to relate to a first offender earning £100 per week – is less extensive for each class of offence. Thus for theft, Court Z's suggested approach is 'From shop £75–150; other £50–150; from employer, consider prison; if in position of trust, £100–200; pedal cycle, £50–150'. Court Z does, however, provide a starting point for a wide range of less frequent offences, and also indicates specific local policies in dealing with some offences such as the use of threatening words or behaviour in a context of 'soccer hooliganism'.

My reason for referring to these first, faltering steps towards sentencing guidance in various magistrates' courts is not to criticise them. Although they show that there is a long way to travel before workable, effective and systematic guidance is developed, they point to two important elements in the process. One is that reflection on existing sentencing patterns gives a good grounding for the development of guidance: magistrates will assess their present practices and will discuss them with a non-sentencer (the justices' clerk), who may adopt a questioning approach to current practice and should be apprised of any Court of Appeal decisions which are relevant. The other is that the guidance may be seen to evolve rather than to be imposed *ab extra*: since the guidance is devised by representatives of the justices for the use of their own bench, one would hope that criticism would be more constructive and the process of change less painful than in more formal settings. These two elements are important but not, of themselves, sufficient. On the other hand, I would not go so far as some of the American jurisdictions in using opinion polls and surveys to establish a ranking of the relative gravity of offences (von Hirsch, 1982, pp.197–9). There are difficulties in accepting the opinions of persons who may not have reflected adequately upon the problems at hand, some of which would test even the most accomplished moral philosopher, and there are also difficulties in devising a survey which yields the fine detail which is necessary if guidance is to be practical and effective (Ashworth, 1983, pp.301–5; Levi and Jones, 1985). Indeed, not only members of the general public but also those involved in law enforcement may have an inaccurate impression of the realities of certain kinds of crime. It is easy to slip into modes of thought about, say, residential burglary which take a few well-publicised features and judge all incidents labelled as 'burglary' as if they share those features. Research into the characteristics of burglary and its effects on the victims could therefore make an important contribution to the grading of offences, by establishing a firm factual basis for judgments about the effects of the crime in its different manifestations. Relatively few English studies of particular crimes are available (though see Maguire, 1982; Walsh, 1978; Levi, 1981) and this is a fruitful direction for further research.

Another way in which research could help to provide a firm foundation for sentencing guidance is by producing statistics on the correlation between levels or types of sentence and various features of offences. In a sense this covers much the same ground as sentencers' impressions of their own practices, such as those which form the basis of the guidance drawn up by magistrates' courts Y and Z. But there are good grounds for believing that sentencers are not always fully aware of their own practices, and might not be able to commit them to paper accurately (see Ashworth *et al.*, 1984, pp. 50–6). Detailed statistics of the kind necessary to assist in the present task have rarely been gathered, but there is one small field in which the statistical techniques have been applied promisingly. Home Office research on sentencing for sexual offences in 1973 was based on a study of crime reports and other official returns, and the authors were able to correlate sentencing levels with factors such as the presence or absence of consent, the ages of victim and offender, whether there had been any previous relationship between the parties, whether or not force was used, whether the crime was completed or merely attempted, and so on (Walmsley and White, 1979). This kind of information on the objective relationship between these factors and sentencing would be invaluable in the process of drafting guidance for the crimes studied – unlawful sexual intercourse with under-age girls, homosexual offences and incest. However, its main limitation is that it is information about practice, and there may be respects in which that practice diverges from the principles laid down by the Court of Appeal. This problem is explored further at a later stage in this Chapter; it should not be taken to diminish the need for detailed sentencing statistics of the kind produced by the Home Office study of sexual offences.

In order to grade offences, therefore, it would be ideal to have some detailed sentencing statistics for each kind of offence, some wider studies of particular crimes and their effects on victims, and a knowledge of any principles laid down by the Court of Appeal which deal with relative gravity. It would be too much to expect that a coherent picture would emerge from this exercise in any one particular area of criminality: there would inevitably be judgments and choices to be made, and so the process must to some extent be normative rather than merely empirical. Bearing in mind the difficulties, let us now proceed to the next stage. How should the guidance be formulated? Should one aim for a large number of sub-divisions of each offence, reflecting all the major variations in factors? Should one adopt a more restrained approach, with a small number of sub-divisions and a long list of permitted or forbidden aggravating or mitigating factors?

As a means of considering the issues in concrete terms, let us take the offence of theft, the crime for which English courts have to pass sentence more than any other (non-motoring) offence. The most obvious way of sub-dividing thefts is according to the value of the property stolen, but it is not difficult to think of other factors which assume greater importance in cases where they arise, e.g. whether the offender occupied a position of trust in relation to the property, or whether the property was known to be stolen from someone who could ill afford the loss, with which some would contrast a theft from a large company (see Ashworth, 1983, pp. 181–8). As soon as one forsakes the comfortable simplicity of a ranking according to the value of the property, conflicts and choices press forward. The great temptation, when asked whether stealing goods worth £100 from a supermarket by shoplifting should be ranked higher or lower than a theft of £10 by a person in a position of trust, is to say: 'It depends'. And so it does. But it does *not* depend on an infinite number of factors, and in effect the question *is* answered every day by courts all over the country. My guess, in the absence of sufficiently detailed statistics, is that the very few small thefts by persons in positions of trust,[1] who are invariably first offenders, are regarded as more serious than the ordinary run of supermarket thefts by first, second or even third-time offenders. There is certainly some appellate authority which suggests that the In/Out line between custodial and non-custodial sentences is reached sooner by the 'breach of trust' offender (see, for example, *Upton* (1980), *Bibi* (1980) and *Barrick* (1985)). It therefore appears that the position of trust generally out-weighs the value of the property stolen, although there must be points at which the value of the property taken in breach of trust is so small, or the property stolen in an ordinary case is so high, as to place limits on the general proposition. Fixing those points will be awkward, but in an evolving process of guidance that should not give rise to embarrassment.

Another aspect of the problem is whether it is desirable to use existing categories of offence as the basis for new guidance, or whether it would be better to be more specific in some spheres. For example, English law has a single offence of theft with a maximum penalty of ten years' imprisonment, yet most of the thefts which come before the courts are at the lower end of the scale. The initial aim should be to concentrate attention on the lower echelons and to draw distinctions there. There might be a separate group of subdivisions for theft from shops, for example, which distinguished planned offences from the deliberate and the impulsive, or systematic thieving from the isolated act, as well as incorporating a scale referable to the value of the property taken. Theft in breach of trust, too, might be the subject of a separate scale. Some might argue that pickpocketing should be treated separately, as should meter thefts, keeping over-payments, and so on. In preparing this paper I lack the detailed information necessary to make definite proposals about the number of sub-divisions appropriate for theft but my provisional view is that there should be separate scales for certain types of theft (shoplifting, for one), and that each scale should incorporate variations in the value of the property and the degree of planning or system. Apart from that, there should be available general lists of aggravating and non-aggravating, extenuating and non-extenuating factors. If these were combined with a more rigorous approach to the giving of reasons for sentences, progress would surely be made towards a more structured approach to sentencing.

Before introducing a possible tabulation of those factors, however, there remains another major issue to be tackled. How can the scale for one offence be related to that for another? How, for instance, might the scales for theft be related to those for burglary and for handling? Comparison of the maximum penalties might suggest that handling ought generally to be regarded as more serious than theft, yet in court Y a small handling is treated as less serious than a small theft. This conflict is more apparent than real, because one can imagine why handling by a professional 'fence' might be regarded as more serious than theft of the same property, whereas buying a small item in a public house suspecting that it has been stolen may be less culpable than the actual stealing. Once again, more detailed information about the manifestations of these crimes and about actual sentencing practice would give a firmer basis for discussion. The comparison between theft and burglary raises another kind of difficulty: there is evidence that burglary of a dwelling house often causes distress to the householder which assumes greater significance for the victim than the loss of property involved. Of course there is a wide variation within each offence category, and a burglary may amount to nothing more than a 'walk-in' theft (e.g. taking a radio-cassette player from an unattended kitchen), which does not cause significant distress. For more serious burglaries, however, these psychological effects are sometimes severe and prolonged (Maguire, 1982, Ch. 5). Should the potentiality of psychological harm be regarded as raising the gravity of all residential burglaries? Or should this element only aggravate where the burglar knows or suspects that the premises are occupied at the time, as by breaking into a house at night whilst the occupants are asleep? The psychological effects may indeed be more strongly correlated with the characteristics of the victim (e.g. the greater vulnerability of older women who live alone) than with the presence or absence of the victim at the actual time of the burglary. Can we assume that burglars know of the severe psychological effects which are probable with victims of particular kinds? It might appear both strange and unworkable to treat the beliefs of each individual burglar as determinative on this issue. Another solution would be to treat residential burglars as a general class, viewing their offences as more serious because of the risk of psychological harm − though the risk varies according to the type of victim. This is one interpretation of the position at which the Court of Appeal appears to have arrived (*Hardman* (1982)), and which also suggests an answer to the next question − how much more grave? There seems to be a widespread view that burglary of a dwelling house is considerably more serious than theft involving a similar amount. The broad sentencing statistics do not bear out such a marked distinction as the Court of Appeal has suggested, but a more detailed analysis of sentencing might reveal the factors which lead courts to impose non-custodial measures when the Court of Appeal has so strongly favoured custodial sentences for this offence. Once this analysis has been completed, it would be possible to place the range of existing sentences alongside the ranges for theft, and to consider any apparent inconsistencies.

To conclude this discussion of approaches to the grading of offences, I invite attention to Table 3. I am perhaps being somewhat pessimistic in constructing such an extensive table: ideally it would be possible to incorporate a number of these variables into the scales of gravity for at least some offences, but I recognise that opposition of the idea of guidelines which are too tightly drawn might bring about recourse to a fairly extensive list of aggravating, mitigating and excluded factors. Table 3 deals with a wide range of factors, with references to further discussion for those who find the tabulation too stark or question-begging (cf. von Hirsch, 1982, p. 206). The concept of 'extenuating factors' is limited to matters relating to the offence. Personal mitigating factors are dealt with in the following section of this Chapter. In almost every instance, the strength of the factor will vary somewhat in individual cases. But that is not a telling argument against an attempt to give guidance; and, if sentencers are able to

TABLE 3[a]

Aggravating factors	Non-aggravating factors
Concerted offending by a group (p. 199) Systematic criminality for profit Offence was planned or (less significantly) was deliberate (p. 152) Knowledge that the victim belongs to a specially vulnerable group (e.g. children, or the elderly, pp. 162, 182)	Consequences of conduct which the offender did not foresee or knowingly risk (p. 155; and *Krawec* (1984))
Committing an offence against someone who, as the offender believes, is attempting to enforce the law (p. 158) Offence committed by a law enforcement officer (p. 159) Breach of position of trust held by the offender (p. 194) Use of a weapon with which the offender had unlawfully forearmed himself before the incident (p. 164) Use of a firearm (p. 166) Violence used in the course of other criminality (p. 160) Other offences which the offender asks to be taken into consideration Offence forming part of a course of criminal conduct (p. 162)	Ease of committing the crime (p. 197)

Extenuating factors	Non-extenuating factors
Offence committed impulsively (p. 153) Offence committed under significant provocation from the victim (p. 167; and Wasik, 1982) Offence committed under considerable pressure (not amounting to the defence of duress) (Wasik, 1983) Offence committed against a corporation (p. 186) Offender played only a minor or a passive role in the crime	Offence was an attempt or conspiracy which in fact caused no harm: perhaps slight mitigation may be permissible (Cross, 1981, pp. 151–7)

Note (a) All page references are to Ashworth, 1983, unless otherwise stated.

indicate the weight they have attributed to certain factors in arriving at the sentence in a case, real progress could be made.

The characteristics of the offender

In many of the American jurisdictions which have adopted guidelines or presumptive sentences, the offender's prior criminal record is the principal or even the only characteristic of the offender which is allowed to influence sentence. The preponderance of English authorities favours the view that the gravity of the current offence sets a ceiling above which the sentence cannot go, that a first offender should receive a substantial concession for his good record, and that a lengthening criminal record should lead to a progressive loss of mitigation (Ashworth, 1983, pp. 109–12). Unfortunately this appears not to be the position in sentencing practice. Although there is no detailed statistical study, some courts seem to increase a persistent offender's sentence beyond what is proportionate to the gravity of the latest offence, and the Court of Appeal has occasionally approved this course (Ashworth, 1983, p. 213). This divergence between practice and the general principle is facilitated by the absence of clear ceilings, especially in relation to less serious forms of offending. Indeed, one of the critical choices for those who draw up sentencing guidance is whether to make allowance, when setting the ceilings, for offenders with a substantial record of previous convictions. My strong view is that it would be wrong to choose levels of sentence simply on the basis that they should be sufficiently high to cater for the offender with a bad record. The proper starting point is the gravity of the particular offence: if it is at the lower end of the scale − say, theft of £100 with no aggravating factors − the court should not have access to a disproportionately high sentence simply because the offender has several previous convictions for dishonesty. The matter is, however, one for debate, not least because of the divergence between the leading principles and what appears to be frequent practice (for discussion see von Hirsch, 1981; Ashworth, 1983, Ch. 5 and the chapter by Wasik in the present volume).

Even if the leading English principles win the day, there is much more to be resolved. Previous convictions may be for offences of varying gravity. Courts surely make some rough qualitative assessments of previous records now, and it would be undesirable if any new guidance were to preclude qualitative assessment. An offender with only minor previous convictions should, generally speaking, be treated more leniently than an offender with a more serious record (von Hirsch, 1982, p. 201). Just as the 'ceiling' principle shows respect for the quality of the present crime, so the principle of progressive loss of mitigation should be applied in a way which reflects the 'quality' of previous convictions. How might quality be assessed? Crude measures would be whether the offence was tried summarily or on indictment, and whether it resulted in a custodial or non-custodial sentence, but neither of those is sufficiently accurate. If, however, a new sentencing structure were to have recognised sub-divisions of offences and bands of sentence for each, one advantage would be to give a clear impression to later courts of how each sentencing court assessed the seriousness of each offence. Of course, the more variations and elements of 'fine-tuning' which one wishes to allow for, the more complicated any set of guidance becomes. The most robust among the 'just deserts' theorists would doubtless view this pursuit of fine distinctions as obsessive and unprofitable, whereas the typical English defence is that any sentencing guidance requires 'sophistication'.[2] I believe that these distinctions may be worth drawing. If the present offence is theft of goods worth £50 from a supermarket, it should hardly matter what the quality of the previous convictions is — whether they be other thefts, woundings or even murder (von Hirsch, 1982, p. 202, n. 140). However, if the present offence is a serious wounding, it would surely be right to regard a previous record of theft and handling rather differently from a history of criminal assaults.[3] Another relevant variable is the periodicity of previous convictions. An offender with a significant conviction-free period should be treated differently from one with an unbroken succession of convictions (Ashworth, 1983, pp. 225–6; von Hirsch, 1981, p. 616): a person is entitled to credit for a gap in his criminal record, although the quantum of the concession cannot be expressed simply. Lastly, after how many convictions should an offender reach the 'ceiling' for the offence? It is surely unnecessary to leave room for courts to distinguish between the offender with forty and one with forty-one previous convictions: the statistics show that after five convictions an offender is about ninety per cent likely to reoffend (Philpotts and Lancucki, 1979), and my suggestion is that in general the ceiling should be reached after five convictions. After that, there is no more mitigation to be lost.

How might all these principles be expressed and implemented?

In order to take full account of all the differences indicated, it would be necessary to construct a complex numerical framework which assigned a score to each previous conviction, and with provision that totals of a certain level would deprive the offender of a certain proportion of mitigation. The practical difficulties of such an elaborate framework have led von Hirsch to propose a rather crude weighting which is able to give some extra effect to particularly serious previous convictions (von Hirsch 1981, pp. 620–1); the Minnesota guidelines ignore the qualitative differences entirely, in view of the problems of incorporating them into a tabulation, and simply refer to the number of previous convictions (von Hirsch, 1982, pp. 201–2). My suggestion is that two methods should be given a trial in any English guidance. For offences of medium gravity the offence tabulation would take the form of a grid, with previous convictions 0 to 5 showing different recommended sentences, and with a strong indication that the tabulation should only be used in conjunction with principle (d) below. For all offences other than the most serious, the guidance would indicate a recommended penalty and the ceiling for the category of offence, and the sentencer would be directed to apply the four principles set out below when considering the effect of previous record. That approach allows flexibility and therefore tolerates a loss of effectiveness when compared with the Minnesota system; there is therefore scope for courts to misapply the principles. However, the most important decision within the scheme being proposed here is the setting of the ceiling for each category of each offence. Once the ceiling is established, the sentencer should then take account of the principles set out below, in considering the effect on the sentence of the offender's previous record:

(a) no matter how bad an offender's previous record, his sentence should not exceed the ceiling provided for the offence of which he is now convicted;

(b) where the offender has no previous convictions, he should be given substantial credit for his good record;

(c) where the offender does have some previous convictions, the general principle should be progressive loss of mitigation; in other words, with only one or two previous convictions he should receive a significant concession, but this should be progressively diminished. An offender with five or more previous convictions can expect no reduction of his sentence below the ceiling, unless his record falls within (d) below;

(d) in assessing the effect to be given to previous convictions, the court should (i) accord less weight to convictions for relatively minor offences than to convictions for offences of a similar or higher gravity than the present, and (ii) accord less weight to convictions which have been followed by a significant period free from convictions.

These principles are equally applicable to magistrates' courts, although they would there be used primarily for non-custodial rather than custodial sentencing. In fixing the level of a fine, for example, the court should have regard to these principles. The second principle seems to be applied frequently, whilst the first and third principles have important implications for decisions in relation to the most severe sentence which magistrates' courts may pass.

Now for the English sentencer this is merely the beginning of a discussion of the relevant characteristics of offenders. Part of the tradition of English sentencing lies in the discretion allowed to the court to reflect a whole range of mitigating factors, examples including where the offender is young or very old, where his health is poor, where he has shown genuine remorse for what he has done, where he has suffered extreme social deprivation, where the offence followed a period of family disturbances or financial worry, where the consequences of the offence have already been considerable, and so on. On a strict view of 'just deserts' theory, such factors should not be allowed to enter into sentencing decisions. Some have no bearing on culpability; others appear to do so only inasmuch as they are put forward as the reason for the commission of the offence and are therefore tied to a particular form of rehabilitative sentence. One of the main concerns of 'just deserts' theory is that the sentencing decision should not be affected by social judgments upon and about offenders: von Hirsch argues strongly against basing sentences on the offender's 'past non-criminal choices' (von Hirsch, 1982, p. 204), and the Minnesota guidelines expressly forbid the use of race, sex, employment, educational attainment, marital status, residence, or living arrangements as aggravating or mitigating circumstances (von Hirsch, 1982, p. 203).

Would it be possible to preserve the sentencer's discretion to take account of factors such as age, ill-health, remorse etc. whilst excluding from consideration 'status' factors such as those forbidden by the Minnesota guidelines? There seems no reason why this should not be attempted. The Minnesota example could be followed in drawing up a list of excluded 'status' factors, and there could then be a list of other factors of personal mitigation which might properly be taken into account by the sentencer. The offender's age is clearly a crucial matter if he is under seventeen, or aged seventeen to twenty, because English law provides some separate measures for those age-groups. It would probably be desirable to provide separate guidance for courts when dealing with a young offender: only in this way could the different measures and different policies be properly implemented. I would certainly not suggest that the decision as to what factors should appear in the 'mitigation' list would be straightforward: there are several conflicts to be resolved before a conclusion can be reached (Ashworth, 1983, p. 297). For example, the effect of a guilty plea has been much discussed in England, where courts tend to regard the plea as a mitigating factor in itself. The main reason for this appears to be expediency: it is thought necessary to offer defendants an incentive to plead guilty, so as to reduce the burden on trial courts. However, the effects of this concession may be deleterious to individual rights, and there are grounds for questioning whether the factual assumptions behind the English practice are sound (Ashworth, 1984b, Ch. 9).

Choice of sentence

English law provides a vast range of alternative measures for adult, young adult and juvenile offenders. Few of the relevant legislative provisions contain guidance on the use of the measure, and it is fair to say that, for the bulk of non-custodial measures, the Court of Appeal has made little progress towards the articulation of criteria which could guide sentencers. The result is that there remains considerable scope for judges to take quite different views of the purpose and appropriate use of given measures (Ashworth *et al.*, 1984, p. 29), and research into the use of different measures in thirty magistrates' courts revealed wide variations (Tarling, 1979). How can some degree of order be brought to bear on the use of these sentences?

I propose to leave custodial sentences out of account at present: they will be discussed later. The main problem in providing guidance on the use of non-custodial measures is their sheer variety, but, since no radical changes in the sentencing structure are to be contemplated in this exercise, the problem has to be tackled. One possible approach would be to arrange all the non-custodial measures in order of relative severity. To this there are two principal drawbacks: (a) there is a considerable range of severity within certain measures, such as the fine (which may go to hundreds or even thousands of pounds) and the community service order (from forty to 240 hours' work); and (b) some of the measures ought not to be forced into the strait-jacket of 'relative severity'. Indeed, to take up the second point, I suggest that three measures should be set apart from the others: deferment of sentence, the probation order and the hospital order. Each of these should only be considered in a particular case in which the court has received evidence that the offender has a need which the particular measure might be expected to deal with. For the hospital order, the nature of that evidence is fixed by statute. The probation order has been undergoing change, as the approach of individual casework is being joined by the use of day-centres and their various facilities. A precondition of the use of these orders will usually be the receipt of a recommendation from a probation officer that this offender can be expected to benefit from this kind of treatment.

Another difficulty in arranging non-custodial measures schematically concerns the compensation order. This may now be imposed either as the sole order upon an offender or in addition to any other measures. In principle the court should consider making a compensation order wherever injury, loss or damage has been caused to a victim. Whether an order is made should depend on the court's ability to assess the appropriate sum, and the offender's ability to pay. However, since the law allows a court to make a compensation order as the sole method of dealing with an offender, it must somehow be related to the other measures and my suggestion would be to place it alongside the fine, which it is supposed to replace in these cases. The compensation order must also be listed with the other ancillary orders, such as restitution orders, forfeiture orders and disqualification from driving, in a separate category of orders which may be added to most (though not all) other measures.

Having indicated that deferment of sentence, probation orders, hospital orders and compensation orders should be dealt with separately, how should the main group of non-custodial measures be presented? Both court Y and court Z present their guidance chiefly in terms of levels of fine. It might be argued, in their support, that the fine is the most frequently used measure and that a court would rarely need to consider an alternative unless there were a report or other representations in favour of an alternative measure. To use the fine as the basic 'currency' of a system of guidance would certainly have the merit of simplicity. Its primary disadvantage, particularly in times of recession, is that many offenders have limited means, and any system which appears to favour the fine might result in the unfair treatment of certain kinds of offenders. However, there are approaches such as the 'day fine' which could be introduced to remove those disadvantages, without altering the character of English sentencing (Ashworth, 1983, Ch. 7). It would certainly be necessary to articulate the general principles applicable to the fine. Moreover, the proposal is only that the fine should be the *basic* 'currency' of recommended starting points for *most* offences. On the one hand it would not preclude a court from selecting another measure if that were thought more appropriate to this offender. On the other hand, it would be possible to indicate that a particular offence is viewed seriously by indicating that a substantial community service order should be considered, without having to rely upon fines or imprisonment to cover all forms of offence.

Even if the fine were regarded as the starting point for most offences, it would be necessary to indicate the kinds of reasoning which would justify the court in selecting an alternative measure. In broad terms of relative severity, one might say that absolute and conditional discharges are less severe than the fine; at present the statute gives virtually no guidance on the kinds of case for which they are appropriate, and it would be important to develop some descriptive guidance on the proper use of each measure. The same approach should be adopted in dealing with the two measures which are more severe than the fine and yet less severe than immediate imprisonment – the community service order and the suspended sentence. Both the legislature and the courts have made some clear statements in this sphere, about patterns of reasoning which ought or ought not to be adopted (see Ashworth, 1984a). This is not to overlook the disputes about these patterns of reasoning: clearly it is not possible in the space of this article to resolve all the issues which would need to be resolved before any guidance could be formulated. What is proposed, however, is that the level of guidance could be significantly improved by providing more detailed descriptions of the purposes and proper uses of the various measures, and indicating patterns of reasoning which are generally correct or incorrect.

This structure of sentencing guidance, based on the fine and moving out towards the various alternatives which may be relevant in particular situations, will clearly not be sufficient for the less numerous but more serious kinds of offence. For them, custodial sentences may have to be considered. Custodial sentences, like financial penalties, have the advantage that they can be finely calibrated so as to reflect fairly subtle differences in the gravity of offences. Unlike fines, however, they are subject to deduction and alteration by the executive, through the operation of remission and parole. It is hardly surprising that many of the American jurisdictions which have turned to guidelines have restricted or even removed their parole arrangements: the chaos which reigns over the actual length of sentences served in England strongly supports the need for this. Any thorough-going sentencing system must have a firm distinction between judicial and executive powers to determine the length of sentences. It is hardly too dramatic to suggest that in England the sentences pronounced by the courts are sometimes almost meaningless, in terms of the time actually served: with the advent of section 33 of the Criminal Justice Act 1982, the executive has outmanoeuvred the judiciary and has gone a long way towards introducing virtually automatic parole for all sentences between eleven and twenty-four months. Nothing more can be said about this in the present context, save that the terms of imprisonment recommended in any guidance will refer to the nominal term and may bear little relationship to the term actually served.

How should the framework of custodial sentences be established? What levels of prison sentence should be regarded as appropriate? The answers here must be along the same lines as the general approach: the aim is to reproduce those levels which represent present practice, as modified by present authority. But there is an additional factor of cardinal importance: custodial sentences require prisons and other buildings to house the inmates, and when those buildings become overcrowded – especially if the buildings are old and the facilities poor – conditions may become so inhumane as to justify a reduction in the level of sentences so as to relieve the prisons. As von Hirsch and Hanrahan have argued, the state's duty to refrain from cruelty and inhumanity should be treated as overriding the duty to punish offenders as much as they deserve (von Hirsch and Hanrahan, 1976, p. 40). There has been some judicial recognition that this would be the proper course (*Upton* (1980); *Bibi* (1980)), but it is doubtful whether English courts would go far towards a reduction in the lengths of custodial sentences on this ground. Minnesota is one of the American jurisdictions to have taken prison capacity as a constraint on the levels of imprisonment prescribed by the guidelines (von Hirsch, 1982, pp. 176–80), but I see dangers in this approach. Of course, at a basic level any system of sentencing guidance would be unworkable if it took no account of prison capacity and indicated a use of custody with which the prisons simply could not cope. But more prisons could be built, and in so far as levels of custody are related to the availability of facilities rather than other measures, it seems that sentences could become longer simply because a particular government was willing to spend more money on providing the facilities. This is a vicarious form of executive sentencing which we would do well to avoid. There is a humanitarian argument in favour of reducing levels of imprisonment to the extent that prison conditions are inhumane, but that does not lead inexorably to a general principle that prison capacity should be the determinant of sentencing levels.

How, then, should the levels be set? According to the scheme outlined here, the levels should be determined by examining the statistics of current sentencing practice, in conjunction with guidance laid down by the Court of Appeal. It would be a mistake to treat the gross statistics as a sufficient starting point: the Advisory Council on the Penal System adopted this as the basis for their system of lower 'normal maximum' sentences (A.C.P.S., 1978, Ch. 9), but their approach was convincingly criticised for its suppression of qualitative differences in sentencing levels (Thomas, 1979). In drawing up guidance for particular types of offence it would clearly be essential to examine these qualitative differences and to consider the factors which lead to sentences of particular lengths in particular cases. Once again, reference may be made to the Home Office research on sentencing for sexual offences, which was able to correlate sentencing levels for those offences with various factors which were present or absent in different cases (Walmsley and White, 1979). When the correlations have been established, it would be necessary to consider them in conjunction with Court of Appeal judgments before formulating the guidance. The need to do so was recognised in the Home Office study, and a good example is provided by the Court of Appeal's practice in recent years of quashing custodial sentences for consensual buggery with a practising homosexual in a public lavatory – for which some judges still impose a substantial custodial sentence (e.g. *Tosland* (1981), *Dighton* (1983), *Bedborough* (1984)). Lord Lane also referred in his *Bibi* judgment to 'minor cases of sexual indecency' as a group of offences for which sentencing levels might be significantly lowered.

In other spheres of offending, however, the divergence between practice and declared principles is of the opposite kind. The Court of Appeal has made several statements to the effect that burglary of residential premises should invariably attract an immediate custodial sentence, even for a first offender, and yet the courts continue to use non-custodial measures for about one-half of all those convicted of this offence. One reason for this is that some offences falling within the legal category of 'burglary' are clearly non-serious. Another probable reason is that most burglars are young, and therefore there are separate principles of sentencing which militate in favour of a restricted use of custody and a wider use of non-custodial measures. It is not apparent that the interaction of the various sentencing principles has been considered by the Court of Appeal, and this may be a sphere in which an attempted restatement of sentencing principles would have to adopt a normative approach. It should be recalled, however, that there is a general case for having separate guidance in respect of offenders under twenty-one: the measures available to English courts for those under seventeen and for those aged seventeen to twenty are so different from the adult sentences that a single system would be unsatisfactory.

Between those offences for which custody is the invariable response and the many others for which custody is rarely proper there lies an extensive group of offences for which the In/Out decision is crucial. One set of decisions concerns exactly how to draw the In/Out line. Another set of decisions concerns the so-called alternatives to custody, which may be relevant in these instances. In placing the In/Out line there is a theoretical choice between a steep dispositional line, which attributes great significance to the number of previous convictions and less to the actual offence on this occasion, and a flat dispositional line, which accords priority to the gravity of the offence over the length of criminal records. Von Hirsch describes the Minnesota choice as a line which 'is flat at the left, and hinges up at the right': its effect is that those convicted of 'intermediate-level offences' who have long criminal records would receive imprisonment – a concession to the incapacitative rationale which was thought necessary in order to ensure the political acceptability of the guidelines (von Hirsch, 1982, pp. 189–90). It seems probable that a dispositional line based on English practice and principle would be relatively steep, for there is a tendency to ascribe considerable weight to previous record even if the current offence is a relatively minor theft. My own views are firmly against this, and my hope would be that detailed statistics would reveal English sentencing practices to be so diverse on this matter as to require a fresh decision to be taken. It is important to keep a sense of proportion, and for various non-serious cases of theft, handling and taking cars, etc., there is an argument in favour of stating clearly that a custodial sentence should not normally be imposed, no matter how bad the previous record.

An additional problem stemming from the recent proliferation in English sentences is the availability of at least two alternatives to custody which ought to be considered by a court which has to make an In/Out decision. The suspended sentence and the community service order must be worked into the guidance, as Lord Lane CJ made clear in *Clarke* (1982). What is lacking is full descriptive guidance on the kinds of offender for whom these sentences ought to be used: there are judicial statements suggesting that they should be seriously considered for an offender with a good record who has committed a single offence of some gravity, but this is a small group of offenders and the intention is surely that the sentences should be more widely used. Once again, as with non-custodial sentences generally, guidance should be drawn up.

Conclusions

I have attempted to give some idea of the steps which might be taken to 'codify' the English sentencing system. The advantage of doing this would be to increase the volume and detail of guidance available to magistrates and judges in the English criminal courts, whilst preserving their discretion to deal with individual cases in an individual way, upon reasons given. In putting together this sketch of what might be possible, I have borne in mind a melancholy English maxim – the more novel the proposals, the less likely they are to win acceptance or to have practical impact. There is a parallel between my position and that of the team of academic lawyers who have recently, under the auspices of the Law Commission, drafted parts of a possible criminal code for England and Wales (Law Commission, 1985). I would propose, however, to be more explicit about the distinction between restatement and reform. Any attempt to codify the rules and principles of sentencing would inevitably involve more than a restatement, because in so many respects the practices of English courts are diverse and the Court of Appeal's judgements are inconsistent.

Even the more ambitious reformers in America, working in states sufficiently progressive to entertain the possibility of sentencing guidance, have had to genuflect towards political pressures. In England the problem of securing acceptance is more acute because of the immense power wielded by the judiciary. Yet the judiciary may now be starting to realise that its power over the time an offender spends in custody is slipping away. Even a Conservative government thought it necessary to introduce a new means of executive release of prisoners, by section 33 of the Criminal Justice Act 1982, thereby effectively shortening many prison terms for non-grave offences when the judges had signally failed to do so. If the judges do not move to put their own house into order, there is an increasing possibility that Parliament or the Executive will do so.

This Chapter amounts to little more than a brief sketch of the proposed guidance. It recommends as its main feature the offence tabulation, sub-dividing offences into categories and indicating recommended sentences. For serious offences there would be a grid showing a range of recommended measures according to the number of previous convictions, from none to five. For less serious offences it might be preferable to leave courts to use a number of alternative measures, but it would remain necessary to indicate both a recommended normal penalty (e.g. for an offender with one previous conviction) and a ceiling above which the sentence should not go. For both approaches, the court should have regard to the principles relating to previous record. Having located the offence in the offence tabulation, the sentencer would then have to consider further matters. There would be the list of aggravating and extenuating factors, which would help the sentencer to decide whether to go higher or lower than the recommended penalty. There would be the list of mitigating factors, to be considered in conjunction with any representations made on behalf of the offender. There would be the guidance on non-custodial measures, to be considered in conjunction with any report on the offender by a probation officer (or, where appropriate, psychiatrist). And, lastly, there would be principles of totality of sentence – not discussed in detail above (see Ashworth, 1983, Ch. 6), which would give guidance on whether the sentence should be concurrent or consecutive, and on how the court should assess the totality of consecutive sentences, for cases in which an offender is sentenced for more than one offence. It is envisaged that guidance of these kinds should be addressed to the Crown Court and to magistrates' courts, and attention would have to be paid to the practices and particular problems of each.

To reach even the initial stage proposed in this paper, which may appear monumentally unambitious to many reformers, considerable research and thought would be necessary. Detailed research on sentencing, as described above, would have to be undertaken so as to provide the working basis for the offence tabulation. Guidance on the appropriate use of the various non-custodial measures would have to be drawn up, a task which would be difficult but would demonstrate the problems which courts often have. It is heartening that some magistrates' courts have taken their own initiative towards developing guidance, and that some counties have tried to develop uniform policies on such matters as the relationship of community service orders to custodial sentences.[4] These initiatives confirm that guidance may be seen as a practical response to practical needs, and that the whole enterprise cannot be dismissed as academic and American – two strongly condemnatory adjectives in the vocabulary of some English sentencers. It is a *controlling* exercise, since it aims to structure sentencing discretion and to produce relatively uniform reasoning towards more uniform sentences. But it would not involve the elimination of discretion, and it would preserve the court's power to respond to peculiar combinations of factors in particular cases. So long as the court gave reasons for departing from the recommended sentence, there could be a meaningful review of the sentence and material leading to the evolution of the guidance by revision.

Notes

1   By 'very few' I refer to the number prosecuted. It is likely that many such offences go unreported and that employers deal with them by dismissing, warning or demoting the culprit.

2   cf. the ironic use of this concept by the Advisory Council on the Penal System, Appendix C, when arguing that the new American reforms of sentencing structure would be inappropriate in England.

3   There is a trace of these distinctions in the principles relating to activation of suspended sentences: see Ashworth (1983), pp. 241–247.

4   It could be argued that these initiatives have been taken because of local needs and that the benches involved would reject the very idea of national guidelines. The response must be to challenge the benches to identify any particular local factors which justify a different sentencing approach. Differences in income levels should not be relevant (because of the principle that courts should take account of offender's means), unless a set of standard

fines is established. This seems to be the case with motoring fines, for the Magistrates Associations *Suggestions* accept that a good reason for local variation would be that the average rates of pay are locally higher or lower than average. But would a special bench policy be a 'good reason' for variation? Surely not.

References

Advisory Council on the Penal System (1978) *Sentences of Imprisonment: A Review of Maximum Penalties*, London, HMSO.

Ashworth, A. J. (1982) 'Reducing the prison population in the 1980s: the need for sentencing reform', in *A Prison System for the 1980s and Beyond*, London, NACRO.

Ashworth, A. J. (1983) *Sentencing and Penal Policy*, London, Weidenfeld and Nicolson.

Ashworth, A.J. (1984a) 'Techniques of guidance on sentencing', *Criminal Law Review*, 519.

Ashworth, A. J. (1984b) *The English Criminal Process: A Review of Empirical Research*, Centre for Criminological Research Occasional Paper No. 11, University of Oxford.

Ashworth, A. J., Genders, E., Mansfield, G., Peay, J. and Player, E. (1984) *Sentencing in the Crown Court*, Centre for Criminological Research Occasional Paper No. 10, University of Oxford.

Cross, R. (1981) *The English Sentencing System*, (3rd. ed.), London, Butterworth.

Galligan, D. (1981) 'Guidelines and just deserts; a critique of recent trends in sentencing reform', *Criminal Law Review*, 297.

Law Commission (1985) *Codification of the Criminal Law*, Law Commission No. 143, London, HMSO.

Levi, M. (1981) *The Phantom Capitalists*, London, Heinemann.

Levi, M. and Jones, S. (1985) 'Public perceptions of crime seriousness', *British Journal of Criminology*, 25, 234.

Maguire, M. (1982) *Burglary in a Dwelling*. London, Heinemann.

Philpotts, G. J. O. and Lancucki, L. B. (1979) *Previous Convictions, Sentence and Reconviction*, Home Office Research Study 53, London, HMSO.

Tarling, R. (1979) *Sentencing Practice in Magistrates' Courts*, Home Office Research Study 56, London, HMSO.

Thomas, D. A. (1979) 'The Advisory Council and maximum penalties', *Modern Law Review*, 42, 309.

Thomas, D. A. (1983) 'Sentencing discretion and appellate review', in Shapland, J. (ed.) *Decision-Making in the Legal System*, British Psychological Society, Issues in Criminological and Legal Psychology Occasional Paper No. 5, 61.

von Hirsch, A. (1981) 'Desert and previous convictions in sentencing', *Minnesota Law Review*, 65, 591.

von Hirsch, A. (1982) 'Constructing guidelines for sentencing', *Hamline Law Review*, 5, 164.

von Hirsch, A. and Hanrahan, K. (1979) *The Question of Parole*, New York, Ballinger.

Walmsley, G. R. and White, K. (1979) *Sexual Offences, Consent and Sentencing*, Home Office Research Study 54, London, HMSO.

Walsh, D. P. (1978) *Shoplifting*. London, Macmillan.

Wasik, M. (1982) 'Cumulative provocation and domestic killing', *Criminal Law Review*, 29.

Wasik, M. (1983) 'Excuses at the sentencing stage', *Criminal Law Review*, 450.

Cases

Barrick (1985) 7 Cr. App. R. (S). 142.

Bedborough (1984) 6 Cr. App. R. (S). 98.

Bibi (1980) 2 Cr. App R. (S). 360.

Clarke [1982] 1 W.L.R. 1090.

Dighton (1983) 5 Cr. App. R. (S). 233.

Hardman (1982) *The Times*, Nov 10; (1983) 147 J.P.N. 59.

Krawec (1984) 6 Cr. App. R. (S). 367.

Tosland (1981) 3 Cr. App. R. (S). 365.

Upton (1980) 71 Cr. App. R. 102.

7 Martin Wasik

Guidance, guidelines and criminal record

Few people would be likely to argue with the proposition that a defendant's criminal record is an important determinant of his sentence. There are numerous assertions to this effect in the texts on sentencing, where criminal record is said to be 'of the greatest significance' (Devlin, 1970, p. 46), 'an important factor in sentencing' (Nicholson, 1981, p. 211) and that which 'often ... turns the scale in one direction or another' (Walker, 1985, p. 44). The Streatfeild Committee regarded it as 'obvious and clear' (1981, p. 8) that full details of the defendant's criminal record should always be made available to the sentencing court and it seems that sentencers themselves regard the receipt of this information as being of very great significance, second only perhaps to details of the current offence (Hogarth, 1971, pp. 231–235). Studies of sentence decision-making in England (Kapardis and Farrington, 1981) and in the United States (Green, 1961, Green, 1964, Tiffany et al., 1975, Greenwood et al., 1976) indicate that sentencing outcome is crucially affected by prior record. The modern American sentencing guidelines movement selects the defendant's criminal record (or 'criminal history score') as one of the key determinants in sentencing (von Hirsch, 1976, 1981). In some American jurisdictions criminal record has traditionally been given greater weight by sentencers even than the nature of the current offence (Johnston et al., 1973, Minnesota Sentencing Guidelines Commission 1984, Ch. 1).

What is remarkable, given all this, is the lack of analysis of precisely what information about a defendant's prior record is relevant to sentence selection, and in what ways that influence is manifested. In short, the relation between sentencing and prior record remains obscure, despite virtually unanimous acceptance of the importance of the assocation between the two. It may be said that there is hardly any guidance for judges and magistrates on the issue, comment in the appellate cases tending to be 'tangential and obtuse' (Samuels, 1985). Sentencers are presumably expected to appreciate intuitively the significance of the information which they are given and to tailor their sentencing accordingly. Reference in the standard works which a sentencer might consult is rare and unhelpful. The English sentencer's pocket guide, *The Sentence of the Court* (Home Office, 1978) does not mention the matter. The latest edition of Brian Harris' *Criminal Jurisdiction of Magistrates* (Harris, 1984) contains no specific discussion of prior record. David Thomas's *Principles of Sentencing* (Thomas, 1979) is more helpful, though even there only nine pages from over four hundred are devoted to the issue of the prior record of the defendant.

Clearly, detailed empirical investigation would be required to determine what use is actually made by sentencers of information provided for them relating to the defendant's prior record. The purpose of the present essay is to foreshadow such an investigation by examining a number of factors which are potentially relevant in linking a defendant's previous record with the sentence for the current offence.

What makes a difference?

In spite of the lack of direct authority on the relevance of prior record to sentencing in England a number of indirect indicators may be found. These are implicit in statutory provisions, such as the Rehabilitation of Offenders Act 1974 which, taken together with a Practice Direction issued by the Court of Appeal in 1975 and a Home Office Circular of the same year, means that old or 'spent' convictions should only exceptionally be taken into account in sentencing. A different Home Office Circular now allows for the citing of formal cautions as part of the defendant's criminal record, even when he is sentenced as an adult, but a series of appellate decisions disallows sentencing on the basis of alleged but unproven past wrongdoing, so that prior arrests or prior acquittals cannot be cited to sentencers or used by them in sentence selection. Admitted offences are, however, frequently taken into consideration. Appellate decisions often make reference to the significant mitigating factor of a defendant's clean, or relatively short, record. The existence of a substantial conviction-free 'gap' prior to the current offence in the record of a persistent offender is also a matter of mitigation, it being contrary to principle to take the cynical view that the defendant has merely avoided detection for the relevant period. By implication from these and other matters, it is suggested that *eight* factors of prior record emerge as likely to be perceived by the sentencer as relevant.

1 *Number of previous convictions*

That the sheer number of previous convictions is regarded as important in itself is supported by several observations of the way in which prior record information is provided for and handled by sentencers. Formal police cautions should now be presented to the court at the same time as previous convictions, but 'care must be taken to present cautions separately so that the distinction between cautions and convictions is clear' (Home Office, 1985). Findings of guilt when the defendant was a juvenile and convictions followed by nominal sentences (notwithstanding the wording of section 13 of the Powers of Criminal Courts Act 1973) are also included. Spent convictions are included, although they should be specially marked. On the other hand, it is clear that number alone is not the governing factor. Research by Shapland indicates that sentencers generally do not require that a defendant's full criminal record be read out in court, requesting 'last three or four only' (Shapland, 1981) as reflecting previous convictions generally regarded as relevant. Official guidance (Home Office, 1973) suggests that previous convictions should not be read out if they 'are either so stale or so different from the current offence as to make them of little relevance'. There seems to be a clear working assumption on the part of police and court personnel that some previous convictions are more relevant than others. The common practices of prosecuting sample counts and taking offences into consideration tend to distort the number of previous convictions appearing on a record.

One of the observations which appears most frequently in the appellate cases which mention prior record as relevant to sentencing is the aphorism that 'a man must not be sentenced on his record' (see, e.g., *Queen* (1981)). This has been taken to mean that the relevance of previous convictions is not a primary one, in the sense of fixing the appropriate sentence. The sentence level is primarily determined by the seriousness of the current offence. Occasionally, then, the current offence will be so serious that even a completely clean record will be irrelevant (for example, *Bailey* (1982)). These cases apart, the defendant's criminal record is relevant to the extent that if he has no previous convictions he is generally entitled to substantial mitigation as a first offender (Thomas, 1979, pp. 199–200). If, however, there are previous convictions, the mitigation is less impressive and, ultimately, non-existent. This theory has been described as 'progressive loss of mitigation' (Ashworth, 1983) and is generally thought to be preferred by the English Court of Appeal to the simpler notion of increasing sentence on each reconviction having regard to lengthening record ('cumulative sentencing'). The real difference between the two theories is that in the former the notion of a 'ceiling' for the current offence must be kept firmly in mind, while on the latter view there need in the end be no proportionality between the current offence and the sentence imposed. In *Cohen* (1984) the first approach was followed, and a five-year prison sentence imposed on a man with a long record for similar offences of petty deception was reduced to six months in order properly to reflect the seriousness of the most recent offence. A similar line was taken in *McPherson* (1980) where a fifteen month prison sentence was reduced so as to allow immediate release of a persistent petty thief. The 'progressive loss of mitigation' theory is a rather loose one, however, with the ceiling for many offences remaining vague and the question of how much mitigation should be regarded as lost upon each reconviction being unexplored by the courts at anything but a very general level. Many writers suggest thta, whatever may be the theory of the matter, in practice a record of previous convictions 'is an aggravating consideration' (Walker 1985, p. 44; Nicholson 1981, p. 212) and that something much closer to cumulative sentencing is applied, as would be suggested by the preliminary work of Fitzmaurice and Pease (1986).

2 *Similarity of previous offences to the current offence*

In support of the importance of similarity there is the practice, approved by Home Office Circular, of reading out in court only selected offences from the record. This Circular provides, inter alia (Home Office, 1973): 'When the previous offence is for a traffic infringement, previous convictions of offences outside the traffic field will not usually be relevant. More generally, previous offences of a class different from the current offence may be able to be ignored (e.g. in the case of theft, no reference may be necessary to a previous conviction of a sexual offence).'

On the other hand, it is striking that one of the few statutory provisions to deal specifically with the relevance of previous convictions, the extended sentence provision designed to deal with persistent serious offenders under section 28 of the Powers of Criminal Courts Act 1973, does not require repetition of similar offences for eligibility for the sentence.

Some recent appellant cases where the very different nature of the earlier offending has been held to render the record wholly or in part irrelevant are *Silver* (1982) (conviction for manslaughter, earlier record of traffic offending irrelevant), *Williams* (1983) (defendant convicted of offence of dishonesty; the court took note of a 'record of dishonesty' but regarded an earlier conviction for rape as 'not material'), *Cawser* (1980) (convicted of rape; 'a man with a bad record; it is, perhaps, fair to say, that there is only one incident in his record of a sexual nature'.) And see *Dodsworth*, below.

3 *Frequency of reoffending*
There are a number of indications that frequency of past offending is relevant in sentence selection. Convictions become spent under the 1974 Act after the relevant 'rehabilitation period' has expired. If an offence is committed during the rehabilitation period, the first offence is not lived down until the rehabilitation period for the second offence has ended. Frequent offenders, therefore, have few or no spent convictions. Frequency is a criterion for the imposition of an extended sentence. The existence of a conviction-free gap prior to the current offence is regarded as a significant mitigating factor (Thomas 1979, pp. 200–202). A recent example is *Bleasdale* (1984), where Hobhouse J. commented: 'What has to be said in favour of this appellant is that since serving that sentence (in 1978) he has kept out of trouble. This is an important feature in his favour … This appellant did make [an] effort, clearly, and between 1978 and 1982 he succeeded.'

A case combining this factor with the previous one is *West* (1983), where the defendant was convicted on two counts of assault. The court, while noting West's 'indifferent record', changed a custodial sentence to one of community service on the basis that the last conviction for violence 'was some nine years ago, when he was in his twenties'.

4 *Seriousness of previous offences*
Previous offences which were visited with severe sanctions (custodial sentences of thirty months or more) are never spent under the 1974 Act.

All indictable offences committed by the defendant should necessarily
appear in his criminal record, but summary convictions contained in
local police records may not appear (Walker 1985). Seriousness of
past offences is a criterion for the operation of the extended sentence.

In *Dodsworth* (1984) the defendant was convicted of the rape of
a girl aged twelve. The fact that the defendant had been convicted
of attempted rape in similar circumstances in 1979 was regarded as
highly significant, '... so plainly this is a man who has to be punished
and punished severely and from whom the public is entitled to expect
protection for a considerable length of time'.

5 *Previous sentences*

Full details of previous sentences received should be included in the
criminal record, such as the amount of any fine, the duration of any
custodial or non-custodial sentence, or number of hours community
service and any alteration as the result of an appeal. The date of release
from the last custodial sentence (if any) is also given. Where the
defendant has not previously served a custodial sentence, the sentencer
is obliged by statute to satisfy himself that custody is now essential
(Powers of Criminal Courts Act 1973, s. 20; Criminal Justice Act
1982, s. 1). The Home Office Circular of 1973 suggests that there are
a number of other situations in which previous sentences received by
the defendant must be regarded as relevant: (Home Office 1973):
'Previous offences and sentences which bear on statutory sentencing
requirements may need to be cited if the court contemplates a sentence
to which one of the requirements is relevant.'

Some sentences are dependent upon the existence of an earlier
decision of a sentencing court (e.g. punishment for breach of a conditional order).

Also the court might, for example, find it necessary to cite a finding of guilty
of an offence, in a different class from the current offence, in respect of which
an offender had been placed on probation but had failed to comply with the
requirements of the order, in order to make it understood why the court was
not considering a probation order in the current case. Similarly, it may be
necessary where the court is considering imposing a custodial sentence to cite
a previous sentence of imprisonment, regardless of the nature of the offence.

Previous sentences handed out to a particular offender are
sometimes referred to, especially where the offending pattern has
continued. In *Tremlett* (1984) the defendant was convicted of
assaulting a bus conductor. The Court of Appeal noted that in

Tremlett's record similar assaults had been punished by way of fine in 1979 and suspended prison sentence in 1980. According to the Court, 'He does not on this occasion fall to be dealt with for those offences but what has happened in the past indicates strongly that it is high time that this appellant was brought to his senses'. An immediate custodial sentence was imposed. Conversely, where it appears from the defendant's record that he has complied with earlier sentences, such as conditional orders, a 'jump' to a more severe kind of sentence should not be made in the absence of more serious law-breaking (Thomas 1979, pp. 204–205). Shapland (1981) found that a common ground for mitigation was the beneficial effect upon the defendant which a particular sentence was said to have had in the past.

6 *Staleness of previous convictions*
The same circular also provides: 'It may only rarely be necessary to take into account a single, isolated offence more than, say, ten years (or even five years) previously.'

This appears to be concerned with the staleness of certain offences on a criminal record. The Rehabilitation of Offenders Act 1974, as applied to sentencing by the Practice Direction of 1975, reflects a similar view. A complex set of rehabilitation periods is laid down in the Act, where heavier sentences are tied to longer rehabilitation periods (see Walker, 1985 for extended discussion). The implications for sentencers of the Circular and the Act taken together seem to be that stale offences are of less significance in the criminal record than recent offences, that minor offences become stale more quickly than serious offences and that offences visited with severe penalties (custodial sentences of more than thirty months in the Act) never become stale.

Broadly in line with this is section 16(2) of the Children and Young Perons Act 1963 which provides that in proceedings against a person who has attained the age of twenty-one, findings of guilt made against him when he was under the age of fourteen shall be disregarded 'for the purpose of any evidence of previous convictions'. Oddly, though, such information should still be incorporated in the antecedents (Practice Direction, 1975).

In *Cole* (1983), the defendant was aged twenty-seven at the date of conviction. A 'very ancient conviction as a juvenile ... can be disregarded for present purposes', said the Court of Appeal.

7 *Age of defendant when he received previous convictions*

The age of a defendant is often an important consideration in sentencing in England, and can operate as a significant mitigating factor, particularly where it is associated with other factors. Thomas (1979, p. 195) suggests that youth continues to have some value as a mitigating factor throughout the early twenties and sometimes as late as thirty. An aspect of this is that if previous convictions were recorded against a defendant at a young age, they may be regarded as less relevant later.

Antecedents generally contain the age of the defendant, and his age at the time of the commission of each earlier offence is evident from the list of previous convictions. Findings of guilt are included but convictions under the age of fourteen are generally so marked. If the defendant was under seventeen when convicted, certain of the rehabilitation periods under the 1974 Act are halved.

8 *Previous record as allowing character inference*

Certain offences in a criminal record are regarded as 'obviously revealing' (Devlin, 1970) in some way about the defendant, indicating that there must be 'something wrong' (Samuels, 1985) and suggesting a particular line of enquiry for the court, or a particular mode of disposal. Examples would be a previous history of offences of arson or sexual offences (e.g. *Brown* (1985)). An example given by Devlin (1970) indicates that sometimes a criminal record will allow character inferences to be made where the offences contained therein would not otherwise appear particularly relevant to the current conviction: '... some benches have been observed to regard it as highly relevant in some offences of dishonesty that a young offender has a record of the less serious motoring offences ... as being indicative of a complete disregard for the rules.'

Shapland's research (Shapland 1981, pp. 70–71) shows that mitigation advanced by lawyers on behalf of their clients often refers to previous convictions. Apart from the obvious benefit to the client of a clean or virtually clean record, mitigation was often advanced to try to show the character of the defendant in a better light than at first appeared from a perusal of his previous law-breaking. She says (1981, p. 70):

Previous convictions ... will tend to show that the offender is of little moral worth ... Mitigating factors concerned with previous convictions will either assert that, contrary to the virtual offender normally considered by the court, this particular offender has few or no convictions; or that his previous offences were of a minor nature; or as he is not a persistent offender the present offence does not fall into a train of similar offences. In these cases the offender is attempting to adjust the virtual picture of himself painted by the police.

In *Loosemore* (1980) the Court of Appeal made the general observation that a sentencer should deal with the defendant on the basis of his offence and not on the basis of his 'feckless character and general behaviour'. There are numerous examples, however, where the Court may be seen to drawn an inference as to character from the list of previous convictions. An example is *Smith* (1982), where it was said to be 'clear from Smith's record that he is a man who sees no reason at all why he should not poach if he has the time and the opportunity', and *Bowater and Davies* (1980) where the Court inferred from the record that the defendant was a man well acquainted with dishonest methods of dealing in scrap metal.

Perhaps the classic instance of English courts drawing character inferences is in the use of 'last-chance probation' in an attempt to break a cycle of repeated offending, where repeated custodial sentencing is perceived by the sentencer as 'ineffective'. Recent examples are *Hammond* (1982) and *Bradley* (1983).

Guidance or guidelines?

To what extent are the eight factors identified above capable of being refined and encapsulated in appellate guidance or sentencing guidelines? Traditionally, the Court of Appeal in England has been reluctant, when hearing appeals against sentence, to travel much beyond the instant facts of the case to provide general guidance for sentencers. Recently, however, this has begun to change, with an important series of 'guideline' judgments providing more generalised assistance for sentencers on important questions of sentencing policy, such as prison overcrowding, or dealing with particular types of case, such as sentencing in serious drug offences in *Aramah* (1983) (for a discussion of recent developments see Ashworth, 1984). The Court of Appeal has not so far addrressed the general issue of interpretation of prior record in a similar way, but in principle it would seem that some ground-rules should be capable of being drawn and indeed must be enunciated if we are to have anything approaching consistent decision-making. As the Lord Chief Justice has commented in his seminal speech in *Bibi* (1980): 'We are not aiming at uniformity of sentence; that would be impossible. We are aiming at uniformity of approach.'

To what extent can there be such uniformity of approach in relation to the interpretation of prior record? In order to achieve uniformity, we have to move away from the still prevalent notion in England that sentencing is a matter of intuition, towards the articulation of general rules and relevant exceptions.

The first substantial difficulty is that prior record may be taken account of for one of two very different reasons. It may be looked at in order to provide a basis for some kind of predictive assessment of the defendant's likely future behaviour or response to sentence, or it may be considered as a dimension of the defendant's culpability against which his punishment is to be measured. Some of the eight factors identified above primarily reflect the predictive approach, some primarily reflect the culpability approach, but nearly all are capable of reflecting both.

Criminal record and prediction

Some writers have argued that whenever previous convictions are taken into account by the sentencer, a predictive rationale of sentencing must be operating. Take, for example, Fletcher (1978, p. 466): 'The contemporary pressure to consider prior convictions in setting the level of the offence and of punishment reflects a theory of social protection rather than a doctrine of deserved punishment. The rule of thumb is that recidivists are more dangerous and that society will be better served if the recidivists are isolated for longer terms.'

Whilst the correctness of this view will be challenged in a moment, it is certaintly true to say that previous convictions are more obviously relevant to the sentencer working on a predictive rather than a just deserts basis.

Let us consider the implications of prior record for the predictive approach. To start with, the *number* of previous convictions recorded against a defendant is generally regarded as being the best available predictor of future offending. The research evidence is that the more convictions recorded against a defendant, the greater the likelihood that he will be reconvicted. An English research study (Philpotts and Lancucki, 1979) found that 29% of males having no previous convictions who were convicted of standard list offences in January 1971 were reconvicted within six years. The percentage of offenders who had one previous conviction when convicted in January 1971 who were reconvicted within six years was 54%. If they had two to four previous convictions the figure rose to 70% and for those with five or more previous convictions, 87% were reconvicted within six years. A sentencer working on a predictive rationale would, therefore, require a full and accurate account of the defendant's previous law-breaking. A number of American jurisdictions allow the sentencer to have reference to the defendant's 'arrest record' as well as previous convictions, on the (surely debatable) basis that this more clearly establishes a criminal 'pattern of conduct', and there is some research evidence that the number of the defendant's prior arrests was a very important determinant of sentence in pre-guideline America (Hawkinson 1975: Johnston *et al.*, 1973).

The predictive sentencer would require information about prior record in order to implement one or more of a variety of approaches (for fuller discussion see Ashworth 1983, Ch. 5). He might well seek to deter or incapacitate the individual offender by a severe sentence, perhaps relatively early in his perceived criminal career, as a 'nip in the bud'. The severe sentence would be seen as more likely to prevent the offender (through deterrence, or perhaps through reform) from continuing his life of crime. Evidence of repetition of *similar* offending, and *frequency* of repetition, would inevitably tend to reinforce the predictive sentencer's view, even though the statistical evidence is that repetition of a particular type of offending in the past is not a particularly good indicator that similar offending will continue in the future.

The English research study referred to above (Philpotts and Lancucki, 1979) also examined the likelihood of reconviction of certain types of offence given the offence with which the offenders in the sample were convicted in January 1971. A person convicted of an offence involving violence, for example, was found to be considerably more likely to be reconvicted of violence than any other offender, but the violent offender was still considerably more likely to be reconvicted of a property offence than an offence of violence (1979, Table 4.3). Thus for offenders of twenty-one or over who were convicted of offences of violence in January 1971, 58% were not reconvicted, 15% were first reconvicted for an offence of violence and 27% were first reconvicted for an offence against property. With regard to the *age* of the defendant when the previous offences occurred, recent Home Office Research (1985) shows that the earlier a defendant's first conviction occurs, the more likely he is to be reconvicted. Yet this must be set against the fact that of all males first convicted before the age of sixteen, some two-thirds are not reconvicted at all within two years (Pease 1985). The *seriousness* of previous convictions seems, from the earlier observations from the writers to be regarded as a reason for taking a tougher line on sentencing. Yet the statistical evidence is that, in general, crimes of serious personal violence and sexual molestation are the *least* likely to be repeated. The drawing of *character inferences* from the prior record would seem to be rooted in a predictive rationale. The sentencer is making a 'diagnosis', based on what the defendant has done in the past, geared towards his needs and the best perceived way of amending his conduct for the future, such as trying to break into a cycle of offending through 'last chance probation'. It will be seen from this last example that, exceptionally on the predictive approach, a poor record could form the basis for a lenient sentence in order to pursue some therapeutic objective.

Systematic guidance could in theory be drawn up for sentencers along the lines of statistical prediction of likely reoffending on the basis of past record, in reliance on research such as that outlined above (see also Whinery *et al.*, 1976; Home Office, 1985; Farrington and Tarling, 1985). There is insufficient evidence of this kind available for it to be done now and there are uncertainties and contradictions in the work which has been done, but it could in principle be achieved. Such an exercise would be not dissimilar to the work which has been done in this country and the United States on 'parole prediction scores' (see Nuttall *et al.*, 1977; Gottfredson, Wilkins and Hoffman, 1978). In England and Wales the parole prediction score is based upon sixteen variables, including the nature of the offence for which the prisoner was sentenced, the number of his previous convictions, the number of his previous imprisonments, any gap prior to the latest conviction, his age when first found guilty and his age when convicted of the current offence. There are, however, numerous problems with the predictive approach. Firstly, in the vast majority of predictive studies carried out, whilst criminal record taken together with other predictive factors has been strongly associated with subsequent recidivism, the association between each of the variables and future offending has been found to be weak. A high rate of error in prediction almost always occurs, both in failing to identify those who did return to crime and in mistakenly identifying those who did not (for a summary of the evidence available see Floud and Young (1981)). Secondly, efforts to improve predictive accuracy involve the collection of information about the offender going far beyond his actual criminal record. In important recent work on predictive sentencing by Greenwood (1982) matters identified as predictors include the defendant's history of drug use and his employment status, as well as the number of his previous convictions and his age when first convicted. Collection of such 'soft' data may well be objected to on grounds of its likely inaccuracy and its invasion of privacy (see von Hirsch, 1986 and the counter-arguments of Wilkins, 1985).

Criminal record and 'just deserts'

The recent history of sentencing reform in America, the resurgence of the notion of 'just deserts' and the introduction of sentencing guidelines in so many states has been fully described elsewhere in this volume. One of the most difficult matters for the just deserts theorists to resolve has been the relevance of the defendant's previous convictions to the current sentence. Some writers have argued that such a theory cannot support more severe sentences for persistent offenders and that the reasoning employed in taking account of them must be covertly preventive (Fletcher, 1978; Singer, 1979). Most recently, Wilkins (1985) has claimed that it is 'because we know that prior convictions are prognostic of future criminality that the strict retributive model is, to most persons, unacceptable'. Such criticism has provoked an important response from Andrew von Hirsch, the leading proponent of the just deserts view.

In *Doing Justice* (von Hirsch, 1976), two main arguments were advanced for taking account of prior record in computing culpability. The first was that (at p. 85): 'A repetition of the offence following ... conviction may be regarded as more culpable since [the actor] persisted in the behaviour after having been forcefully censured for it through his prior punishment.'

The second was an 'evidentiary' one that the more often the defendant is convicted and punished, the more sure we can be that he is actually guilty. In a later article (von Hirsch, 1981) he seems not to pursue the latter claim (wisely, perhaps, for it apparently confuses 'evidence of greater culpability' with 'greater culpability'. He does, however, provide the fullest account yet available of the relevance of previous convictions within just deserts theory.

It is argued by von Hirsch that when a person commits some misdeed in everyday life, he may plead that his misconduct was uncharacteristic of his previous behaviour. This plea relates to an inference which is normally drawn from (a) a judgment about the wrongfulness of an act to (b) the disapproval directed at a person. The actor is claiming in mitigation that though this act was wrong he should not suffer full obloquy for it because the act is out of keeping with his customary standards of behaviour. Logically, this plea carries greatest weight when the actor has not committed the misdeed before and it becomes progressively less persuasive with repetition of the wrongdoing. This analysis is then transferred to sentencing. It is clear that the resultant model is very similar, though drawn in more detail, to the 'progressive loss of mitigation' theory, outlined above. It entails that the defendant's criminal record is not appropriate to justify endless successive increases in penalty, but is primarily a means of achieving sentence reduction for those with clean or nearly clean records. The clarity of von Hirsch's model, especially as set out in his 1981 article, provides us with an excellent opportunity to examine the eight factors which were identified above as potentially relevant to prior record in the English sentencing context, to see to what extent they might be compatible with a just deserts sentencing framework.

The first consideration is *number* of previous convictions. It will be recalled that on the basis of predictive sentencing, number provided the best available indicator of future offending. The greater the number of previous convictions, the greater the risk of reoffending and the more pressing the need for appropriate preventive sentencing. In 'just deserts' sentencing, however, number is relevant is only a strictly limited way. The defendant is entitled to mitigation for the first few offences, and then the mitigation is exhausted so that the defendant is visited with the full penalty of the law. The obvious question is how many repetitions can occur before the force of the mitigation is lost? Von Hirsch concedes that he has 'no ready answer' to this question, being content to suggest 'a certain limited number of repetitions' (1981, p. 616). We may, for the purposes of argument, select five (as Andrew Ashworth suggests in his Chapter, above). The crucial point is that after those five convictions, reconviction would not attract greater severity. Von Hirsch calls this a 'closed criminal history score'. If we take the Minnesota Sentencing guidelines as an example, we see (Appendix to this volume, below) that the defendant is assigned one point for every felony conviction prior to the current conviction. The guidelines have a closed criminal history score in that after six or more previous convictions, the presumptive sentence in the right-hand column of the grid remains unchanged with, for example, twenty-four months representing the 'ceiling' for an offence in seriousness category (I).

It must be obvious, however, that in taking account of prior record on a just deserts calculus, number cannot be all there is to it. What of the *similarity* or otherwise between the current offence and offences appearing in the record? Surely similarity ought to be relevant, for it confirms in the starkest possible manner that such misbehaviour is characteristic of the defendant. Von Hirsch is less forthcoming on this point, but in *Doing Justice* (von Hirsch 1976, p. 86), he argued that previous convictions might lose some of their significance if they were for crimes 'sufficiently dissimilar' to the present one. Of course, the significance of this must depend upon the level of generality at which similarity is identified. Von Hirsch now suggests that the criterion is whether the current act and the prior criminal conduct are 'similar in the basic principles they violate' (von Hirsch 1981, p. 616). In arguing that 'white-collar swindle' is similar to 'other frauds', 'outright thefts' and 'acts of force', since these all 'involve wilful injury' (p. 617), it is clear that he identifies similarity at a fairly low level. The effect of this is to decrease the relative importance of similarity in the criminal record and increase the relative importance of number. In the Minnesota guidelines no particular importance is attached to repetition of similar offences. It seems that this may have been for fear of introducing great complexity into the calculation of the criminal history score (von Hirsch 1982, pp. 201–202).

What about the *staleness* of previous convictions? Again, in *Doing Justice* it was argued that provision should be made 'for the decay of offenders' criminal records, with convictions long past being disregarded' (1976, p. 87). This is because the more distant the conviction the less plausible it is to claim that such acts are characteristic of the defendant's conduct. The Commission introduced a 'decay factor' into the Minnesota guidelines in this respect. Thus prior felony convictions do not count towards the criminal history score if ten years have elapsed since the date of discharge from or expiration of the sentence, providing that the defendant remained free of conviction during that period. There is also the question of the *seriousness* of the previous convictions. According to von Hirsch (1981, p. 620):

... the quality of the record should count. Someone convicted of his first serious crime would be entitled to plead that such gravely reprehensible conduct has been uncharacteristic of him, and hence that he deserves to have his penalty scaled down — even where he has a record of lesser infractions. Where the current crime is serious, in other words, the criminal history should take into account the gravity of the prior convictions as well as their number.

If, on the other hand, the current offence is less serious than some offences which appear on the record, it would seem that the defendant has shown that offending of a nature at least as serious as the current offence is not untypical of him and the argument for mitigation is much less strong. In the Minnesota guidelines relative seriousness is taken into account in computation of criminal history scores, but only to a limited extent. If a previous offence was punished only by way of a fine it will be accorded less weight. If the fine was $100 or less, the conviction does not count at all. Yet the distinction remains crude in that all previous convictions resulting in custodial sentences attract one point, whether the offences were in fact serious or relatively trivial.

Frequency of repetition does not as such form part of von Hirsch's scheme, though, as we have seen, he advocates giving less weight to older convictions. On the face of it, rapid repetition of offending would seem relevant to desert, as underlining the characteristic nature of the behaviour, and it is perhaps odd that specific provision is not made for it. In the guidelines, adoption of the 'decay factor' takes account of it to some extent. The Commentary states that 'a person who was convicted of three felonies within a five-year period is more culpable than one convicted of three felonies within a twenty-year period'. Yet, it is not clear that the ten-year 'decay factor' for felonies would operate in either of these cases, assuming the convictions to be evenly spaced.

On a just deserts view, the *age* of the defendant does not qualify as a mitigating factor as such, though it could be relevant indirectly, such as through the issue of degree of participation in the offence (e.g. where a young person was led by experienced offenders into a criminal enterprise). The relevance of the defendant's age to his culpability is a matter which has not so far been adequately dealt with by the just deserts theorists. It is, however, taken account of in the Minnesota guidelines, where for an offender who is under twenty-one when sentenced, only half a point is ascribed to him for each prior felony conviction occurring after his sixteenth birthday. Previous convictions for less serious offences committed as a juvenile are disregarded. Once the offender attains the age of twenty-one, a nominal one point will be left on his record to indicate to the court the existence of convictions as a juvenile. If he has one such prior conviction, the resultant half-point will be disregarded. It is difficult to discern the rationale upon which the Commission proceeded in weighting these factors.

It is apparent from the just deserts model that what is taken to matter is the legal classification of previous convictions, rather than *previous sentences* served by the defendant. The emphasis upon convictions seems also to ensure that in 'just deserts' theory, in contrast to predictive sentencing, no attention should be given to 'arrest records' or alleged but unproven law-breaking (see von Hirsch 1981, p. 608 et. seq.). These limitations are reflected in the Minnesota guidelines. On the other hand, as we have seen, the guidelines refer to sentences served rather than to offence seriousness when drawing the fairly crude distinctions in assigning points to take account of seriousness of previous offences.

Recently, Walker has criticised von Hirsch's analysis of the relevance of prior convictions by questioning the implications of the 'out of character' plea. He says (1985, p. 44):

The principal defect of his justification, however, is its failure to distinguish clearly between punishing because punishment is deserved and punishing because punishment expresses disapproval. If his argument is to hold water it must be carried to the length of saying that recidivists should be punished not merely to express disapproval of their character but because the sentencer is entitled to punish them for that character. The Court of Appeal sometimes allows evidence of good moral character – such as bravery – to mitigate sentence ... but to generalise from this to a policy of sentencing people for their moral character would be a leap into a bog without boundaries.

If Walker is right in this vividly-expressed criticism, it seems that factor number eight, above, whereby information about prior record can be used by the court in drawing *character inferences* must be regarded as being within von Hirsch's theory. Yet this factor must surely be confined to predictive sentencing, having no possible place in just deserts theory. A closer reading of just deserts theory, however, reveals that it does not have the wide implications which Walker claims for it. 'Just deserts' relates to punishment for the current offence, though if that offence is the first, there is some room for leniency in the way in which it is sentenced. In no sense, therefore, could this amount to 'sentencing people for their moral character'. As von

Hirsch says, it must be a mistake to assume that using prior law-breaking in judging someone's actions 'must rest on a whole-life notion of good or bad character' (1981, p. 609). Perhaps, though, von Hirsch's use of the words 'typical' and 'characteristic' to describe the assessment to be made of the defendant's record in the light of the current offence is unfortunate in tending to suggest an assessment being made of the overall moral standing of the person. It is quite clear from the context of the discussion that this is not what is meant.

Conclusions

It seems beyond doubt that while the importance of taking account of the defendant's previous convictions is universally recognised in English sentencing practice, there is great confusion over the precise relevance of items of information contained in such records. The theory of progressive mitigation, which is akin to just deserts, appears to be gaining prominence in English writings, reflecting the majority of observations of the Court of Appeal. On this view, as we have seen, good record is a matter capable of constituting mitigation but poor record is not an aggravating factor. Yet one of the leading writers on English sentencing, Nigel Walker, while accepting this position in theory, says that 'it would be more realistic to acknowledge that in practice a record with previous relevant convictions is an aggravating consideration' (Walker 1985, p. 44). A leading practitioner, Sheriff Nicholson, says that 'previous good character is not so much a mitigating factor, but rather an essentially neutral one, whereas previous bad character is certainly an aggravating factor' (Nicholson 1981, p. 212). An attempt has been made in this Chapter to separate out two strands in English sentencing in relation to prior record — 'predictive' sentencing and 'just deserts'. It has been argued that these approaches are in tension with each other, often entailing contrary inferences from facts about a defendant's previous record. So long as English sentencing retains both approaches in this context, its attitude to the relevance of prior convictions is bound to be incoherent.

A powerful case has been made in several of the Chapters of this book for the adoption of guidelines based on just deserts into English sentencing practice. As far as the relevance of prior convictions is concerned, the attractions of such an approach are considerable. First, as reflected in the theory of progressive loss of mitigation, it allows us to break with the open-ended approach of increasingly severe sentencing which ultimately bears no relation to the seriousness of the last offence. Secondly, it provides us with an agenda of matters relating to previous convictions which ought to be taken into account in every sentencing decision (*number, seriousness, similarity, staleness*, etc.). While it will be clear from the foregoing discussion that there is still room for debate about which factors should be included, the respective weight to be assigned to each, and the practicability of including them within a workable scheme, the attraction of sentencing guidelines is that they offer us a framework within which sentencers are constrained to a 'uniformity of approach'. Of course the issues are difficult to resolve, because sentencing is a complex form of decision-making, but the resultant model offers the great attraction of coherence, a quality clearly lacking in current English sentencing practice.

References

Ashworth, A. J. (1983) *Sentencing and Penal Policy*, London, Weidenfeld and Nicolson.

Ashworth, A. J. (1984) 'Techniques of guidance on sentencing', *Criminal Law Review*, 519.

Devlin, K. (1970) *Sentencing Offenders in Magistrates' Courts*, London, Heinemann.

Farrington, D. P. and Tarling, R. (eds.) (1985) *Prediction in Criminology*, Albany, State University of New York Press.

Fitzmaurice, C. and Pease, K. (1986) *The Psychology of Judicial Sentencing*, Manchester University Press.

Fletcher, G. (1978) *Rethinking Criminal Law*, Boston, Little, Brown.

Gottfredson, D. M. *et al.* (1978) *Guidelines for Parole and Sentencing*, Lexington, Heath.

Green, E. (1961) *Judicial Attitudes in Sentencing*, London, Macmillan.

Green, E. (1964) 'Inter and intra-racial crime relative to sentencing', *Journal of Criminal Law, Criminology and Police Science*, 55, 348.

Greenwood, P. W. *et al.* (1976) *Prosecution of Adult Felony Defendants*, Santa Monica, Rand.

Greenwood, P. W. (1982) *Selective Incapacitation*, Santa Monica, Rand.

Harris, B. (1984) *Criminal Jurisdiction of Magistrates*, Chichester, Barry Rose.

Hawkinson, T. (1975) 'The effect of pre-trial release, race and previous arrest on conviction and sentencing', *Creighton Law Review*, 8, 930.

Hogarth, (1971) *Sentencing as a Human Process*, University of Toronto Press.

Home Office (1978) *The Sentence of the Court*, London, HMSO.

Home Office (1973) Circular 17/1973.

Home Office (1985A) Circular POL/85; 1/19/1 of Feb. 18.

Home Office (1985B) Statistical Bulletin 7/85 *Criminal Careers of those born in 1953, 1958 and 1963*, Home Office Statistical Department, Tolworth Tower.

Johnston, B.L. *et al.* (1973) 'Discretion in felony sentencing – a study of influencing factors', *Washington Law Review*, 48, 857.

Kapardis, A. and Farrington, D.P. (1981) 'An experimental study of sentencing by magistrates', *Law and Human Behaviour*, 5, 107.

Minnesota Sentencing Guidelines Commission (1984) *The Impact of the Minnesota Sentencing Guidelines: Three Year evaluation*, St Paul, Minnesota.

Nicholson, C.G.B. (1981) *The Law and Practice of Sentencing in Scotland*, Edinburgh, Green and Son.

Nuttall, C. *et al.* (1977) *Parole in England and Wales*, Home Office Research Study 38, London, HMSO.

Pease, K. (1985) 'What risk of reconviction for juveniles?', *Justice of the Peace*, 149, 329.

Philpotts, G.J.O. and Lancucki, L.B. (1979) *Previous Convictions, Sentence and Reconviction*, Home Office Research Study 53, London, HMSO.

Samuels, A. (1985) 'The effect of previous convictions on the sentencing decision', *Justice of the Peace*, 149, 550.

Shapland, J. (1981) *Between Conviction and Sentence*, London, Routledge and Kegan Paul.

Singer, P. (1979) *Just Deserts: Sentencing based on Equality and Desert*, University of Chicago Press.

Streatfeild Committee, (1961) *Report of the Interdepartmental Committee on the Business of the Criminal Courts*, Cmnd. 1289, London, HMSO.

Thomas, D.A. (1979) *Principles of Sentencing* (2nd ed.), London, Heinemann.

Tiffany, L.P. *et al.* (1975) 'A statistical analysis of sentencing in federal courts', *Journal of Legal Studies*, 369.

von Hirsch, A. (1976) *Doing Justice*, New York, Hill and Wang.

von Hirsch, A. (1981) 'Desert and previous convictions in sentencing', *Minnesota Law Review*, 65, 591.

von Hirsch, A. (1982) 'Constructing guidelines for sentencing: the critical choices for the Minnesota Sentencing Guidelines Commission', *Hamline Law Review*, 164.

von Hirsch, A. (1986) 'Deservedness and dangerousness in sentencing policy', *Criminal Law Review*, 79.

Walker, N. (1985) *Sentencing Theory Law and Practice*, London, Butterworths.

Whinery, L.H. (1976) *Predictive Sentencing*, Lexington, Heath.

Wilkins, L. (1985) 'The politics of prediction' in Farrington, D.P. and Tarling, R. (eds.) *op. cit.*

Cases

Aramah (1982) 4 Cr.App.R.(S) 404.
Bailey (1982) 4 Cr.App.R.(S) 15.
Bibi (1980) 2 Cr.App.R.(S) 177.
Bleasdale (1984) 6 Cr.App.R.(S) 177.
Bowater and Davies (1980) C.S.P. A9.2(f).
Bradley (1983) 5 Cr.App.R.(S) 363.
Brown (1984) 6 Cr.App.R.(S) 335.
Cawser (1980) 2 Cr.App.R.(S) 31.
Cohen (1984) 6 Cr.App.R.(S) 131.
Cole (1983) 5 Cr.App.R.(S) 218.
Dodsworth (1984) 6 Cr.App.R.(S) 187.
Hammond (1982) 4 Cr.App.R.(S) 148.
Loosemore (1980) 2 Cr.App.R.(S) 172.
McPherson (1980) 2 Cr.App.R.(S) 4.
Queen (1981) 3 Cr.App.R.(S) 245.
Silver (1982) 4 Cr.App.R.(S) 48.
Smith (1982) 4 Cr.App.R.(S) 219.
Tremlett (1984) 6 Cr.App.R.(S) 199.
Walsh (1980) 2 Cr.App.R.(S) 224.
West (1983) 5 Cr.App.R.(S) 206.
Williams (1983) 5 Cr.App.R.(S) 244.

Sentencing and measurement: some analogies from psychology

It is said that the Rake's Progress of psychology started when she lost her soul. Then she lost her mind, then her consciousness, and now all she has left is her behaviour, of which the less said the better. If the subject matter of psychology is behaviour, then judicial sentencing is fair game for the psychologist's attention. Yet the psychologist's concern with sentencing seems to have been slight and selective. Perhaps the largest literature concerns individual differences among judges and the effects such differences have upon sentencing practice. It is strange that the psychology of individual differences (ideographic psychology) has been applied more than nomothetic psychology (the study of general principles of behaviour), because it is difficult to see how ideographic psychology can help develop or reform sentencing practice. Can we envisage a state of affairs in which judges are excluded from practice because of a particular set of attitudes or personality traits which influence their sentencing? Nomothetic psychology, on the other hand, might well be able to identify general problems and issues in sentencing, and suggest general remedies. Some of the possibilities have been spelled out by Catherine Fitzmaurice and myself elsewhere (Fitzmaurice and Pease, 1986).

In this Chapter, ways will be suggested in which a psychologist might approach sentencing issues as though sentencing were like any other piece of behaviour which involves the person as a measuring instrument. The reasoning is necessarily speculative. The purpose of the Chapter will have been achieved if the reader sees the relevance of the concepts employed to sentencing practice. A bonus will be the recognition of how plausible it is to see descriptive sentencing guidelines as the sort of mechanism for sentencing reform which would have resulted from a psychological approach on the lines which follow.

In short, this is one psychologist's view of how sentencing could and should be approached. The perspective has implications for all aspects of sentencing, including sentence review.

The strange world of sentencing

Imagine a naive psychologist (called Psyche) who wishes to do her doctoral thesis on judicial sentencing. She has the advantage over psychologists already working in the field of a complete ignorance of criminal justice, and an utter disregard for the conventional accounts by judges of what they are doing when they sentence. The first thing Psyche notices about sentencing is what an extraordinary activity it is, even when it is not accompanied by strange custom and ritual and eighteenth-century dress. People listen to accounts of the actions of other people, and proceed to match these actions to punishment. The aspects of the action which are relevant to punishment choice are not made explicit. The punishments are expressed in units (usually of time or money) which bear no obvious relation to the actions. The way in which the response is arrived at is ineffable. There is no debate about the mechanisms of scaling, simply the observation that the occasional response is 'wrong', or that there are wide differences in punishments awarded to overtly similar acts. A rhetoric of 'principles of sentencing' exists. These principles are only evident from the words which accompany sentence. There is seldom any way of inferring sentencing principles from sentencing practice.

Faced with a situation of this kind, Psyche seeks clarification by applying concepts familiar from other parts of her discipline. She seeks insight in the field of psychological testing. The classic concepts of test theory are those of reliability and validity.[1] Validity concerns the capacity of an instrument to measure what it sets out to measure. Reliability refers to the capacity of an instrument to measure whatever it is measuring consistently. An instrument can be reliable without being valid. The converse is not true. For instance, tape-measures provide a reliable measure of something. That is to say, almost all tape measures will come up with the same measures of difference between people, and will keep on doing so. The tape-measure is reliable. If, however, what it is measuring is described as intelligence, the test is not valid. If it is described as height, it is. While the issue seems ludicrous in the example, it is not so when one has to deal with the measurement of personality traits like aggression or professional aptitude – nor with sentencing.

Looking over research on sentencing, Psyche remarks that there has been more concern with the *reliability* of sentencing than with the *validity* of sentencing. Studies of sentencing disparity and attempts to reduce that disparity, she opines, are rather like attempts to produce a set of judges who behave as consistently as tape-measures. The trouble seems to be a relative indifference as to whether what is measured is height or intelligence! (I should clarify that this particular criticism is of psychologists, not judges, although Psyche is too naive to care whom she offends.) Psychologists have accepted too readily the characterisation of sentencing issues by those in the criminal justice system with too little concern about the *nature* of the sentencing task. This is reflected in an imbalance in the literature between the analysis of individual differences in sentencing (unreliability), of which there is a good deal, and the study of factors with which sentencing practice tends to co-vary (studies of validity) of which there is very little in the psychological literature. Psyche concludes that since a reliable test can be produced which is invalid, but a valid test cannot be produced which is unreliable, the proper search should be for judges to operate a valid system of sentencing. She concludes that it would be a waste of her time to risk creating the sentencing equivalent of a tape-measure test of intelligence.

Now committed to approaching sentencing as a problem in psychometrics, Psyche muses about the concept of validity. She talks to some judges about how she might examine valid sentencing, and finds them determinedly eclectic, self-confident (as she expected, having read Ashworth *et al.*, 1984) and referring to the 'mental mixer' of sentencing considerations (see Fitzmaurice, 1981). She reads the literature on sentencing principles, and returns to her intellectual base to consider techniques of validation.

Two related and basic methods of validation should be mentioned. One is known as *criterion-related* validation, the other as *construct* validation.

Criterion-related validation

In criterion-related validation, groups are distinguished which are known to differ in the variable of interest. For instance, if one wanted to develop a test of hairdressing aptitude for school-leavers who wanted to be hairdressers, ask them a large number of questions, wait several years, identify those who had turned into particularly skilled hairdressers, and go back and find the test items which they had answered differently from other children at school-leaving age. These questions are those which are *valid* predictors of hairdressing skill. This kind of validation is relevant to sentencing insofar as sentencing has a utilitarian purpose. Let us take incapacitation as an example of such a sentencing purpose. Valid incapacitative sentencing exists to the extent that those so sentenced, upon release, commit further offences of the kind which incapacitation was designed to prevent. There are some complications in the analogy here which should be made explicit. Figure 1 attempts to do so. It distinguishes:

(a) Those tests which best predict reconviction (like the valid questions in the hairdressing potential test described and the social variables identified by West (1982) and Blumstein *et al.* (1985) as predictors of criminality).
(b) The actual selection of school-leavers as apprentice hairdressers or of penal sentence.
(c) Outcome.

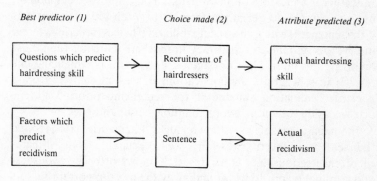

Figure 1 The hairdressing analogy to utilitarian sentencing

If sentencing were utilitarian in purpose, the kind of validation which would be best suited to the problem would be criterion-referenced validation, which assesses the extent to which a test predicts on outcome.

Construct validation

Criterion-referenced validation was the first technique of relevance to sentencing. The second is construct validation. In this, what is validated is a concept or theory. For example, H.J. Eysenck's concept of extraversion–introversion (Eysenck, 1977) was validated by reference to the pattern of relationships which it exhibits with other behaviours. Starting with a theory of individual differences in brain function, Eysenck predicts that extraverts ought to differ from introverts in a variety of ways, including smoking more, preferring the radio on louder, and having different susceptibility to optical illusions. He developed a personality test (the Maudsley Personality Inventory) to assess extraversion–introversion. If all the predicted relationships actually emerge from use of the test, both the concept and the test of extraversion–introversion are validated. The test can be used to scale extraversion.

The characteristic extraversion–introversion has some useful parallels with sentencing issues. You cannot see introversion, but you can see the sequelae of introversion. The *retributive* sentence is a measure of culpability, in the same way that the Maudsley Personality Inventory is a measure of introversion. You cannot see culpability, but you can predict certain differences between judgments of acts if the sentence is a measure of culpability. Offences inflicting greater injury, loss or damage will attract more severe sentences than those involving less injury, loss or damage, and so on. Is sentencing like this? If it is, what are the implications of viewing matters from a construct validation standpoint for sentencing reform? Psyche brushes aside the sneers about common sense, and goes on.

In sentencing exercises with two judges, Fitzmaurice (1981) found that sentencing severity was fairly well predictable from estimates of offence seriousness. Other research shows offence seriousness and criminal record to be far and away the most important factors in determining sentence. As Fitzmaurice and Pease (1986) observe:

The view of offence seriousness as pre-eminent in determining, along with criminal record, the severity of sentence passed, while consistent with judicial practice, is at odds with judicial reservations about the notion of a tariff ... Nonetheless, it seems clear that the two variables identified are indeed central to sentencing, whatever the complexities, real and imagined, of the principle of taking each case on its merits.

To restate the last few points of the argument: insofar as sentencing is retributive, construct validation is the technique of preference. The pattern of relationships between sentencing and variables linked to culpability encourage Psyche in the belief that current sentencing practice corresponds more (albeit not necessarily very closely) with what would be anticipated from people having retributive rather than utilitarian purposes. In other words, to aspire to valid retributive sentencing goes more with the grain of current sentencing practice than does the aspiration to valid utilitarian sentencing. For this reason, in the remainder of the Chapter, discussion will centre on the steps which are necessary to produce valid (and hence reliable) retributive sentencing practice.

Towards valid retributive sentencing

Psyche is weaned from a narrow psychometric approach. The analogy having served its purpose, she is committed to a particular course based on the construct validation of retributive sentencing, by whatever means seems most appropriate. She concludes that there are two necessary conditions for validation to occur. They are consensus at least at the ranking level of culpability, and agreement, actual or imposed, as to how to scale sentence against culpability judgments. There is a variety of evidence, direct and indirect, that there is *general* social consensus as to relative *offence seriousness*, (see Fitzmaurice and Pease, 1986 Ch. 4), which is the major component of culpability. It will be assumed in what follows that consensus of this kind extends to judgments of culpability, at least at the level of ranking. There are three reasons for making this assumption. The first is that the evidence tends in that direction. The second is that if it were not so, the very possibility of retributive justice would not exist. The third (as if the second were not enough) is that as long as culpability judgments are not wholly random, the course of the argument which follows would be unaffected.

Turning now to the second necessary condition, the fact that people can agree about the relative extent of a characteristic does not mean that they can agree on how it can be scaled. This must be a major problem in dog-shows and beauty contests. Even if each judge ranks all contestants (or offenders) in the same way, how numbers are assigned to the underlying variable (beauty or culpability) is far from clear. For one judge, a doubling of culpability may be reflected in a relatively modest increase in sentence length. For another, a doubling of culpability may be reflected in a tripling of sentence length. Differences of just this kind were identified by Fitzmaurice (1981). Fitzmaurice and Pease (1982) classified judges as 'steep slope' or 'shallow slope' retributivists on the basis of these differences. In short, it is clear that judges do not agree on the time or money equivalents of culpability.

The signs of inconsistent scaling

Just looking at distributions of sentences would persuade Psyche that something strange is going on. For instance, sentences of imprisonment tend to be duodecimal, with multiples of three, six and twelve months appearing often and multiples of five and ten appearing scarcely ever. This contrasts with the situation concerning fines, where multiples of ten are the rule, and of twelve the exception. Money sentencing is decimal. It is difficult to think of orderly scaling under these circumstances. The great Victorian scientist, Sir Francis Galton, argued:

The extreme irregularity of the frequency of the different terms of imprisonment forces itself on the attention. It is impossible to believe that a judicial system acts fairly which acts in this way. Runs of figures like these testify to some powerful cause of disturbance which interferes with the orderly distribution of punishment in conformity with penal deserts.

Further, the gaps between sentences actually imposed get bigger as one goes up the sentencing scale. There are few sentences of four or five months' imprisonment, few of nineteen, twenty, twenty-one, twenty-two or twenty-three months, and few of forty-nine, fifty, fifty-one, fifty-two, fifty-three, fifty-four, fifty-five, fifty-six, fifty-seven, fifty-eight or fifty-nine months! Some light can be shed on this pattern of sentencing (see Fitzmaurice and Pease 1986, Chs 5 and 6) but for present purposes it suffices to say that the scale is not a simple one!

Faced with this sort of problem, Psyche starts to think about score standardisation. If the raw scores on a scale are distributed in an inconvenient way, they are standardised, i.e. they are converted to scores with a known average and a known scatter. Typically, a *mean* score is established, together with a standard deviation score, which by definition means that a known proportion of all cases fall within one unit of scatter of the mean. In this way, one can calculate the score that is exceeded by a given proportion of the population.[2]

The reader may now be aware of the relationship between the procedure described and the development of descriptive guidelines. Descriptive guidelines provide similar information about sentencing as psychological test manuals do about tests developed on the lines described. They relate the way in which a particular sentence (test score) is distributed in a particular category of case (group of people). In that way, one can calculate what the most likely sentence (test score) in a particular category of case (group of people) would be, and how extreme that sentence (score) would have to be so as to be regarded as significantly unusual.[3] The purpose of finding that out in the two circumstances has certain similarities too. In sentencing guidelines, the unusual sentence needs to be identifiable so that the necessary degree of justification may be provided, on the basis that the more unusual the sentence, the more one needs to do to justify it. In psychological test usage, the more unusual the test result, the more interpretive work needs to be done on it.

To summarise the argument, if sentencing were to be conceived as a psychological measuring instrument, with retribution as the preferred sentencing justification and construct validity as the aim of the general approach, what might have resulted would look quite similar to sentencing guidelines. Sentencing guidelines calibrate raw agreement about relative culpability in the same way that standardisation calibrates raw test responses, so that the normal (defined in terms of average *and* scatter) responses in relation to particular target groups can be known and compared, themselves forming the basis of potentially important decisions.

To say that descriptive sentencing guidelines were constructed in ways which arguably enable valid retributive sentencing is not to say that they necessarily provide a desirable approach to sentencing guidance and reform, although it is argued that they do provide necessary information, notably about sentence scatter, which no appellate system does. The significant point is, in the writer's view (and hence in Psyche's), that guidelines are what would emerge from a concern with valid sentencing, not just reliable sentencing. If the primary issue is sentencing validity then guidelines are an appropriate response and appellate guidance alone is not.

Despite the extended analogy, current guidelines have not been based on the full research which would be necessary for the process of construct validation. In particular, judicial consensus about relative culpability is an issue concerning which further research is necessary. This is also true of the problem of the bizarre length patterns of existing sentencing practice (which patterns have persisted over more than a century), and how to incorporate them in sentencing guidelines. In some ways, the development of prescriptive guidelines addresses this issue, albeit in a way of which Psyche would not approve.[4]

Why guidelines are preferable to guideline judgments

It was asserted that guideline judgments in an appellate system do not offer the same advantages for retributive sentence validation as do sentencing guidelines themselves. This assertion should be justified. Guideline judgments do not assume, nor do they attempt to reflect, consensus judicial assessments of culpability. A guideline judgment may cut across agreed judgments of relative severity or suggest differentials which bear no relationship to judicial thought or action. Critically, guideline judgments do not 'calibrate' judges by specifying the range of normal variation. Ashworth (1984) has extrapolated a scale of punishments from a guideline judgment of Lord Chief Justice Lane. It relates street value of a drug consignment to the 'proper' sentence. It runs as follows: £100,000: 7 years; £250,000: 8 years; £400,000: 9 years; £550,000: 10 years; £700,000: 11 years; £850,000: 12 years; £1,000,000: 13 years.

It is interesting that the scaling of sentence against value does not correspond with most judgments on the matter (see Gottfredson *et al.*, 1980, Fitzmaurice and Pease, 1986). For example, does this really mean that a consignment worth £2,500,000 gets you twenty-three years and a consignment worth £1.00 gets you six years and a bit?

Crucially, the judgment does not offer the range within which the normal sentence for a particular street value may vary. Can prior record take the proper sentence for a crime worth £700,000 below 10·5 years or above 11·5 years? Unless information of this kind can be given, *no real guidance is being given*. To the writer's knowledge, no guideline judgment has provided information about the range of acceptable dispersion around the guideline judgment. The most troubling aspect of this is that the Lord Chief Justice seems unaware of what guidance is necessary for valid retributive sentencing to be possible. Psyche has an uphill struggle ahead.

Even were guideline judgments to include information about dispersion, guidelines themselves afford other advantages. Reliable judgments of relative culpability are more likely to be found among a group of judges than in individual judges, however distinguished. Assuming general social consensus about culpability, there are likely to remain individual differences. *General* judgments, enshrined in guidelines, are more likely to coincide with more general views of culpability[5] than are the judgments of one or three Court of Appeal judges. Because guidelines derive from the collective views of brother judges, individual judges may feel more constrained to take them seriously.

In principle, guidelines provide an engine for their own change. Since unusual judgments have to be justified, a range of agreed aggravating and mitigating factors should emerge from the monitoring of reasons for such judgments. These could provide a sound basis for guideline revision and sentence review procedures.

Appellate systems may act to inflate recommended sentences. In the extant system in England and Wales, sentencing courts and the Court of Appeal both have general ideas (what Psyche would call anchors), about the appropriate sentence in a particular class of case. Decisions from the sentencing court will modify the anchor of the Court of Appeal. Decisions of the Court of Appeal will modify the anchors of sentencing courts, if they are known and regarded as relevant. (Ashworth *et al.*, (1984) found that 'although few judges stated that they personally felt a need for more guidance on sentencing levels, a number of judges thought it would be useful to other judges.' The study, unsurprisingly in the light of such sentiments, suggested that many judges have a poor awareness of the principles laid down by the Court of Appeal). If anchors were to be modified in both directions, what would be the consequences for sentencing practice? A hypothetical suggestion is set out in Figure 2. The figure should be read upwards from box A. In box A are given the anchors or starting points for Court of Appeal and Crown Court of eight and six years respectively. The higher initial level of the anchor in the Court of Appeal is predictable from anchoring effects and observed (see McLean, 1980). It is predictable because the Court of Appeal gets to review those sentences argued to be excessive rather than those argued to be too lenient. These sentences form the basis of the Appeal Court's anchor. The Court of Appeal then gets appeal 1 (box B). The sentence appealed is 12. Getting this case itself slightly changes

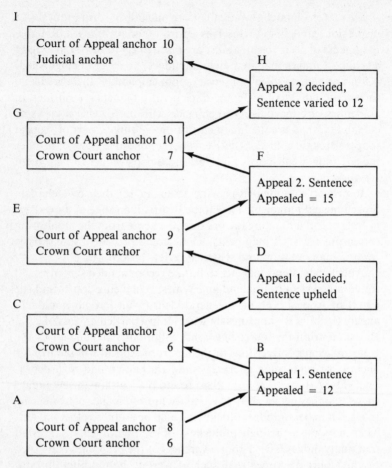

Figure 2   Hypothetical illustration of the operation of anchoring effects on sentencing levels

the Court of Appeal's anchor in the direction of the sentence appealed (box C). Upholding the sentence (box D) feeds back and modifies the Crown Court anchor upwards (box E). This step is the weakest point in the speculation. It assumes that we are talking about judicial anchors in the sense of the average anchor of each judge who comes to hear of a Court of Appeal decision. There is of course no reason for the particular judge who made the judgment that was appealed to modify his anchor. Given that the standard which the Court of

Appeal applies is longer than the average of that of individual judges (as we have seen it is: McLean, 1980) the appeal judgment will move the average Crown Court anchor upwards. A second appeal (boxes F to I), this time upheld, illustrates the process and suggests that, so long as the sentence as modified is not below the average Crown Court anchor, the upward spiral of sentence severity hypothesised is not specific to appeals rejected, although it is strongest in its effect there.

The reader is now entitled to wonder where the real world went. The upward spiral of sentence is not evident in that world. It is submitted that this is because of the virtual irrelevance of Court of Appeal decisions to the general run of sentences, primarily through their remaining unknown. The reason why we should consider the upward spiral is to consider the consequences if the appellate system were ever to operate efficiently. If it did, it is likely that it would function to increase average sentence severity.

The presentation of arguments in favour of descriptive guidelines should be taken in conjunction with the warnings of Tonry in his chapter about the pitfalls of guideline development. However, the kind of information which judges *need* in order to sentence validly cannot be less than is provided in descriptive guidelines. This is a crucial point and should be acknowledged in arguments like that presented by Andrew Ashworth in his Chapter and elsewhere. The way in which guidelines also inform the discussion of sentencing principle is also illustrated in the discussion in Andrew von Hirsch's discussion of the slope of the In/Out line in his Chapter. The other advantages offered by guidelines are sufficiently powerful to be taken seriously in the decision about which avenue of sentencing reform to follow. In short, sentencing guidelines remain an attractive option in the search for just sentencing.

Notes

1   The writer is aware of more recent developments in test theory. However, certainly for presentational reasons the classical (i.e. out of date) formulation is best. Arguably it is also better equipped to deal with the distinctive problems of sentencing.

2   The argument is simplified somewhat here. In fact what Psyche would do would be to transform the sentence lengths so that a normal distribution resulted. It is not thought realistic to suppose that such a transformation would find favour with judges, whatever its advantages.

3   There are differences. In descriptive guidelines, the category of case

is chosen in the knowledge that scores within it are distinctive. This would not be true of test development. The choice of category in descriptive guidelines is crucial (see Michael Tonry's chapter in this volume) but is outside the scope of this chapter.

4   Because it is no part of a psychologist's function to change the attribute under test.

5   There appear to be only very modest age and social class differences, at least in judgments of offence seriousness (see Fitzmaurice and Pease, 1986, Ch. 4).

References

Ashworth, A. J. (1984) 'Techniques of guidance on sentencing', *Criminal Law Review*, 661.

Ashworth, A. J. *et al.* (1984) *Sentencing in the Crown Court: Report of an Exploratory Study*, Oxford, Centre for Criminological Research Occasional Paper No. 10.

Blumstein, A. *et al.* (1985) 'Delinquency careers: innocents, desisters and persisters', in M. Tonry and N. Morris (eds.) *Crime and Justice 6*, University of Chicago Press.

Eysenck, H. J. (1977) *Crime and Personality* (3rd ed.), London, Routledge and Kegan Paul.

Fitzmaurice, C. T. (1981) *On Measuring Distaste in Years: A Psychophysical Study of the Length of Prison Sentences*, M.A.Econ. thesis, University of Manchester.

Fitzmaurice, C. T. and Pease, K. (1986) *The Psychology of Judicial Sentencing*, Manchester University Press.

Gottfredson, S. *et al.* (1980) 'Additivity and interactions in offence seriousness studies', *Journal of Research in Crime and Delinquency*, 17, 26.

McLean, I. (1980) *Crown Court: Patterns of Sentencing*, Chichester, Barry Rose.

West, D. J. (1982) *Delinquency*, London, Heinemann.

Sentencing reform and the structuring of pre-trial discretion

The brief I was given for my contribution to this book was to examine the possible 'up-stream' effects upon decisions taken by police and prosecution authorities in England and Wales that might follow from the implementation of sentencing guidelines or similar schemes for greater control over judicial discretion in sentencing. I certainly intend to try to fulfil these terms of reference, and shall focus especially upon recent moves by the Home Office to introduce greater consistency into cautioning and prosecution decisions. However, I want to locate my discussion within the rather broader context of the study of decision-making in the administration of criminal justice as a whole, and to conclude by outlining a strategy for achieving more integrated decision-making in criminal justice policy and practice. Thus my Chapter is divided into four parts: (a) emergent themes in criminal justice research; (b) the implications of sentencing guidelines for the relocation of discretionary power; (c) cautioning guidelines and the decision to prosecute; and (d) a proposed strategy for integrated decision-making in the criminal justice process.

Emergent themes in criminal justice research

The last two decades have witnessed a spectacular growth of research into decision-making within the criminal justice process, especially in North America and to a lesser extent in Britain. A number of common and interrelated themes have emerged from this research that are of particular relevance to our present concerns, namely (a) *disparity*, (b) *discretion*, and (c) the *system* or *non-system* characteristics of criminal justice administration. Each of these themes has a central part to play in any debate about sentencing reform, and together they comprise an essential agenda-setting framework.

The literature on *disparity* is probably the most extensive and controversial. Apparent, and often very widespread, disparity has been discovered at virtually every decision point in the administration of criminal justice. Yet, despite the extent and scope of empirical research into disparity, comparatively little progress has been made in the fundamental tasks of conceptualising and defining the term. As one recent commentator has said: 'Unfortunately, more than six decades of research have failed to provide precise and generally accepted definitions of sentencing disparity' (Forst, 1982, p. 26). Just because disparity can be stated in such a seemingly straightforward way, i.e. that different decisions are made in similar cases, it easily persuades, especially if it matches the expectations and preconceptions of the audience. But, in fact, any discovery of alleged disparity should be the *beginning* of the intellectual and practical task of resolving the problem, rather than regarded as clear 'proof' of injustice. More specifically, in the context of sentencing for example, the twin problem surrounding disparity is that of the identification of overall *objectives* and of measurable variables that are directly relevant to these objectives. Until these issues are clarified no sensible meaning can be attached to claims that one case is 'the same' as another for the purposes of a particular decision. To quote Martin Forst again:

Anyone who wants to show disparity in sentencing must demonstrate that the different sentences meted out to persons committing the same offence under similar circumstances cannot be justified by reference to some legally relevant variables, that is, to factors that have some rational relationship to the aims of the criminal law. This is a tall order to fulfil, since *the aims of the criminal law are rarely clearly articulated*.

                                   (Forst, 1982, p. 30. Emphasis added).

So the first general lesson to be learned from the research tradition in criminal justice is the need for clearly articulated aims.

The link between disparity and the second theme of *discretion* is a clear and direct one. If decision-makers had to act strictly according to a rule-book and were not allowed any legitimate discretion, then there would be little opportunity for disparity to occur. As a consequence, research that reveals disparity usually either arises out of or has direct implications for a specific concern to control some discretionary power. Furthermore, as more and more decision-stages have become the object of academic scrutiny and research, often leading to experiments in the structuring of discretion by means of formal guidelines of one sort or another, the essential 'resilience' of criminal justice discretion has become all too obvious. The successful reduction or elimination of discretion at one stage often leads to its increased significance at another, so that this process has been described rather graphically as a 'balloon theory' or 'hydraulic model' of criminal justice discretion. For example in this quote from Ozanne: 'Other commentators have suggested that discretion in the penal system is like liquid in a hydraulic system: if you squeeze all discretion out of the sentencing process, it will reappear and augment discretion at other points in the system.' (Ozanne, 1982, p.187)

The implication here is obvious. Any attempt to reform sentencing by reducing the discretionary powers of the judiciary must anticipate the emergence of comparable problems both 'up-stream' and 'down-stream'.

This 'hydraulic model' of discretion is inextricably bound up with the third theme that has pervaded much recent research in criminal justice, namely the 'system' or 'non-system' characteristics of the process(es) being studied. Somewhat inconsistently, many participants in this debate simultaneously deny and assert the existence of a 'system' of criminal justice, contrasting the practical reality of offenders being processed along a human conveyor belt, from police to parole board, with an apparent absence of meaningful communication between the different members of the workforce, or any obvious common goal. A particularly apt example of this kind of thinking is found in an article by Ohlin and Remington (1958). Frank Remington was a leading figure in the pathbreaking survey of the administration of criminal justice in the United States carried out by the American Bar Foundation, that resulted in a number of classic volumes throughout the 1960s (e.g. LaFave, 1965; Newman, 1966; Dawson, 1969; Miller, 1970). He was a tireless advocate of the need for greater integration within the process:

All agencies engaged in the administration of criminal justice must direct their efforts towards the common objective of processing criminal offenders. This, of necessity, requires a degree of integration among their policies and practices ... There is inadequate awareness of the fact that the administration of criminal justice is a single, total process and that, therefore, changing one important aspect may require substantial reorientation of the entire system.

(Ohlin and Remington, 1958, p.496)

More than twenty years later, in Britain, we find two of our own pioneering researchers in this field, Baldwin and McConville, reaffirming the importance of recognising the interaction between the different interlocking parts of the criminal justice process: 'Appreciation of the interactions of the different stages of the criminal process is crucial since, for example, decisions taken at one stage (say when a suspect is in police custody) will as a rule have an important bearing on decisions taken by the suspect and by others at later stages.' (McConville and Baldwin, 1981, p. 2)

A number of different ways of describing and analysing the system elements have been put forward. For present purposes, we simply need to be aware of the realities and ideals inherent in the concept of a 'criminal justice system', which provides the crucial backdrop against which the drama of discretion and disparity is played out! Having set the scene, I now want to examine in a little more detail some of the implications of the sentencing guidelines movement for the displacement or relocation of discretion.

Sentencing guidelines and the displacement of discretion

An intriguing and, it seems, almost integral feature of sentencing reform movements represented by such developments as guidelines, and presumptive or mandatory sentences, is the way they have almost always been associated with the change of emphasis in penal policy from a former allegiance to the rehabilitative ideal to the new favourite of the 'justice model', offering 'just deserts' to convicted offenders. As a result of this rather restricted view of sentencing aims incorporated into many of the reformed decision-making structures, the seriousness of the offence and the offender's previous record have assumed overwhelming significance. There is, of course, no inherent reason why guidelines or other similar approaches to the structuring of sentencing discretion should be based only, or indeed at all, on just deserts principles. As Galligan has said, in his valuable 1981 Criminal Law Review article: 'Although clearly much of the impetus for such procedural reform derives from the just deserts principles, a rule-based system is not a necessary part of a deserts approach; a rule-based system might equally be geared to utilitarian policies.' (Galligan, 1981, pp. 302–3)

However, the clear and consistent message that seems to come from North American sentencing reform movements is that the *nature of the offence* of which the defendant is convicted or to which he pleads guilty is of paramount importance, and the more strenuous the attempts to limit judicial discretion in the choice of sentence for any particular offence category, the more influential becomes *prosecutorial discretion*. Furthermore, by displacing discretion in this way there is no guarantee that the same overall objectives will guide the exercise of discretion at the points in the process which it continues to be allowed to flourish, relatively unchecked. When they considered the merits of determinate sentencing structures many years ago, Ohlin and Remington warned of the likely effects of such 'accommodative responses' in undermining the aims of the system as a whole:

> The natural tendency, under these circumstances, therefore, is for the agencies of criminal justice administration to engage in various kinds of accommo-dative responses to a changed sentencing structure, so that they may continue to perform their customary tasks ... with the usual expenditure of time, effort and money. This may result in a failure to achieve the objectives of the sentencing structure, since these objectives may be regarded as less important than the maintenance of the current administrative equilibrium.
>
> (Ohlin and Remington, 1958, p.496)

When any jurisdiction promulgates guidelines or establishes a system of presumptive or mandatory sentences, defendants and their lawyers are able to predict fairly precisely the likely sentence they will receive on the basis of particular charges, so that there is even more incentive to enter into negotiations with the prosecuting authorities with a view to getting charges dropped or reduced. In these circum-stances, the prosecutor in effect takes over the role of sentencer, in formulating charges and negotiating pleas of guilty, so that if the objectives of sentencing reform are to be achieved it is essential at the same time to control prosecutors' discretion. As Albert Alschuler has put it: 'Under a fixed-sentencing regime, bargaining about the charge would *be* bargaining about the sentence' (Alschuler, 1978, p.507). To recognise the need for simultaneous control of prosecut-orial discretion is therefore an essential step towards successful sentencing reform, although the task of achieving this, if American experience is anything to judge by, is likely to be even more difficult than the control of judicial discretion − as it is exercised less openly, by arguably less well qualified or experienced personnel and 'its exercise may depend less upon consideration of desert, deterrence and reformation, than upon a desire to avoid the hard work of preparing and trying cases' (Alschuler, 1978, p.504).

Turning, then, to the situation in Britain, how important is the role of the police or prosecution authorities in the selection of charges, and what considerations ought to be borne in mind when speculating about possible consequences of the introduction of sentencing guidelines? For England and Wales, as far as I am aware, there is very little systematic information or research evidence either about the selection of charges by the police or about the extent to which 'charge bargaining' takes place between the police or prosecuting solicitors and defendants. Despite the wealth of evidence from the USA, confirming the widespread practice of charge bargaining, the much more flexible sentencing structure in this country may have resulted in bargaining being focussed primarily on an anticipated sentence discount. Thus, in Baldwin and McConville's Birmingham study, *Negotiated Justice* (1977), in only three out of the twenty-two cases identified as clear plea bargaining did the bargain take the form of charge reduction, and 'in none of these cases was any offer or promise held out to the defendant about the consequent sentence to be imposed' (Baldwin and McConville, 1977, p. 29). In a smaller group of sixteen cases in which there were tacit bargains of the 'nod-and-a-wink' type, the offer in half of the cases was in the form of a charge reduction. These figures mean that only in less than ten per cent of this sample of guilty pleaders did implicit or explicit bargains involve charge reductions. In view of the rather small and unrepresentative nature of this study, judgment ought to be reserved on the actual extent of charge bargaining in England and Wales, until further research has been carried out. Personally, I suspect that quite extensive pre-trial charge bargaining takes place between police and lawyers, perhaps especially in the lower courts, with a largely unknown effect on the pattern of sentences subsequently imposed. The recent study of prosecution decision-making by procurator fiscals in Scotland, by Moody and Tombs (1982), seems to confirm the extent of this practice north of the border. In their discussion (Ch. 6) of what they call 'trial-avoidance' arrangements by the negotiation of guilty pleas, they say that these generally focus on charges and 'charge-bargaining', involving either reduction of charge, alternative charges, deletion of charges, or amendment in the wording of charges (Moody and Tombs, 1982, p. 106). They discovered that most fiscals distinguished between the practice of entering charges on a complaint for mainly evidential reasons and those put in purely as bargaining counters: 'Virtually all fiscals positively disapprove of including charges as bargaining-counters only' (Moody and Tombs, 1982, p. 111). Nevertheless, despite the apparent frequency of such trial-avoidance arrangements, the authors reached the conclusion that where pleas were negotiated the accused stood to gain very little in terms of a material reduction of sentence.

In the light of the vociferous concern in the United States with the way the restriction of judicial discretion has in effect transferred the sentencing decision to the prosecutor, who can largely determine the charge(s) on which a guilty plea is then negotiated, in Britain there has so far been a remarkable lack of interest in studying police decisions in the actual formulation of charges. This may be due to a realistic appreciation of the fact that, ultimately, the precise charge(s) on which a person pleads (or is found) guilty makes very little difference to the final sentence imposed, with the suspicion that 'reading through' charges occurs as much in this country (despite being frowned upon by the Court of Appeal) as in others with less sentencing discretion. Nevertheless, this topic should not be neglected as it is likely to be of increasing importance with the changes in the prosecution system. In fact, it could be argued with some plausibility that the police approach to charging is determined above all by a desire to get a conviction on more or less any charge that bears a reasonable relationship to what they believe the accused is in fact guilty. Just as the 'resource charge' in the earlier stages of police action against suspects is now well known (having been documented in England by Mike Chatterton), so it is merely an extension of this to envisage the entire charging process to be aimed primarily at securing a conviction. The impressive Canadian studies carried out by Richard Ericson, with their wealth of ethnographic detail, have shown the many practical purposes for which police in that country use their control of the charging process. 'Multiple charging' is used to ensure a conviction on at least one charge, acting as a 'lever' to a guilty plea; charges can also be used to persuade suspects into giving information about activities unrelated to their present arrest and charge; sometimes the purpose of a police charge is to legitimate police investigations with the suspect in custody:

When detectives decided to charge a suspect they did so with careful con-sideration of what bail-related controls they wanted placed upon the person up to the point of his conviction, and with strategic planning as to how the construction of charges would maximise the chance that the accused would be convicted and receive a sentence within a predictable range.

(Ericson, 1981, p. 165)

The goal of convicting the offender is more likely to be achieved if there are a number of charges available from which to 'lever' a guilty plea ... The patrol officer's concern is less often with the specific offences charged than with the fact that the charges laid serve to assert control over a troublesome individual. In this light, officers are content to get a conviction on *something* (although not just anything) among a number of charges they had laid.

(Ericson, 1982, p. 178)

In summary, the charges available to patrol officers provide a framework which predictably ensures that convictions will be forthcoming, although what the conviction will be on and its link to sentencing are open to situated elements and discussions among the police, lawyers, and crown attorneys.

(Ericson, 1982, p. 191)

Here is an almost uncharted area of decision-making between police, lawyers and prosecuting authorities that we have hardly begun to explore, but which no serious attempt at sentencing reform can afford to neglect.

At a practical level it could be argued (and indeed has been extensively so argued in the American literature) that too much importance need not be attached to charge bargaining in a system that allows considerable discretion to sentencers, because experienced sentencers will not just look at the official charge as convicted but will decide upon an appropriate sentence in the light of the 'real offence' behind the legal label. Many advocates of sentencing guidelines and presumptive sentencing have warned against taking offences at face value, but have insisted on 'reading through' the official record to obtain as accurate picture as possible of the nature and seriousness of the offence committed. This was brought out particularly well by Leslie Wilkins and his colleagues in their report on the feasibility study for sentencing guidelines in the States in 1976. In order properly to assess offence seriousness for guidelines purposes they said it was essential to have more information than 'the mere statutory label of a plea-bargained conviction', although this did raise questions in their minds 'as to whether or not a part of the plea bargain was being improperly taken away from the defendant without the defendant's knowledge' (Wilkins *et al.*, 1978, p. 8). They argued that in any introduction of sentencing guidelines 'real offence' sentencing would have to be made far more explicit than it had been in the past.

This same issue has been taken up by other scholars, as it has implications not only for 'up-stream' decision-making but for 'down-stream' reliance on the official record of offences by parole boards. Ira Blalock, in the volume edited by Forst, says:

Discretion exercised at the prosecutorial and trial court level poses a serious problem for parole boards using structured discretion. The term-setting agent, whether the parole board or the sentencing judge or perhaps both, has to read through the bargain if equity and fairness in term-setting are going to prevail ... If the purpose of guidelines is to introduce a consistency in dealing with similarly situated offenders, then the actual offense behaviour becomes more important than the crime title. This raises a concern over what data elements will be considered when classifying an offender.

(Blalock, 1982, p.106)

The dangers and possible pitfalls of a unilateral introduction of arrangements for structuring sentencing discretion without serious thought both to the objectives of the exercise and the effects on how decision-makers both earlier and later in the process may exercise their particular discretion emerge pretty clearly from the accounts and critiques of the American experience of the last decade or so. If we are to profit from this experience, as much attention needs to be focussed on ways of structuring the decisions to charge, prosecute or caution an offender as on the sentencing decision itself. Do the recent Home Office initiatives in drawing up guidelines for cautioning and prosecution suggest that we have begun to tackle the problem in the right way?

Cautioning guidelines and the decision to prosecute

Considerable progress has been made in the last few years towards the structuring of the discretion of police forces to caution or prosecute juvenile offenders. Are these developments likely to stimulate and complement similar initiatives for sentencers, parole boards, etc., or are they likely to be of only marginal value in the context of radical sentencing reform?

It would certainly be true to say that they derive from and are intended to solve very similar problems of disparity and discretion to those that are the target of sentencing reform. The relevant recommendations of the Royal Commission on Criminal Procedure (1981) were based not only on an appreciation of research findings but on principles that few would wish to find fault with: fairness, openness, and efficiency.

We believe the time has come for the use of the formal caution to be sanctioned in legislation and put on a more consistent basis.

(Report, 7.59)

A statutory prosecution service will promote a greater measure of openness and accountability and will stimulate, and provide the forum for, the development of agreed and consistent criteria for the exercise of the discretion to prosecute.

(Report, 8.6)

The Home Office (1984) consultative document, *Cautioning by the Police*, rejected the idea of a statutory basis for cautioning as too rigid, and instead put forward a set of draft guidelines for the cautioning of juveniles and adults that were eventually circulated in their final form in February 1985 (as Home Office Circular 14/1985), to replace the existing guidelines for juveniles (HOC 70/1978) and to supplement the Attorney General's guidelines on *Criteria for Prosecution* (HOC 26/1983), as far as adults are concerned. The brief discussion that follows will concentrate upon the final version of the guidelines, with cross-references to the earlier draft and the consultative document as necessary.

Juveniles
The importance of a clearly stated presumption in favour of cautioning was stressed in the consultative document, as research showed that 'forces which have left a wide area for discretion whether or not to caution tended to have *low* cautioning rates' (Home Office, 1984, p. 8). The guidelines therefore open with a general statement that juveniles should not be prosecuted unless it is absolutely necessary: 'As a general principle, in the case of first time juvenile offenders where the offence is not serious, it is unlikely that prosecution will be a justifiable course' (para. 1). They then set out a two- or three-stage process for cautioning decisions:

(a) *criteria for a caution*, evidential and procedural, must be met in full (viz., likelihood of conviction, admission of offence, parental consent to cautioning);
(b) *immediate decisions*, based on the seriousness of the offence and the offender's record (a caution for a second or subsequent offence is not ruled out);
(c) *further considerations*, taking into account the interests of the aggrieved party, the offender's previous character and/or family circumstances, and whether the offence was committed in a group (although 'this should not prevent the consideration of each member of a group of offenders on an individual basis').

If these guidelines are adhered to by police forces throughout the country, there should be greater consistency at this vital early stage and probably a slight increase in the proportion of offenders diverted from prosecution. Apart from the initial criteria that must be met before a caution is considered, which are essentially of a legal and procedural nature, is it possible to identify any principles underlying the selection of factors to be taken into account in reaching the final decision? And, if so, how might these principles relate to the sentencing decisions that will be taken in the cases of those subsequently found guilty by the courts?

The opening sentence of the guidelines enunciates a major 'preventive' element underlying the decision as to whether or not to prosecute a juvenile offender: 'It is recognised both in theory and in practice that delay in the entry of a young person into the formal criminal justice system may help to prevent his entry into that system altogether'. Despite the unequivocal nature of this statement, it is not at all clear precisely what 'theory' or 'practical experience' is being referred to. It seems to support the 'labelling' perspective, whereby the more formal the labelling of an offender as an official delinquent the more likely is that offender to recidivate. It is difficult to see how this justification of non-prosecution, as helping to prevent future offending, can be interpreted as supporting other principles such as deterrence, reformation, denunciation etc. The invocation, in the following sentence, of 'the public interest' and 'the interests of the juvenile concerned' is somewhat more equivocal, seeming to imply the obvious point that prosecution may well be against the personal interest of offenders, but using the 'public interest' positively to *justify* cautioning rather than its more usual negative role of *denying* a caution as being '*against* the public interest' (on which, more below!). In any case, what is really intended is unfortunately hidden by a well-worn official phrase.

Considering the 'first-tier' factors to be taken into account in the 'immediate decisions' whether or not to caution, the primacy of the nature of the offence and the offender's record confirm that the main principle here is that of 'just deserts', with its linked elements of harm or suffering and the offender's wilfulness or blameworthiness. The consultative document rejected the idea of giving a precise list of offences suitable for cautioning, on the grounds that this 'would not in itself provide any sensible guide to the seriousness of the offence' (para. 5.10, p. 15), but was rather more specific than are the final guidelines on the types of harm envisaged. This will inevitably allow considerable latitude for the interpretation of the degree of seriousness (either in the instant offence or in the past record) that merits or rules out a caution. The 'further considerations' that come into play when no decision can be reached on the basis of the initial assessment of offence seriousness or just deserts are a curious mixture. Unlike the draft guidelines which placed the offender's circumstances first in the list of 'second-tier' factors, and gave more details of the relevant aspects under this heading, the final guidelines relegate this category to second place, preceded by a much longer section on the interests of the aggrieved party, and followed by a consideration of how to handle decisions on groups of offenders. This last category recognises the just deserts argument (supporting the 'need for consistency and equity'), but also indicates the possibility of individualised decision-making. There is no indication in the final guidelines as to *why* or *how* an offender's circumstances may be relevant. The consultative document, on the other hand, had stated that 'all these points bear on the other factor identified in the Attorney General's guidelines, *whether the offence is likely to be repeated*' (Home Office, 1984, para 5.13, emphasis added), and, although the draft guidelines did not repeat that crucial phrase, what they included about the attitude of the offender and his/her parents clearly indicated that the primary concern was the likelihood of further offending. The final reordering, pruning and lack of explicit justification for taking into account an offender's circumstances severely weaken the impact and rationale of these guidelines for juveniles, and, in this respect at least, offer an inadequate model for sentencing guidelines.

Adults

For adults, unlike juveniles, there is no general presumption that cautioning will be the normal course. However, the new guide-lines endorse the principle in the Attorney General's guidelines that criminal offences should not automatically be the subject of prosecution: 'In general, prosecution should only take place where there is sufficient evidence to support a prosecution and the public interest requires it. Where there is sufficient evidence, but the public interest does not require prosecution, a formal caution may well be appropriate' (para. 1). Here again, therefore, we find the sequence of initial (evidential and procedural) criteria that must be met, followed by a range of other considerations, broadly grouped into

(a) 'humanitarian-sympathy' cases, and (b) 'not in the public interest' cases. As in the Attorney General's guidelines, it is suggested that sympathetic consideration should be given to the elderly or infirm, young adults, and other persons 'at risk', such as those suffering from some form of mental illness or under severe emotional stress. Prosecution for members of these groups is not ruled out, as the seriousness of the offence or the need for a stronger deterrent effect may indicate that a caution is inappropriate. The main principle appears to be humanitarianism, although in the case of young adults (aged seventeen to twenty years) there is a similar justification to the general (preventive/labelling) justification for cautioning juveniles − namely that 'a criminal conviction early in adult life may have a significant effect on the prospects of the person concerned' (para. 2). In the case of adults who do not fall into one of these categories, prosecution may not be justified 'in the public interest', if account is taken of the seriousness of the offence and the offender's previous record and character. Relevant indicators include the likely penalty on conviction, the value of property stolen, and the circumstances surrounding certain offences, such as sexual offences involving willing parties, and 'victimless' offences. For adults, as for juveniles, the possibility of a *second* caution is not precluded, 'especially where the offence is trivial or of a different character to the earlier offence, or where the earlier offence was trivial, or where there has been a reasonable lapse of time since the previous decision' (para. 6). The only common feature that might appear to justify the label 'not in the public interest' for the above circumstances seems again to be that of just deserts − or a belief that public opinion would not be affronted if it became known that such cases had *not* been prosecuted! Nevertheless the use of this vague, omnibus term 'public interest' merely serves to avoid the issue of a clear statement of principle, that could easily be understood and fairly applied. In a situation such as the cautioning of adults, where a majority will in fact *not* be cautioned but prosecuted, the attachment of the phrase 'where the public interest requires it' is unlikely to provide much real guidance to the decision-makers. Indeed it could be argued that the whole thrust and objective of any criminal justice policy should ultimately be the public interest, so that to use this phrase in a narrow and unexplicated way serves only to obfuscate and not to educate.

Andrew Sanders is similarly very critical of the conception of 'public interest' as reflected in the Attorney General's guidelines on criteria for prosecution, in his article in the January 1985 *Criminal Law Review*; he claims that it is limited in scope, includes factors that are either too vague or subject to manipulation by the police, and is largely irrelevant when the charging rather than the summonsing process has been invoked (Sanders, 1985, p.17). In his view the likely result of guidelines of this kind will be to discourage rather than encourage cautioning, and to perpetuate inconsistency in decisions relating to the prosecution of adults. The findings of one of the rare studies of the cautioning of adults in England, by David Steer (1970), confirms that such decisions were generally in line with the sort of factors covered by the guidelines, including victims as willing parties, insufficient evidence, and the complainant declining to prosecute. The more subjective factor of 'offender's circumstances' was the main reason in about a fifth of his cases, and included the old, the mentally ill, and those with other extenuating circumstances. He found that previous good character was not *per se* a sufficient reason to caution, and indeed 'circumstances were occasionally such that offenders with as many as ten or more previous convictions were still dealt with in this way' (Steer, 1970, p.46). 'Just deserts' played a part, in that offences of a trivial or technical nature often resulted in a caution, and the tendency in group offences was for all offenders to be treated alike, either all cautioned or all prosecuted.

The more recent Scottish study by Moody and Tombs (1982) has added an important comparative dimension. As in England, so in Scotland, certain primary legal criteria must usually be met before the decision to prosecute (or not) is taken; but there are also various 'extra-legal' factors taken into account in the 'marking' decision by procurator fiscals, described by the authors in the following way:

> It is generally accepted that there is also another facet of the marking task which does not relate to purely legal criteria but involves consideration of an individual's circumstances and motivation for committing a crime ... This extra-legal dimension is regarded as particularly relevant in certain types of cases such as domestic violence. It permits the fiscal to exercise not only legal but also moral judgment.
>
> (Moody and Tombs, 1982, p.52)

Interestingly there are few formal rules governing decisions at the marking stage in Scotland, and it was reported that most fiscals would be totally opposed to the introduction of standard instructions, placing a high value as they do upon their professional tradition of individualised decision-making. Decisions 'not to proceed' are taken in less than ten per cent of all cases, and tend to be restricted to those instances 'where a case falls outside the fiscal's definition of *real* crime' (Moody and Tombs, 1982, p. 60). Once again we find the phrase 'safeguarding the public interest' being used as the keystone of the procurators' approach to their task — so much so that it was incorporated into the title of the book!

The picture that emerges from this examination of the new guidelines for the cautioning of offenders in England and Wales is one of an official reluctance to enunciate clear principles and policies for the guidance of the decision-makers, preferring instead to leave them with considerable discretion, both in the interpretation of objectives and the assessment of relevant factors. To be fair, some progress has been made, particularly with regard to juveniles, and there are a few lessons that might be learned for wider applicability to sentencing reform and the structuring of discretion at other stages. For example, where there is a clear presumption in favour of a particular course of action (e.g. cautioning of juveniles), and the vast majority of decisions are made in line with that presumption, then it tends to be easier to formulate reasons that might justify a departure from that presumption, rather than trying to explain the positive justification for acting in accordance with the presumption. Secondly, the fewer the choices that are open to the decision-maker the easier it should be to establish effective guidelines. Thirdly, where a decision involves procedural, legal or evidential factors these can be separated from the other 'non-legal' elements of the decision which may introduce moral/value judgements or wider policy considerations.

To return to the main concern of this paper, do these developments have any direct relevance for sentencing reform and the possible introduction of guidelines at that later stage in the process? To the extent that sentencing guidelines may be based on some form of just deserts principles, in which assessment of the seriousness of the offence plays a central part, they will have much in common with cautioning/prosecution guidelines. There ought to be a uniform approach to the assessment of offence seriousness, for although sentencing guidelines will require many more graduations of seriousness, the 'bottom line' of seriousness below which offenders will be diverted from prosecution sets the standard and determines the intake to the sentencing stage. Likewise, to the extent that sentencers may continue to consider a variety of other factors, in relation to a variety of penal aims, there always needs to be an explicit acknowledgement of these underlying assumptions and objectives, consistent with the way these same factors may have influenced earlier decisions.

A strategy for integrated decision-making in criminal justice

Being realistic, as far as this country is concerned, it is likely that any progress towards sentencing reform and the structuring of discretion at other stages in the criminal justice process will take place in a piece-meal fashion. The recent guidelines for prosecution and juvenile cautioning are typical examples, as are the guidelines for parole introduced in 1975 – despite the fact that these have been somewhat overtaken by the parole policy changes of the last eighteen months. However, this should not deter us from persistent and critical scrutiny of the developments that are taking place, or from setting out ambitious blueprints for the direction in which we feel criminal justice decision-making should be moving. This is what I want to attempt in this final section, in the hope that the exercise will not be seen as too idealistic, and perhaps some direct action might flow from some of the ideas I shall be floating. The three main elements of the proposed strategy are the primacy of *articulated policies*, a recognition of the *interrelatedness of the different decision-stages*, and the introduction of *model structures for decision-making*, to maximise the likelihood of consistency.

Articulated policies

There is nothing original in the assertion that reform in criminal justice must begin with a clarification of policy objectives. Explanations of disparity have almost always placed as much emphasis upon disagree-ment over objectives as upon disagreement over the methods to achieve particular objectives. Most of the authors in the recent American volume on *Sentencing Reform: Experiments in Reducing Disparity* (Forst, 1982) reiterated the primacy of policy determination as a precondition for any successful reform. To quote just a couple of examples:

Without an internally consistent statement of policy to guide the system, each sentencer becomes an independent policy-maker who is free to choose a theory or purpose of punishment that seems to suit the circumstances in a particular case. In short, there is sentence disparity in our penal system because there is disparity in our sentencing policies.

(Ozanne, 1982, p. 183)

... it is not the case that determinacy or more general efforts to structure discretion require or preclude any particular sentencing philosophy. Once a decision to structure the sentencing decision is reached, however, the choice of goals matters a great deal. A clear, explicit statement of the aim or aims of the system should precede its design. Where there is more than one aim, there should be a rank ordering or some indication of priority. This is necessary because the traditional goals of sentencing are in potential conflict ... Where there is no agreed-upon balance of objectives, there is bound to be confusion in the design of the system.

(Hanrahan and Greer, 1982, p. 40)

Nearer to home, Galligan has also expressed the need for articulated policies:

The crucial point is that within any system along these lines there must be a ranking of penal goals and values. Deserts is the central guiding principle and other goals may be pursued within the deserts ranges and above or below those ranges for reasons that are objective and open to scrutiny ... Such a system has the virtue of forcing policy choices into the open rather than concealing them under the camouflage of deserts. Finally, there is no reason in principle why penal policies cannot be ranked in order of importance, nor is there any reason for not having fairly clear criteria for their application.

(Galligan, 1981, p. 306)

Why, then, with so much apparent agreement, is it in fact so rare for penal policies to be articulated in such a way that they command public support and can be applied in a consistent manner? Fundamentally, no doubt, it is because of the apprehension and expectation in official circles that it would be impossible to achieve consensus on overall policies, and a consequent unwillingness to grasp the nettle of attempting to articulate policies that would inevitably be unpopular in some quarters. However, in my view, if this process were to be linked with a parallel exercise in the structuring of decision-choices, in the light of stated policy aims, there might be more chance of winning some measure of public support. As it is at present a wide range of penal aims are proclaimed as legitimate, with no indication of priorities, or proper guidance on how they should be applied to particular cases. Another reason for the lack of progress in the articulation of policy is that most attention has been paid to the sentencing decision, which, in terms of policy choices, raises some of the most intransigent problems of all. There would be great value in a strategy that approached this central issue by considering 'up-stream' and 'down-stream' policy options at the same time, as these are often rather less complicated in terms of the range of policy options, and could offer solutions or 'leverage' for the structuring of sentencing discretion.

To ask questions systematically about the primary aims of each group of decision-makers in turn (albeit in full awareness of their place in the wider on-going process) could result in useful answers emerging, even if they were rather more limited than the questions and answers about sentencing. The work of Joan Jacoby in her study of prosecutors showed how this might work in practice. Having asserted the primary need for identifying policy at the outset, she constructed a typology of policies, in relation to which the discretion of prosecutors could be structured towards the implementation of any particular balance of policy priorities: 'When one evaluates the performance of the prosecutor, and more broadly the direction of all criminal justice activity, the first task is to determine what the prosecutor is attempting to do; the second is to assess how well he is performing; the third is to see whether the community agrees with him.' (Jacoby, 1979, p.95)

Raising questions in this way about what particular decision-makers are attempting to do must be the starting point; but the official answers to those questions must not necessarily form the sole criteria on which future policy and practice is based. There must be a forum for the authoritative resolution of the legitimacy and desirability of competing aims. At every stage there must be an opportunity for open discussion of alternative objectives, to test the validity of a particular group's perspective on the exercise of their discretion. Conflicts should not be swept under the carpet, nor should guidelines adopt a conservative or 'cosmetic' approach that allows disparities to continue unchecked.

Interrelatedness of decision-stages

The fact that the different decision-stages in the criminal process are interrelated in practice and ought to be even more so in terms of guiding principles, should not in my view rule out the possibility of the co-existence of a certain amount of differentiation in primary working concerns. I like the notion of the different criminal justice agencies each having a sphere of influence or 'domain', but with a degree of overlap in physical, economic and political terms that make them more like a confederation than a group of sovereign states. McDonald described the situation as follows:

The traditional formal view of the division of labour among criminal justice agencies is misleading. Legal pronouncements about the clear distinction between the functions of these agencies obscure the reality of the overlapping and constantly changing roles they perform. It is more useful to regard each component of the criminal justice industry as having a domain, i.e. a claim to control performance of certain parts of the process. These claims are always open to negotiation ... Furthermore, changes in the way one organisation performs its part of the work will cause changes in the way other components perform. Encroachment on domain and the forcing of changes in the performance of one's function will be resisted if vested interests are at stake.

> (McDonald, 1979, pp. 45–6)

The dangers of the traditional 'domain' theory could be largely eliminated by a greater openness and accountability in the articulation of policies, and the establishment of comprehensive guidelines and standards for the implementation of those policies at all levels. Such an outcome would be even more likely if similar procedures were adopted at every stage in the process. Quoting Blalock again:

One way to help improve the image of the guidelines and the parole board, and to increase the likelihood of equity and uniformity in prison terms is to provide standards, guidelines, or rules at the front end of the system i.e. at the arrest, prosecution, and sentencing levels ... Standards should be adopted at all decision points in the sanctioning system. We could start by requiring prosecutors to explain on the record why charges have been dropped. A prosecutor should be required to explain the original arrest, indictment, and subsequent charges pleaded to and explain the reasons and bargains that resulted in dropped charges.

> (Blalock, 1982, pp. 107–8)

Model structures for decision-making

A final element in the strategy for structuring discretion would be the introduction of model structures for the application of agreed principles. To avoid the *retrospective* 'fitting' of criteria or guidelines to decisions that have already been arrived at, it is essential for the decision-task to be broken down into a series of two-way decisions of the in–out/yes–no variety, for each of which there would be clear criteria for how to proceed to the next step in the process. Decisions in which the final choice is itself a simple two-way (e.g. bail/custody, charge/summons, caution/prosecute, parole/prison) should in theory lend themselves to greater consistency than the more complex multi-choice decisions, such as sentencing. However, the steps to a single option outcome may themselves be quite complicated, whereas a decision that has a choice of several options might be broken down into a relatively simple set of intermediate stages, e.g. a 'tariff ladder' should be relatively easy to construct, indicating criteria for progressing from one rung to the next, or transferring to a different set of criteria to arrive at a goal that is not 'just deserts'.

The success of such a dichotomised decision-making structure would be further enhanced by the authoritative establishment of a clear 'presumption' in a particular direction at each stage, with the onus very much on those wishing to depart from the 'presumed' decision taken in the majority of cases. Virtually all of the successes that have been achieved so far in this country have been associated with the spelling out of a clear presumption – as in the legislative provision in the Bail Act for bail decisions, the administrative extensions of juvenile cautioning, and the increase in the granting of parole to the 'less serious' offenders from the mid-1970s onwards. The lessons of these success stories should be built upon in future developments.

A way forward?

It would be foolish to deny the many obstacles in the way of substantial reform of criminal justice policy and practice along the lines suggested. Attempts to introduce a completely new tradition of decision-making along much more structured lines will inevitably encounter all sorts of opposition. The strength of feeling with which judges have been prepared to defend their traditional independence is just one example of what is likely to be encountered, with slight variations, in most of the groups concerned – reflecting either the strength of occupational culture (such as in the police service), the professional practices of lawyers, or the treasured principle of individualised judgment that is commonly found in decision-making bodies selected for their personal and/or 'representative' qualities. A way must be found of convincing members of all these different groups that professional competence and valued expertise do not lie solely in the preservation of past practices, but in a willingness to recognise that overriding considerations of justice and fairness might often involve the subordination of purely personal or narrow professional interests for the sake of an equally expert application of agreed principles and recommended guidelines. Home-based research has an invaluable contribution to make to the process of education and persuasion, by revealing the nature and consequences of existing decision-making practices. Close collaboration with the decision-makers themselves, and open discussions with them about the validity and implication of such research, are essential prerequisites for bringing about change. More research and better communication between researchers and practitioners are not enough on their own. Initiative and commitment at the top levels must also be forthcoming, from chief officers, professional associations, and the relevant departments of central government. There is little hope of successful co-ordination or integration without positive direction from independent sources external to each group of decision-makers.

The centrality of sentencing in penal policy has meant that both in the USA and in Britain the main focus of attention has been on policy setting and monitoring bodies such as sentencing commissions. So far, attempts to push ideas of this kind to the forefront of public and professional debate in Britain do not appear to have met with a very positive response in official quarters, despite the persuasiveness with which the case has often been put, especially by Andrew Ashworth (1983; 1984). Particularly surprising, perhaps, was the government response to the suggestions in the fourth report from the Home Affairs Committee, *The Prison Service* (House of Commons, 1981) that there should be an urgent investigation into the best means of establishing a National Criminal Policy Committee. The report found it 'self-evident that changes in policy and administration in one part of the criminal justice system often have far-reaching effects elsewhere in the system ... Police prosecution policy considerably affects the work of the courts, which in turn determine to a great extent the work of the probation and aftercare service and the prison service' (para. 106). In order to achieve a more integrated criminal justice system (especially from a resource and planning perspective), it considered that a national criminal justice policy should be formulated and kept under review. A number of alternative ways of achieving this were considered but found wanting (e.g. Ministry of Justice, expanded Advisory Council on the Penal System, Royal Commission on the Penal System), before putting forward the idea of a National Criminal Policy Committee as 'a structural means of filling the lacunae in English criminal policy making' (para. 117). It would operate through influence, without changing the constitutional position of either the judiciary or chief constables, and would therefore have to command the fullest confidence among administrators, the judiciary and the police (para. 118). The government's

considered (?) response to this recommendation was short, to the point
of terseness, and dismissive:

... the Government doubts the effectiveness, as an aid to policy-making, of
setting up standing advisory bodies with wide general terms of reference ... The
Government does not believe that establishing a single all-purpose advisory
body charged with the 'planning' or 'construction' of criminal justice policy
would simplify the process or improve the product.

(Home Office, 1981, p.21)

There are few grounds for thinking that the political climate has
changed sufficiently (if at all) during the last few years to hold out
much hope of any significant shift in the government's view on this
matter, but nevertheless some new initiative ought to be tried. As I have
said on another occasion, I am attracted by many of the ideas that have
been proposed, particularly along the lines of sentencing commissions
with broader remits than just sentencing guidelines, drawing on a wide
range of expertise and commanding widespread authority among
criminal justice professionals (Bottomley, 1983). If the government
had not shown itself so opposed to standing advisory committees, a
body could be established called a *Standing Commission on Criminal
Justice* or, with a more trans-Atlantic flavour, *National Commission
on Criminal Justice Policy and Standards*, with responsibility for
establishing and co-ordinating general policies and guidelines for
decision-making, for setting standards and monitoring the working of
the system at all levels. It could also incorporate research and consult-
ancy functions and act as a clearing house for the dissemination of
relevant information. As an interim step might it be worth considering
the formation of an *ad hoc* committee of interested individuals and
organisations to enquire into the feasibility of some such co-ordinating
organisation for the future? There are certainly impressive precedents
from the United States, where similar unofficial groups have had considerable impact on criminal justice policy (e.g. American Friends Service Committee, 1971; Von Hirsch, 1976). Whether such a committee
would be likely to exert the necessary public and political influence in
Britain of the late 20th century is another question altogether!

References

Alschuler, A.W. (1978) 'Sentencing reform and prosecutorial power:
a critique of recent proposals for "fixed" and "presumptive" sentencing',
Univ. of Pennsylvania Law Review, 126, 550.

American Friends' Service Committee (1971) *Struggle for Justice*, New York, Hill and Wang.

Ashworth, A. (1983) *Sentencing and Penal Policy*, London, Weidenfeld and Nicholson.

Ashworth, A. (1984) 'Prosecution, police and public: a guide to good gate-keeping', *Howard Journal of Criminal Justice*, 23, 65.

Baldwin, J. and McConville, M. (1977) *Negotiated Justice: Pressures to Plead Guilty*, London, Martin Robertson.

Blalock, I. (1982) 'Parole guidelines', in M.L. Forst (ed.) *op. cit.*

Bottomley, A.K. (1983) 'Criminal Justice Policy and Principles of Penal Practice', unpublished paper, Howard League Annual Conference, Oxford, September, 1983.

Dawson, R.O. (1969) *Sentencing: the Decision as to Type, Length and Conditions of Sentence*, Boston, Little Brown.

Ericson, R.V. (1981) *Making Crime: A Study of Detective Work*, Toronto, Butterworths.

Ericson, R.V. (1982) *Reproducing Order: A Study of Police Patrol Work*, University of Toronto Press.

Forst, M.L. (ed.) (1982) *Sentencing Reform: Experiments in Reducing Disparity*, Beverly Hills, Sage.

Galligan, D.J. (1981) 'Guidelines and just deserts: a critique of recent trends in sentencing reform', *Criminal Law Review*, 297.

Hanrahan, K.J. and Greer, A. (1982) 'Criminal code revision and the issue of disparity', in M.L. Forst (ed.) *op. cit.*

Home Office (1981) The Government Reply to the Fourth Report from the Home Affairs Committee, Session 1980–81 HC 412, *The Prison Service*, London, HMSO.

Home Office (1984) *Cautioning by the Police: A Consultative Document*, London, Home Office.

House of Commons (1981) Fourth Report from the Home Affairs Committee, *The Prison Service*, HC 412, London, HMSO.

Jacoby, J.E. (1979) 'The charging policies of prosecutors', in W.F. McDonald (ed.) *op. cit.*

La Fave, W.R. (1965) *Arrest: the Decision to Take a Suspect into Custody*, Boston, Little Brown.

McConville, M. and Baldwin, J. (1981) *Courts, Prosecution and Conviction*, London, Oxford University Press.

McDonald, W.F. (ed.) (1979) *The Prosecutor*, Beverly Hills, Sage.

Miller, F.W. (1970) *Prosecution: the Decision to Charge a Suspect with a Crime*, Boston, Little Brown.

Moody, S.R. and Tombs, J. (1982) *Prosecution in the Public Interest*, Edinburgh, Scottish Academic Press.

Newman, D.J. (1966) *Conviction: the Determination of Guilt or Innocence Without Trial*, Boston, Little Brown.

Ohlin, L.E. and Remington, F.J. (1958) 'Sentencing structure; its effect upon systems for the administration of criminal justice', *Law and Contemporary Problems*, 23, 495.

Ozanne, P. A. (1982) 'Judicial review: a case for sentencing guidelines and just deserts' in M. L. Forst (ed.) *op. cit.*

Royal Commission on Criminal Procedure (1981) *Report*, Cmnd. 8092, London, HMSO.

Steer, D. J. (1970) *Police Cautions – A Study in the Exercise of Police Discretion*, Oxford, Basil Blackwell.

Sanders, A. (1985) 'Prosecution decisions and the Attorney-General's guidelines', *Criminal Law Review*, 4, 19.

Von Hirsch, A. (1976) *Doing Justice; the Choice of Punishments*, New York, Hill and Wang.

Wilkins, L. T. *et al.* (1978) *Sentencing Guidelines; Structuring Judicial Discretion*, Washington DC, US Dept. of Justice.

Sentencing reform and the Probation Service

In 1983 126,470 social enquiry reports (SERs) were prepared' for England and Wales courts at a cost of some £14 million. This is self-evidently a good thing and yet while the industry is flourishing it is difficult to disagree with Ashworth (1983, p. 416) that 'the dynamics of SERs and sentencing are difficult to assert.' Probation officers are routinely expected to embark on their enquiries with little or no clarification of their consumers' expectations and with only implicit assumptions of the courts' requirements, either because reports are prepared before trial, as in virtually all Crown Court cases (twenty-eight per cent of SERs), or because magistrates only rarely give an indication of their reasons for the request. The Home Office's most recent guidance circular (Home Office, 1983) is largely content to refer back to Streatfeild (Streatfeild Report, 1961) despite wide acknowledgement that the 1961 concept of the SER can no longer be sustained (Bottoms and McWilliams 1979, p. 185).

This blindfold exercise doubtless reflects the lack of a coherent jurisprudence of sentencing (Rutherford, 1984) but how has the Probation Service tolerated this haphazard drift? Is it simply our capacity to survive and even enjoy ambiguity and confusion, taking comfort from a vague sense of importance while being on the side of the angels, or the belief that this uncertain arena provides the most productive scope for humanitarian intervention, or that the present lack of structure permits us to function with minimum challenge or scrutiny?

The aim of this Chapter is to support the arguments for a more rational, principled sentencing structure, as healthy for the Service and its rationale, and to consider the implications for our contribution to reformed sentencing policy. Changes will make more exacting demands on the Service, and at the same time should offer a greater measure of fairness and power to the defendants who endure our attentions.

As sentencing dilemmas primarily hinge on the questions: 'What is taken account of?' and 'What is then done?', it is unsurprising that the SER is customarily viewed as fulfilling the tasks of *informing* and *proposing*, with the larger share of attention being paid to the latter. The interrelationship between these roles receives less attention, as if they are an assumed, complementary bond, whereas in fact this is a far from easy juxtaposition.

Informing the courts

It is almost axiomatic that probation officers subscribe to the 'sophisticated' English approach of giving sentencers the discretion to take account of a wide range of factors, past, present and future, rather than to the crude, blinkered and sterile categorisations of a strict 'justice' model. In terms of such sophisticated demands, what have probation officers got to offer?

The Streatfeild Committee, echoed by current Home Office guidance, assumed that SERs could pour useful information into the 'reservoir of assumptions and judgments about morality' (Ashworth 1983, p. 201) in the construction of culpability and blameworthiness.

The offence

Streatfeild seemed to believe that the details of the crime were straightforward. The facts 'are readily made known to the court' by the prosecution and 'no other special arrangements are necessary'. Yet the Home Office request that SERs contain 'information about the circumstances of the offence and the offender's attitude towards it'.

There is not a neat divide between the central core and secondary detail of an offence, and in any event Shapland's (1981) work reveals the lack of procedural scope in guilty pleas for even the basic facts of the case to be properly clarified. Yet a full exploration of culpability would require a subtle analysis of a range of complex and often subjective considerations (see further the chapter by Ashworth, above, in the current volume):

(a) How the crime was committed: degree of skill exercised, how acquired, ease and accessibility of target, degree of planning or

spontaneity, role of offender as instigator or fringe member, any element of entrapment, degree of additional 'nuisance'.
(b) 'Imperfect' defences: questions of duress, self-defence, protection of others, defence of honour, provocation, intoxication (See Wasik, 1983).
(c) Misunderstanding/ignorance of the law.
(d) Other aspects of immediate motivation: need for food, shelter, transport, money etc.
(e) Result: harm caused, value of property, actual gain to defendant, use of proceeds, effect on the victim.
(f) Immediate consequences for defendant: degree of shock, any injuries sustained or other forms of 'natural punishment', reaction of significant others e.g. spouse.
(g) Circumstances of apprehension and subsequent attitude: extent of co-operation, restitution, feelings for victim, regard for criminal process, appreciation of predicament.

This is not intended to be an exhaustive list, but they are all issues which probation officers encounter in SER preparation, many of which defendants will frequently feel have not been properly examined or acknowledged by other professional participants, and which will not necessarily be placed before the court, other than through the SER.

A clear illustration of demand arises out of the recent Court of Appeal guidance in *Barrick* (1985) on fraud offences in breach of trust. Lord Lane listed circumstances which would properly be taken into account, including: quality and degree of trust given, use to which proceeds were put, effect on victim, impact on fellow employees, the strain of any excessive responsibility.

Previous convictions

The report should adequately cover the criminal history of the defendant'
(Home Office, 1983)

Whatever the weight to be given to past offending, the implication is that SERs should address past misconduct, and presumably that only makes sense if the details are known and analysed. Again we know from Shapland's work that this detail is not at present readily available to courts via other routes.

Criminal 'tendencies'
While this issue is not explicitly referred to in the Home Office
Circular of 1983, Streatfeild suggested that the probation officer
should note such factors, for example: 'that a young offender has
collected a number of hangers-on who could shortly become a
determined criminal gang which could be stopped if the defendant
was removed from contact with the others for a substantial period.'
(para. 337)

Such information about 'general reputation and associates' has
caused some problems for compilers of police antecedents and has
been ruled unsound unless based on clear, first-hand information
(Shapland 1981, p.29). The same problems apply to the offending
records of other members of the offender's family, a feature of some
SERs.

Wider issues of culpability
There is a tendency to distinguish culpability as such from the broader
consideration of personality, character, and social background (see
Ashworth 1983, p.422) yet the Circular asks probation officers to
assess these issues as 'relevant to the court's assessment of culpability'
(para. 2.i).

Most SER writers would see blameworthiness as directly linked to:
'those basic economic, material (*and emotional*) factors which set the
limits of an individual's opportunities, and the strengths and weaknesses of the way he has learned to assimilate, make sense of and
operate within the limits of structure.' (Raynor, 1980, p.82; italics
mine)

This is certainly more familiar home ground for the SER, what
the individual brings to the invitational edge of crime, with different
capacities for judgment and restraint, ability to withstand pressure,
availability of alternative legitimate opportunities and outlets.

'Moral bookkeeping'
Nigel Walker (1980) has raised the relevance of past meritorious
behaviour, such as war service, community action, compassionate
behaviour etc. Is this legitimately an exploration of the defendant's
capacity for pro-social behaviour and conformity, beyond merely the
avoidance of criminal convictions, possibly to counteract or set in
context the swamping stigma of deviance arising from prosecution?
This data tends to arise somewhat fortuitously in SER interviews,

and hence the subsequent surprises that can occur in Community Service assessment of an individual's strengths and abilities.

After the event

If culpability arises in the frame of circumstances leading up to and including the immediate events of the offence, what of subsequent action, attitude and intention? Possible issues include whether the defendant has sought or intends to make amends, receive treatment, change associates or life style, or demonstrates a change of conscience or acknowledges a need for change. This may be viewed cautiously as possibly being manipulated by the defendant as 'impression management' or 'remedial work', or as very speculative and uncertain.

If more principled sentencing requires closer, clearer attention to distinguishing features, such as outlined above, how will this degree of thorough information reach the court? To what extent wil the police or public prosecutor tackle this broad survey or how much should be expected as part of 'the deeper study of the offender better entrusted to the probation officer' (Streatfeild, para. 326)?

Probation officers and offending behaviour

There is little expressed lack of confidence about probation officers' ability to contribute information about offending, despite the evidence that detailed knowledge and clear thinking about offending has not featured impressively in SERs or probation records (Perry, 1974; Scarborough, 1985). Raynor, seeking to acknowledge the proper demands of the justice model, states:

> It is only by understanding as far as possible the offender's own view of the offence and its circumstances that we can begin to think about what he intended and how far he had a clear understanding of what was going on. The basic facts of the offence as presented through police evidence are often deficient in this kind of information. This kind of exploration may be more easily carried out by social workers with some training and experience in helping people express their views and feelings than by other court personnel whose preoccupations are often different.
>
> (Rayner, 1980, p. 82)

In the recent final report of the Inner London Service Demonstration Unit (Harraway *et al.*, 1985), the team, who chose to focus experimentally on taking-and-driving-away and burglary offences, indicate how their SER practice investigated the details of how vehicles had been entered, how much skill was required, how acquired, how vulnerable the target, what damage was done, and a similar range of questions about break-ins.

Attention has also been drawn to the implications of the criteria in Criminal Justice Act 1982, S1(4) for the use of custodial sentences for young persons. Does this require 'that report writers must carefully consider the concepts of 'seriousness' and 'protection' in relation to the type and number of offences, the harm inflicted on persons and property', as Whitehead and MacMillan (1985) suggest? Or in what other way is the court to gain help in weighing these criteria, other than by its own implicit judgment, which has so far been given such elastic and unbridled rein? The Inner London Demonstration Unit claim that they were able to use their offence material to counteract the bald appearance of apparently serious crimes, to show how little skill or forethought was involved in vulnerable targets.

Certainly probation officers are becoming more alert to offending behaviour, particularly as a central focus for supervisory attention, day-centre programmes etc., acknowledging the previous avoidance of this issue, and following the lead in juvenile intermediate treatment towards the use of the 'correctional curriculum'. A recent influential text out of the social skills training stable is McGuire and Priestley's *Offending Behaviour* (1985), which offers a variety of techniques for getting offenders to explore their crimes and related values and beliefs. The authors indicate, however, that they offer these methods as private, voluntary exercises, designed to inform the individuals concerned and those they accept help from. 'They must be placed under the control of those who are trying to change themselves.' This cannot be subsumed readily or at all into the enforced and public SER process, with their multiple post-sentence applications in institutions and elsewhere (Shaw, 1981).

What empirical evidence we have for the way in which probation officers understand and interpret offending comes from Pauline Hardiker's studies (1977, 1979) in Leicestershire. She suggests that report writers tend to take either an 'action' (offence the inevitable result of biological, psychological or social characteristics) or an 'infraction' (free-willed choice to break the law) perspective, and bring preconceived assumptions to bear, such as that the more serious or more repeated the crime, the less likely can it be the product of natural choice.

If courts are to increase their demand for accurate, systematic information relevant to sentencing, will probation officers be asked to fulfil the role of 'offence analyst'? If so then that would seem to require a different order of skills and practice than is currently available. Would, for instance, victims need to be routinely interviewed as is common in many United States jurisdictions, not so much with a view to exploring mediation opportunities, as is now tentatively being tried in South Yorkshire, but in order to assess issues of premeditation, sophistication, use of threats and possible victim precipitation (see the Wisconsin guidance quoted in Perry, 1979, p. 31). This would demand a major switch from predominantly offender-centred practice, but would also have more fundamental implications for the way in which SERs are used to persuade sentencers along a particular course.

Offering proposals

The evolution of and controversy surrounding 'recommendations' in SERs is familiar (see Harris, 1979) if unresolved. Of fresher significance is the potential status and value of this feature of reports, if the information before the court points with clearer consistency towards a particular disposal zone.

Perhaps the greatest liability the Probation Service currently bears is the excess burden of responsibility for reducing the prison population. Thus the Home Secretary, responding to the latest rise in custodial measures, called in August 1985 for the Probation Service to 'do all that it can to provide non-custodial alternatives to imprisonment', echoing his *Criminal Justice Working Paper* (Home Office, 1984) which suggested diversion from custody of 'persistent and serious offenders'.

This challenge to the Service masks and fudges the essential issue of 'In' or 'Out', so clearly confronted in North American sentencing reform. As Bean, after Christie, has warned (1981; p. 161) this shelters the courts in a stagnant lagoon, believing that greater expertise will attain utilitarian goals, rather than facing clear moral choice. Rutherford trenchantly argues (1984; p. 168) that alternative measures are a consequence, not a pre-condition of contracting the prison system, and that the real hope of reducing incarceration is a 'deep end' strategy on the use of custody, rather than expecting the 'alternatives' industry to manufacture major solutions.

Whether the courts actually believe the rhetoric of 'alternatives' is doubtful. The results of intensive efforts such as the Hampshire initiative to persuade courts to reduce the prison population (Smith *et al.*, 1984) are not encouraging, either as regards attitude change or sentencing practice. Perhaps the most fervent true believers are within the Service, in self-inflicted travail, tilting at 'heavy end' windmills and bidding for extra resources. The Service is clearly faced with a dilemma that it either shoulders a responsibility which it may well not deliver on, or else feels a worrying sense of marginality. If, however, sentencing can come to terms more explicitly with the 'In Out' issue, then the Service can be restored to participating intelligently in that calculation and then servicing various community-based disposals.

That calculation would firstly contain an evaluation of the impact and differing effect of various disposals upon the defendant (see Ashworth 1983, Ch. 7; Bottomley, 1980). As Harris (1985) suggests, SERs 'should contain an assessment of the likely social consequences of possible sentences, particularly custody when it is being considered'. These considerations include:

(a) effect on defendant and significant others of loss of liberty;
(b) prospective custodial experience in the light of offence, defendant's health and sensitivities, previous occupation, past experience etc.;
(c) effect on accommodation, employment and income of different disposals;
(d) future prospects in the wake of particular disposals.

Secondly, the SER could indicate the viability of particular non-custodial disposals, described by Raynor (1980) as a 'contractual' approach. This means providing a breakdown of what undertakings defendants are prepared to give, should they be allowed continued liberty, how feasible and realistic these are and whether any help or supervision might be provided in trying to sustain them. This can cover the range of non-custodial disposals from discharge to deferment, but with particular reference to Community Service (CS) and probation orders.

Raynor sees this as being prepared in full consultation with and with the consent of the defendant, as the offer of a 'plausible alternative to the retributive tariff sentence'. This promotes the misleading idea of the 'exception to the rule', rather than the sensible and incremental use of an extended scale of community-based, penal demands, whether a promise of good behaviour over a set period, performance of work, undertaking an educational assignment, or the payment of a financial levy.

Advising or manipulating?

Having taken stock of the different ingredients which might constitute the SER, the question arises whether it is a digestible recipe. Doubt has already been expressed as to the extent of probation skills, and may also be raised in terms of practice congruence. Hardiker's research clearly points to the tactical judgments that shape and determine report writing. She identified that probation officers adopted a variety of roles:

(a) Advising sentencers – a relatively straightforward description of the offender's circumstances or a diagnosis or prognosis of his criminal behaviour; offence moderately serious; offender in low need: non-supervisory sentence recommended.
(b) Leaving to classical justice – offence serious; acknowledgement of inevitability of a tariff sentence: custody or nothing recommended. Reports may either play up an offender's incorrigibility and life stresses or omit mitigating evidence.
(c) Manipulating towards a 'social work' outcome – most often occurs when attempts are made to keep the offender out of prison. Great needs and vulnerability stressed, response to supervision played up, life difficulties played down or omitted.

No wonder then that Curnock and Hardiker say that her findings are 'problematical' and have profound implications for the structure and content of SERs (1979, p. 97). Though she reported that officers saw themselves as advising sentencers in eight per cent of their reports, others have felt that the reporting role contains a fundamental ambiguity, involving a struggle to maintain 'the tenuous mythology of objectivity.' Powell states that 'report writing is about getting a result and getting results involves the use of strategies' (1985: 27): 'The effectiveness of the "strategist" role rests on the continuing credibility of the pose as "professional expert" or "servant of the court".' (Pearce and Wareham 1977: 102) As probation officers feel increasingly bound to promote non-custodial outcomes and to write reports in which the 'recommendation' flows logically from the fore-going information, the stance of manipulator towards social work-based disposals is likely to be more identifiable.

The undesirability of pursuing such camouflaged posing is faced by Bottoms and McWilliams who in their proposals for a more coherent probation function suggest that the SER should have an explicit diversionary role, recommendations being made only with the client's consent. Harris (1980) has warned that this transforms the SER into a mitigatory document, a tactical plea negotiated between worker and client as the lightest recommendation on which both can agree. He suggests that this would effect a major change in the Service's role in court, and could lead to a reduced take-up of recommendations, and a consequent increase in custodial sentences.

Such fears fit with the critical if not well-substantiated findings of the Home Office Research Unit that officers select from available information to support their arguments and place the offender in the best possible light, omitting unfavourable details (Thorpe, 1979). Thus it is sometimes suggested that whereas reports frequently describe the defendant as a follower or 'easily led', very few indicate leadership and responsibility for instigation. However, it is often far from clear whether a particular element lies in mitigation or aggravation; what connotations it carried can depend considerably on the nature of the audience and their social proximity to the defendant. Thus who is to say what interpretation should be placed on e.g. the defendant's claim to have committed an offence of assault out of loyalty to his friends who felt aggrieved by the victim's conduct?

It would be incorrect, of course, to assume SERs contain a clear bias towards positive or mitigating material. In a recent survey of SERs recommending community-based disposals prepared on young persons entering detention centre, in the majority of reports 'negative' comments outweighed the 'positive' (Millichamp *et al.*, 1985). What was noticeable were the misleading phrasing and haphazard weighting of such material, linked to vague and unsubstantiated assessment of the defendant's attitude and a wide spread of non-criminal behaviour. Whereas 'statements which indicate that the writer knows about the offence and can put it into a wider context tend to be uncommon'.

We know too from studies of SERs prepared on currently supervised clients that material will be introduced selectively at different points in their offending career, with different attached significance to fit with the pitch for or against continued supervision that the author is making. This is linked to the agenda of organisational self-interest that is pursued simultaneously with the needs of courts and defendants when SERs are written.

Bottoms and McWilliams (McWilliams, 1981) have subsequently suggested that a way out of this conundrum of ambiguity is to develop the two-part SER, the first containing the social information the court requires, the second outlining the possibilities and arguments for non-custodial penalties; the latter would be read as an optional extra, should the court be interested. This neat split may, however, seem. to require an impossible detachment of mind, in that it would be difficult for officers, previously exhorted to write their reports so that the conclusion unfolds naturally from the factual presentation, to prepare Part 1 without seeking to pave the way for Part 2.

The Inner London Demonstration Unit did in fact seek where appropriate to record detail of offending which would emphasise culpability. They wondered if this would in fact promote harsher sentencing. They report that the reverse happened and rarely did a clear statement about the offender's choice to offend affect the court adversely: 'It seemed that the court responded favourably to an SER giving a serious and defined statement about the offence in preference to a lengthy account of the offender's social background.' (Harraway *et al.*, 1985; p.15)

However, this reaction might be explicable because detail in this regard was frequently linked to a broader favourable impression of the defendant, based on their positive attitude towards the offence, the number of contacts between probation officer and client, and an energetic desire for change. Such an impression would cause the writer to make clearer proposals for probation supervision, with detailed plans of what this would seek to achieve. There is also a suggestion that the courts found the blunter detail a refreshing change and responded well. This advantage could not be sustained in circum-stances where the exception became the rule.

Towards 'just welfare'

The fore-going analysis of the problems that can arise in the SERs attempt to link information with recommendation, and the various hypotheses that have been offered to make sense of the probation officer's struggle for authenticity – whether 'second guessing', strategic manipulation, putting forward a tariff-minus-one proposal, or the more complex and disputed 'reverse tariff model' (Hardiker, 1977) – give weight to Harris' argument in the juvenile justice context that sentencing problems have been improperly transferred from court to social worker with unsatisfactory consequences. Harris (1985) proposes instead that the SER, prepared by those who remain centred in social work traditions, values and person-centred skills, should be explicitly geared to (a) an assessment of the likely social consequences of possible sentences and (b) an offer of non-custodial options relevant to the offenders' needs and abilities, to be considered and perhaps taken up by the court, should the principle of 'just welfare' be accepted by the court in the light of the other non-social work considerations on the sentencing agenda. This suggests that close consideration of the offence would be helpful in preparing and writing the SER, not so much to guide the court in how to regard the offence, but in evaluating the offender as actor, and the possible difficulties and needs that it reveals. These may then prompt particular suggestions for disposal by community-based options. Harris is alert to the importance of the principle of limiting welfare measures to the extent appropriate to the culpability of the offence, but he presumably would expect the court to cope with that judgment in the light of the SER author's information about the demandingness of the non-custodial suggestion.

The SER writer is thus relieved of the spurious quest to be 'realistic' and to make doubtful judgments about the seriousness of the offence on a tariff scale. The unreliability of such 'guesstimates', the tendency to over-predict and the possibility that this may in fact influence sentencers upwards are well established. On the other hand, the re-emphasised skill of making imaginative, convincing offers of community-based disposals cannot sensibly be done in a vacuum. Hence the strong desirability that SERs should be prepared not in response to a bald, open-ended request, but with clearer guidance from the court how the sentencing exercise in hand is viewed. Thus the helpful suggestion from the *Magistrate* (Jan. 1984, Vol. 40, No. 1) that courts should identify the issues and areas that they would like investigated, and pass that view on to their colleagues who will read the result.

If Harris is correct, then it would follow that the SER has primary purpose in those cases where courts indicate their willingness to listen to 'just welfare' perspectives. Does this throw into doubt the place of the SER in cases which fall firmly within the 'In' (custody) zone? Probation officers tend to hold to the belief that their reports can still speak usefully about 'impact of sentence' issues, and also sometimes argue that their reports may in fact be serving the hidden, subsequent agenda of prison and parole decision-making. While the first argument is sound, the latter justification is dubious, promoting the undesirable multipurpose use of stale reports (Shaw, 1981). But what of 'low tariff' offending, and the argument increasingly heard that SER resources are squandered on minor, petty cases? Ken Pease has argued (1984) that SERs can make a positive contribution to ensuring that non-custodial measures for trivial offenders should be used to greater and more sustained effect, as an upstream way of making an impact on subsequent In/Out decision-making, depending, of course, on the weight to be assigned to record in reformed sentencing policy.

Some implications for practice and procedure

If reports are then to be prepared purposefully across this spread of circumstances, and report writers are to become increasingly skilled at conceiving imaginative, 'contractual' community measures, there are clear implications for resources, procedure and rights. If the SER is to deliver on 'just welfare', the time spent on careful exploration and explanation would have to be increased, if we are not forced into a quality up – quantity down equation. Secondly, how should the report be received and considered? If sentencing is to become a more rational problem-solving exercise based on an increased pool of information, then how can court room communication channels be improved? Probation officers have tended to feel in a weak procedural position, inhibited by fluctuating local etiquette which Shapland (1981, Ch. 7) identifies as dogging the sentencing process as a whole.

This issue points to the imbalance between trial and sentence in terms of clarity, time and procedural weight. This not only presents problems for the Probation Service in making a more clearly recognised and demarcated contribution, but has left the defendant in a particularly uncertain and exposed position, especially when pleading guilty. If the normal ground rules of the adversarial process tend to become replaced by the inquisitional style of the sentencing arena, the defendant has been highly vulnerable to the contents of SERs with their privileged status – not made under oath, frequent contravention of the hearsay rule, no obligation to provide evidence of disputed facts, seldom challenged, few enforceable safeguards. As Wright (1985) has complained: 'There is no procedure by which a defendant ... can alter the tenor of an SER, nor attempt to exclude any fact or assumption made in it ... Surely some grievance procedure could be incorporated into the court's structure so that the defendant or any of his or her family can express their point of view about them.'

The rights of defendants in SER preparation are far from clear. Are persons obliged to have reports written about them? Keeping of appointments for reports can be a condition of bail, and bail may be refused in order that reports can be secured. Yet to write a report on an unwilling or silent defendant can seem a nonsense, relying on old data or details from third parties. Few decline but more might if the choice was more clear and explicit, if the ramifications of reports were better understood or if the contents were better scrutinised by their subjects.

If the SER is to carry a greater load of responsibility for informing courts or for considering vital questions of liberty and community options, then this has to be matched by a greater obligation of advance disclosure, opportunity for challenge and correction, deletion or alteration of misleading or disputed material. Wright suggests disclosure two weeks before the sentencing exercise and the opportunity for a 'trial' of contentious reports before an independent tribunal of some kind. This kind of safeguard would further add to the time and resources required for preparation and presentation.

Making sense of non-custodial measures

Having surveyed the contribution that probation officers can make to sentencing, it remains to consider how the Service can enhance the clearer standing of those non-custodial measures which it directly administers. As Ashworth's chapter indicates, we lack full descriptive guidance on kinds of cases for which these sentences should be used.

Despite regularly rehearsed arguments that Community Service has no intrinsic tariff character, other than being available only for imprisonable offences, the guidance of the Court of Appeal in *Clarke* (1982), *Lawrence* (1982) and other cases, indicating that CS sits on the In/Out boundary, wins the support of the majority of the Service. Unfortunately, this fine principle is readily abused either by SER authors who find CS a welcome haven for the impoverished client or who promote it in reports as an over-cautious 'second guess'. As a resolution of this dilemma, Pease and McWilliams' proposal (1980) for a two-tier approach to CS, maintaining the upper tier of hours for the *Clarke* kind of judgment, is attractive, but has not found favour with NAPO, which felt this to be an unacceptable pollution of CS's alternative to custody purity. Since it is unlikely that CS across its full range could achieve such purity it would seem better to rationalise it in two coherent segments.

The probation order has been far less easy to locate, on any 'ladder' (Ashworth, 1983, p. 433) or in judicial guidance. There is no hint in *Clarke* of probation as a part of the reasoning process. There is the suggestion in *West* (1975) that probation in its amplified form under P.C.C.A. 1973, s. 3 (condition of mental treatment) could be a direct diversionary measure in the very specialised market of the redeemable mentally disordered offender, and it is not so far removed to contemplate the application of similar reasoning to use of conditions of residence in probation hostels, involving a considerable restriction on the life choices of the defendant. But these types of condition have always been the exception, and somewhat marginal. The attraction of the 'standard' probation order has been its flexibility and lack of precision, and Millard (1982) has written of the probation order's strength in institutionalising the uncertainties and moral dilemmas faced by courts who can pass these on to the Probation Service to handle with pragmatic discretion. Far from being a source of discomfort and secrecy, that discretion should be acknowledged and be explicable and acceptable to lay scrutiny.

However, a major question for the Service now is the capacity of the probation order to stretch up tariff, either by being subject in its 'standard' form to clearer expectations and demands (obligatory attendance at induction group programmes, clear-cut reporting requirements etc.) or in a new wave of additional requirements under Criminal Justice Act 1982, *Schedule 11*. Considerable energy is being given within the Service to the design of programmes which can seem relevant both to sentencers and offenders, based on life-skills training, unemployment, driving and the law, self-assertion, control of temper, choices about alcohol, greater discretion when faced with the temptations of crime, weighing the advantages and disadvantages of offending (i.e. 'crime doesn't pay') etc.

These ideas are very much a response to the crisis of confidence faced recently in social work with offenders. If major change and transformation in individuals is acknowledged to be very difficult to deliver, and the alleged collapse of the 'rehabilitative ideal' is neither to provoke nihilistic cynicism, nor drive us towards increased emphasis on surveillance and segregation within the community, then the educational package has obvious appeal. It offers something reasonably certain and manageable, it is 'demanding' and does not offend notions of 'less eligibility' (hence much reluctance to mix the voluntary participant with the non-voluntary); its delivery and results can be measured and offered as proof of efficiency; it is reasonably limited and clear-cut and does not offend Lord Bridge's principles, as detailed in *Cullen v Rogers* (1982), that the probation order should not contain a custodial element nor allow the unfettered discretion of the probation officer. It thus meets Garland's (1985, p. 262) criterion that progressive penal politics should neither perceive the penal object as 'the responsible individual of the free-market system nor the irresponsible client of the Welfare State'. Clients are in fact given better information and abilities with which to make choices, and should have a clearer notion of where they stand and what the ground rules are.

A constant concern in making sense of the probation order has been the attempt to achieve congruence between issues of need and issues of tariff. There has certainly been a conscious effort within the Service to shift use of probation away from the first time offender, as both wasteful play of a trump card (Harraway *et al.*, 1985) and as possibly having a counter-productive effect in terms of reconviction prospects (Walker, 1983). The necessity of a 'need' dimension has, however, been queried, if probation could simply operate as a form of conditional freedom, backed by reminders and regular offers of help. On the other hand, as the Inner London Demonstration Unit note, 'an ever more enquiring Service is likely to discover an ever greater intensity of need amongst a growing proportion of those who are adjudged eligible for probation'. The Unit's own preference is illuminating. They were particularly inspired by Bottoms' (1983) analysis of a changing style of punishment from 'carcereal' to 'juridical' (i.e. a limited penalty designed to mark and represent societal disapproval, enabling the individual upon completion to continue normal social functioning). The project thus aimed to enhance the probation order as a juridical exercise, with increased use and limited, offence-centred aims (Harraway *et al.*, 1985, p. 42).

This approach can offer real advantages to probationers in terms of the explicitness of what is involved and the offer of help seen as legitimate and rational. These 'justice'-inspired ideas are circulating more prominently in juvenile justice (see Jones, 1983) and are more slowly reaching adult probation. However, the corollary is that by clearer demands and perhaps greater sense of accountability, through project assessments and reports, there is greater expectation of action against defaulters and thus a greater problem over what measures then follow. Those who are wary of such developments see a risk of inflexibility, both in meeting the real needs of the individuals so concerned and in handling their resistance, and the danger of increasingly bringing individuals onto probation territory in offender segregation, rather than promoting the facilitation of integration and outreach into natural community resources. There is additionally the appropriate fear that the Probation Service could paint itself into the corner of creating expectations among sentencers which both diminish the more traditional probation order and prompt sentencers to link individuals to programmes on the basis of assumed need primarily rather than offending career. Thus special probation conditions may follow the way of community service in being attractive means of occupying offenders on the basis of their unemployment, as much as a just measure of penalty.

In conclusion

This Chapter has attempted to outline the complexity of seeking to service 'sophisticated' sentencing, if the potential breadth of relevant issues pertaining to culpability past and prospects future are to be explored. The interweave of culpability and individualisation is intricate; the division of what is inculpatory or exculpatory difficult to assess. Ultimately, it is suggested that it is not appropriate to ask the probation officer to combine congruently the roles of offence analyst and 'just welfare' consultant. One's choice of information invariably reflects one's professional outlook, and the material gets massaged accordingly. To divide the labour, on the other hand, would be an unlikely, time-consuming, and expensive enterprise, and so it seems that SER authors will have to continue an uneasy 'fit' of tasks, requiring a detachment of mind normally only associated with the judiciary.

Beyond those efforts, the question remains on the basis of Hogarth's (1971) investigations, just how much material can the courts handle coherently; to what extent will the judicial mind also massage the material to support or bolster preconceived attitudes and assumptions? If we are to ensure that social enquiry work is a rational contribution to a rational exercise, and not merely offers some symbolic support for the hard-pressed isolated sentencer, then we are heavily reliant on the courts' capacity to integrate us into the process with greater clarity and definition of purpose. And with both Community Service and Probation, while the Probation Service can devise and administer creative helpful and relevant experiences for offenders and comment on their viability for particular defendants, the running, in terms of linking proper disposals to appropriate defendants must come from courts, on the basis of judgments and principles which the Service cannot claim to make. The interrelationship between courts and their probation officers as systems of local criminal justice has not received sufficient research attention (though see Bullock and Tildesley, 1984, for a recent case study). In the partnership that must develop in shaping principles practice, the Service is clearly not just a pliable and passive retainer. Rather, the Service should act as contractor supplying services with more explicit function, subject to closer questioning by the defence, and clearer public accountability.

References

Ashworth, A. (1983) *Sentencing and Penal Policy*, London, Weidenfeld and Nicholson.

Bean, P. (1981) *Punishment*, Oxford, Martin Robertson.

Bottoms, A. (1983) 'Neglected features of contemporary penal systems' in *The Power to Punish*, D. Garland and P. Young (eds.), London, Heinemann Educational.

Bottoms, A. and McWilliams, W. (1979) 'A non-treatment paradigm for practice', *British Journal of Social Work*, 9, 159.

Bottomley, A. K. (1980) 'The justice model in America and Britain: development and analysis' in *The Coming Penal Crisis*, A. Bottoms and R. Preston (eds.), Edinburgh, Scottish Academic Press.

Bullock, W. and Tildesley, W. (1984) *Special Requirements in Probation or Supervision Orders*, Cambridge, Institute of Criminology.

Cohen, S. (1985) *Visions of Social Control*, Cambridge, Polity Press.

Curnock, K. and Hardiker, P. (1979) *Towards Practice Theory*, London, Routledge and Kegan Paul.

Garland, D. (1985) *Punishment and Welfare*, Aldershot, Gower.

Hardiker, P. (1977) *A Probation Intake Team in Action*, Leicestershire Probation and After-Care Service.

Hardiker, P. and Webb, D. (1979) 'Explaining deviant behaviour', *Sociology*, *13*, 1.

Harraway, p. *et al.* (1985) *The Demonstration Unit 1981–1985*, Inner London Probation Service.

Harris, B. (1979) 'Recommendations in Social Inquiry Reports', *Criminal Law Review*, 73.

Harris, R. (1980) *A Flawed Model*, University of Leicester School of Social Work (unpublished mimeo).

Harris, R. (1985) 'Towards just welfare', *British Journal of Criminology*, 14, 31.

Hogarth, J. (1971) *Sentencing as a Human Process*, University of Toronto Press.

Home Office (1983) *Social Inquiry Reports: General Guidance on Contents*, Circular No. 17/1983.

Home Office (1984) *Criminal Justice: A Working Paper*. London, Home Office.

Jones, R. (1983) 'Justice, social work and statutory supervision', in *Providing Criminal Justice for Children*, A. Morris and H. Giller, London, Edward Arnold.

McGuire, J. and Priestley, P. (1985) *Offending Behaviour*, London, Batsford.

McWilliams, W. (1981) 'The probation officer at court: from friend to acquaintance', *Howard Journal*, 20, 97.

Millard, D. (1982) 'Keeping the probation service whole: the case for discretion', *British Journal of Social Work*, 12, 291.

Millichamp, D. *et al.* (1985) 'A matter of natural justice', *Community Care* (13 June, No. 567) 25.

Pearce, I. and Wareham, A. (1977) 'The questionable relevance of research into social enquiry reports', *Howard Journal*, 16, 97.

Pease, K. (1984) 'A five-year plan for probation research', in *Probation: Direction, Innovation and Change in the 1980s*, London, NAPO.

Pease, K. and McWilliams, W. (1980) *Community Service by Order*, Edinburgh, Scottish Academic Press.

Perry, F. (1974) *Information for the Court*, Cambridge, Institute of Criminology.

Perry, F. (1979) *Reports for Criminal Courts*, Ilkley, Owen Wells.

Powell, M. (1985) 'Court work', in *Working with Offenders*, H. Walker and B. Beaumont (eds.), Basingstoke, Macmillan.

Raynor, P. (1980) 'Is there any sense in social inquiry reports?', *Probation Journal*, 27, 78.

Rutherford, A. (1984) *Prisons and the Process of Justice*, London, Heinemann.

Scarborough, T. (1985) 'Knowing what they're in for', *Probation Journal*, 32, 68.

Shapland, J. (1981) *Between Conviction and Sentence*, London, Routledge and Kegan Paul.

Shaw, R. (1981) *Who Uses Social Inquiry Reports?*, Cambridge, Institute of Criminology.

Smith, D. *et al.* (1984) *Reducing the Prison Population*, Research and Planning Unit Paper 23, London, Home Office.

Streatfeild Report (1961) *Report of the Interdepartmental Committee on the Business of the Criminal Courts*, London, HMSO.

Thomas, D. A. (1979), *Principles of Sentencing*, 2nd ed. London, Heinemann.

Thorpe, J. (1979) *Social Inquiry Reports: A Survey*, Home Office Research Study 48, London, HMSO.

Walker, N. (1980) *Punishment, Danger and Stigma*, Oxford, Basil Blackwell.
Walker, N. (1983) 'The effectiveness of probation', *Probation Journal*, 30, 99.
Wasik, M. (1983) 'Excuses at the sentencing stage', *Criminal Law Review*, 450.
Whitehead, P. and MacMillan, J. (1985) 'Checks or blank cheque? Justifying custody of juveniles', *Probation Journal*, 32, 87.
Wright, D. (1985) 'The final word', *Legal Action*, July, 14.

Cases

Barrick (1985) 7 Cr.App.R.(S) 142.
Clarke [1982] 1W.L.R. 1090.
Cullen v *Rogers* [1982] 2 All.E.R. 570.
Lawrence [1982] Crim.L.R. 144.
West 30.7.75; 982/B/75; cited in Thomas, 1979, p.293.

Appendix

Minnesota sentencing guidelines and commentary

Statement of purpose and principles

The purpose of the sentencing guidelines is to establish rational and consistent sentencing standards which reduce sentencing disparity and ensure that sanctions following conviction of a felony are proportional to the severity of the offence of conviction and the extent of the offender's criminal history. Equity in sentencing requires (a) that convicted felons similar with respect to relevant sentencing criteria ought to receive similar sanctions, and (b) that convicted felons substantially different from a typical case with respect to relevant criteria ought to receive different sanctions.

The sentencing guidelines embody the following principles:

1. Sentencing should be neutral with respect to the race, gender, social, or economic status of convicted felons.
2. While commitment to the Commissioner of Corrections is the most severe sanction that can follow conviction of a felony, it is not the only significant sanction available to the sentencing judge. Development of a rational and consistent sentencing policy requires that the severity of sanctions increase in direct proportion to increases in the severity of criminal offences and the severity of criminal histories of convicted felons.
3. Because the capacities of state and local correctional facilities are finite, use of incarcerative sanctions should be limited to those convicted of more serious offences or those who have longer criminal histories. To ensure such usage of finite resources, sanctions used in sentencing convicted felons should be the least restrictive necessary to achieve the purposes of the sentence.
4. While the sentencing guidelines are advisory to the sentencing judge, departures from the presumptive sentences established in the

guidelines should be made only when substantial and compelling circumstances exist.

Determining presumptive sentences

The presumptive sentence for any offender convicted of a felony committed on or after 1 May 1980, is determined by locating the appropriate cell of the Sentencing Guidelines Grid. The grid represents the two dimensions most important in current sentencing and releasing decisions – offence severity and criminal history.

Offence severity
The offence severity level is determined by the offence of conviction. When an offender is convicted of two or more felonies, the severity level is determined by the most severe offence of conviction. Felony offences are arrayed into ten levels of severity, ranging from low (Severity Level I) to high (Severity Level X). First degree murder is excluded from the sentencing guidelines, because by law the sentence is mandatory imprisonment for life. Offences listed within each level of severity are deemed to be generally equivalent in severity. The most frequently occurring offences within each severity level are listed on the vertical axis of the Sentencing Guidelines Grid.

Comment
Offence severity is determined by the offence of conviction. The Commission thought that serious legal and ethical questions would be raised if punishment were to be determined on the basis of alleged, but unproven, behaviour, and prosecutors and defenders would be less accountable in plea negotiation. It follows that if the offence of conviction is the standard from which to determine severity, departures from the guidelines should not be permitted for elements of offender behaviour not within the statutory definition of the offence of conviction. Thus, if an offender is convicted of simple robbery, a departure from the guidelines to increase the severity of the sentence should not be permitted because the offender possessed a firearm or used another dangerous weapon.

The date of the offence is important because the offender's age at the time of the offence will determine whether or not the juvenile record is considered, the date of the offence might determine whether a custody status point should be given, and the date of offence determines the order of sentencing with multiple convictions.

Criminal History

A criminal history index constitutes the horizontal axis of the Sentencing Guidelines Grid. The criminal history index is comprised of the following items: (1) prior felony record; (2) custody status at the time of the offence; (3) prior misdemeanour and gross misdemeanour record; and (4) prior juvenile record for young adult felons.

Comment

The sentencing guidelines reduce the emphasis given to criminal history in sentencing decisions. Under past judicial practice, criminal history was the primary factor in dispositional decisions. Under sentencing guidelines, the offence of conviction is the primary factor, and criminal history is a secondary factor in dispositional decisions. In the past there were no uniform standards regarding what should be included in an offender's criminal history, no weighting format for different types of offences, and no systematic process to check the accuracy of the information on criminal history.

The guidelines provide uniform standards for the inclusion and weighting of criminal history information. The sentencing hearing provides a process to assure the accuracy of the information in individual cases. These improvements will increase fairness and equity in the consideration of criminal history.

No system of criminal history record keeping ever will be totally accurate and complete, and any sentencing system will have to rely on the best available criminal history information.

The offender's criminal history index score is computed in the following manner:

1. Subject to the conditions listed below, the offender is assigned one point for every felony conviction for which a felony sentence was stayed or imposed before the current sentencing.

   (a) When multiple sentences for a single course of conduct were imposed, the offender is assigned one point;

   (b) An offender shall not be assigned more than two points for prior multiple sentences arising out of a single course of conduct in which there were multiple victims;

   (c) When a prior felony conviction resulted in a misdemeanour or gross misdemeanour sentence, that conviction shall be counted as a misdemeanour or gross misdemeanour conviction for purposes of computing the criminal history score, and shall be governed by item 3 below:

(d) When a prior felony conviction results in a stay of imposition, and when that stay of imposition was successfully served, it shall be counted as a felony conviction for purposes of computing the criminal history score for five years from the date of discharge, and thereafter shall be counted as a misdemeanour under the provisions of item 3 below;

(e) Prior felony sentences will not be used in computing the criminal history score if a period of ten years has elapsed since the date of discharge from or expiration of the sentence, to the date of offence of any subsequent misdemeanour, gross misdemeanour or felony, provided that during the period the individual had not received a felony, gross misdemeanour, or misdemeanour sentence whether stayed or imposed.

Comment

The basic rule for computing the number of prior felony points in the criminal history score is that the offender is assigned one point for every felony conviction for which a felony sentence was stayed or imposed before the current sentencing. In cases of multiple offences occurring in a single behavioural incident in which state law prohibits the offender being sentenced on more than one offence, the offender would receive one point. The phrase 'before the current sentencing' means that in order for prior convictions to be used in computing criminal history score, the felony sentence for the prior offence must have been stayed or imposed before sentencing for the current offence. When multiple current offences are sentenced on the same day before the same judge, sentencing shall occur in the order in which the offences occurred.

To limit the impact of past variability in prosecutorial discretion, the Commission placed a limit of two points on computing prior multiple felony sentences arising out of a single course of conduct in which there were multiple victims. For example, if an offender had robbed a crowded liquor store, he could be convicted of and sentenced for the robbery, as well as one count of assault for every person in the store at the time of the offence. Past variability in prosecutorial charging and negotiating practices could create substantial variance in the number of felony sentences arising from comparable criminal behaviour. To prevent this past disparity from entering into the computation of criminal histories, and to prevent manipulation of the system in the future, the Commission placed a limit of two points in such situations. This still allows differentiation between those getting multiple sentences in such situations from those getting single sentences, but it prevents the perpetuation of gross disparities from the past.

The two point limit in calculating criminal history when there are multiple felony sentences arising out of a single course of conduct with multiple victims also applies when such sentences are imposed on the same day.

Finally, the Commission established a 'decay factor' for the consideration of prior felony offences in computing criminal history scores. The Commission decided it was important to consider not just the total number of felony sentences, but also the time interval between those sentences and subsequent offences. A person who was sentenced for three felonies within a five-year period is more culpable than one sentenced for three felonies within a twenty-year period. The Commission decided that after a significant period of offence-free living, the presence of old felony sentences should not be considered in computing criminal history scores. A prior felony sentence would not be counted in criminal history score computation if ten years had elapsed between the date of discharge from or expiration of that sentence and the date of a subsequent offence for which a misdemeanour, gross misdemeanour, or felony sentence was imposed or stayed. (Traffic offences are excluded in computing the decay factor.)

2. The offender is assigned one point if he or she was on probation or parole or confined in a jail, workhouse, or prison following conviction of a felony or gross misdemeanour, or released pending sentencing at the time the felony was committed for which he or she is being sentenced.

   The offencer will not be assigned a point under this item when:

   (a) the person was committed for treatment or examination pursuant to statute; or
   (b) the person was on juvenile probation or parole status at the time the felony was committed for which he or she is being sentenced.

   An additional three months shall be added to the duration of the appropriate cell time which then becomes the presumptive duration when:

(a) a custody status point is assigned; and

(b) the criminal history points that accrue to the offender without
the addition of the custody status point places the offender
in the far right hand column of the Sentencing Guidelines Grid.

Comment
The basic rule assigns offenders one point if they were under some
form of criminal justice custody following conviction of a felony
or gross misdemeanour when the offence was committed for which
they are now being sentenced. Criminal justice custodial status
includes probation (supervised or unsupervised), parole, supervised
release, or confinement in a jail, workhouse, or prison, or work
release, following conviction of a felony or gross misdemeanour,
or release pending sentencing following the entry of a plea of guilty
to a felony or gross misdemeanour, or a verdict of guilty by a jury
or a finding of guilty by the court of a felony or gross misdemeanour.

As a general rule, the Commission excludes traffic offences from
consideration in computing the criminal history score. However, one gross misdemeanour offence − aggravated driving while
intoxicated − is particularly relevant in sentencing cases of criminal
vehicular operation. Because of its particular relevance in cases
of this nature, a custody status point shall be assigned if the offender
is under probation, jail, or other custody supervision following
conviction of aggravated DWI, when the felony for which the
offender is being sentenced is criminal vehicular operation, and
the criminal vehicular operation occurred while under that supervision.

3. Subject to the conditions listed below, the offender is assigned one
unit for each misdemeanour conviction and two *units* for each
gross misdemeanour conviction (excluding traffic offences with the
exception of DWI and aggravated DWI offences when the current
conviction offence is criminal vehicular operation) for which
a sentence was stayed or imposed before the current sentencing.
Four such units shall equal one point on the criminal history
score, and no offender shall receive more than one point for prior
misdemeanour or gross misdemeanour convictions.

(a) Only convictions of statutory misdemeanours or ordinance
misdemeanours that conform substantially to a statutory
misdemeanour shall be used to compute units.

(b) When multiple sentences for a single course of conduct are given pursuant to statute and the most serious conviction is for a gross misdemeanour, no offender shall be assigned more than two units.

(c) Prior misdemeanour and gross misdemeanour sentences will not be used in computing the criminal history score if a period of five years has elapsed since the date of discharge from or expiration of the sentence to the date of offence of any subsequent misdemeanour, gross misdemeanour, or felony, provided that during the period the individual has not received a felony, gross misdemeanour, or misdemeanour sentence, whether stayed or imposed.

(d) A prior misdemeanour sentence shall not be used in computing the criminal history score if a period of ten years has elapsed since the offender was adjudicated guilty for that offence. However, this does not apply to misdemeanour sentences that result from successful completion of a stay of imposition for a felony conviction.

The Commission placed a limit of one point on the consideration of misdemeanours or gross misdemeanours in the criminal history score. This was done because with no limit on point accrual, persons with lengthy, but relatively minor, misdemeanour records could accrue high criminal history scores and, thus, be subject to inappropriately severe sentences upon their first felony conviction.

The Commission also adopted a 'decay' factor for prior misdemeanour and gross misdemeanour offences for the same reasons articulated above for felony offences. If five years have elapsed between the expiration of or discharge from a misdemeanour or gross misdemeanour sentence and the date of a subsequent offence for which a misdemeanour, gross misdemeanour, or felony sentence was stayed or imposed, that misdemeanour or gross misdemeanour sentence will not be used in computing the criminal history score. (Traffic offences are excluded in computing the decay factor.) A ten year limit for considering misdemeanour sentences was adopted.

4. The offender is assigned one point for every two offences committed and prosecuted as a juvenile that would have been felonies if committed by an adult, provided that:

(a) Findings were made by the juvenile court pursuant to an admission in court or after trial;

(b) Each offence represented a separate behavioural incident or involved separate victims in a single behavioural incident;

(c) The juvenile offences occurred after the offender's sixteenth birthday;

(d) The offender had not attained the age of twenty-one at the time the felony was committed for which he or she is being currently sentenced; and

(e) No offender may receive more than one point for offences committed and prosecuted as a juvenile.

Comment

The juvenile history item is included in the criminal history index to identify those young adult felons whose criminal careers were preceded by repeated felony-type offences committed as a juvenile. The Commission held several public hearings devoted to the issue of using juvenile records in the criminal history index. Those hearings pointed out differences in legal procedures and safeguards between adult and juvenile courts, differing availability of juvenile records, and differing procedures among juvenile courts. As a result of these issues, the Commission decided to establish rigorous standards regulating the consideration of juvenile records in computing the criminal history score.

First, only juvenile offences that would have been felonies if committed by an adult will be considered in computing the criminal history score.

Second, the juvenile offences must have been committed after the offender's sixteenth birthday.

Third, juvenile offences will be considered in computing the criminal history score only for adult offenders who had not attained the age of twenty-one at the time the felony was committed for which they are now bein sentenced.

Fourth, the Commission decided that, provided the above conditions are met, it would take two juvenile offences to equal one point on the criminal history score, and that no offender may receive more than one point on the basis of prior juvenile offences. Again, no partial points are allowed, so an offender with only one juvenile offence meeting the above criteria would receive no point on the criminal history score. The one point limit was deemed consistent with the purpose for including juvenile record in the criminal history — to distinguish the young adult felon with no juvenile record of felony-type behavior from the young adult offender who has a prior juvenile record of repeated felony-type behavior. The one point limit also was deemed advisable to limit the impact of findings obtained under a juvenile court procedure that does not afford the full procedural rights available in adult courts.

5. The designation of out-of-state convictions as felonies, gross misdemeanours, or misdemeanours shall be governed by the offence definitions and sentences provided in Minnesota law.

Comment
The Commission concluded that convictions from other jurisdictions must, in fairness, be considered in the computation of an offender's criminal history index score. It was recognized, however, that criminal conduct may be characterized differently by the various state and federal criminal jurisdictions. There is no uniform nationwide characterization of the terms 'felony', 'gross misdemeanour', and 'misdemeanour'.

6. The criminal history score is the sum of points accrued under items one through four above.

Presumptive sentence
The offence of conviction determines the appropriate severity level on the vertical axis. The offender's criminal history score, computed according to section B above, determines the appropriate location on the horizontal axis. The presumptive fixed sentence for a felony conviction is found in the Sentencing Guidelines Grid cell at the intersection of the column defined by the criminal history score and the row defined by the offence severity level. The offences within the Sentencing Guidelines Grid are presumptive with respect to the duration of the sentence and whether imposition or execution of the felony sentence should be stayed.

The line on the Sentencing Guidelines Grid demarcates those cases for whom the presumptive sentence is executed from those for whom the presumptive sentence is stayed. For cases contained in cells below and to the right of the line, the sentence should be executed. For cases contained in cells above and to the left of the line, the sentence should be stayed, unless the conviction offence carries a mandatory minimum sentence.

When the current conviction offence is burglary of an occupied dwelling and there was a previous adjudication of guilt for a felony burglary before the current offence occurred, the presumptive disposition is Commitment to the Commissioner of Corrections. The presumptive duration of sentence is the fixed duration indicated in the appropriate cell of the Sentencing Guidelines Grid. Similarly, when the current conviction offence is sale of a severity level VI drug or sale of cocaine and there was a previous adjudication of guilt for a sale of a severity level VI drug or sale of cocaine before the current offence occurred, the presumptive disposition is Commitment to the Commissioner of Corrections. The presumptive duration of sentence is the fixed duration indicated in the appropriate cell of the Sentencing Guidelines Grid.

Every cell in the Sentencing Guidelines Grid provides a fixed duration of sentence. For cells below the solid line, the guidelines provide both a presumptive prison sentence and a range of time for that sentence. Any prison sentence duration pronounced by the sentencing judge which is outside the range of the presumptive duration is a departure from the guidelines, regardless of whether the sentence is executed or stayed, and requires written reasons from the judge.

Comment

The guidelines provide sentences which are presumptive with respect to (a) disposition – whether or not the sentence should be executed, and (b) duration – the length of the sentence. For cases below and to the right of the dispositional line, the guidelines create a presumption in favor of execution of the sentence. For cases in cells above and to the left of the dispositional line, the guidelines create a presumption against execution of the sentence, unless the conviction offence carries a mandatory minimum sentence.

The dispositional policy adopted by the Commission was designed so that scarce prison resources would primarily be used for serious person offenders and community resources would be used for most property offenders. The Commission believes that a rational sentencing policy requires such trade-offs, to ensure the availability of correctional resources for the most serious offenders. For the first year of guidelines operation, that policy was reflected in sentencing practices. However, by the third year of guideline operation, the percentage of offenders with criminal history scores of four or more had increased greatly, resulting in a significant increase in imprisonment for property offences. Given finite resources, increased use of imprisonment for property offences results in reduced prison resources for person offences. The allocation of scarce resources will be monitored and evaluated on an ongoing basis by the Commission.

In the cells below and to the right of the dispositional line, the guidelines provide a fixed presumptive sentence length, and a range of time around that length. Presumptive sentence lengths are shown in months, and it is the Commission's intent that months shall be computed by reference to calender months. Any sentence length given that is within the range of sentence length shown in the appropriate cell of the Sentencing Guidelines Grid is not a departure from the guidelines, and any sentence length given which is outside that range is a departure from the guidelines. In the cells above and to the left of the dispositional line, the guidelines provide a single fixed presumptive sentence length.

When a stay of execution is given, the presumptive sentence length shown in the appropriate cell should be pronounced, but its execution stayed. If the sentence length pronounced, but stayed, differs from that shown in the appropriate cell, that is a departure from the guidelines.

When a stay of imposition is given, no sentence length is pronounced, and the imposition of the sentence is stayed to some future date. If that sentence is ever imposed, the presumptive sentence length shown in the appropriate cell should be pronounced, and a decision should be made on whether to execute the presumptive sentence length given. If the sentence length pronounced at the imposition of the setence differs from that shown in the appropriate cell of the Sentencing Guidelines Grid, that is a departure from the guidelines.

Departures from the guidelines

The sentences provided in the Sentencing Guidelines Grid are presumed to be appropriate for every case. The judge shall utilise the presumptive sentence provided in the sentencing guidelines unless the individual case involves substantial and compelling circumstances. When such circumstances are present, the judge may depart from the presumptive sentence and stay or impose any sentence authorized by law. When departing from the presumptive sentence, the court should pronounce a sentence which is proportional to the severity of the offence of conviction and the extent of the offender's prior criminal history, and should take into substantial consideration the statement of purpose and principles in Section I above. When departing from the presumptive sentence, a judge must provide written reasons which specify the substantial and compelling nature of the circumstances, and which demonstrate why the sentence selected in the departure is more appropriate, reasonable, or equitable than the presumptive sentence.

Comment

The guideline sentences are presumed to be appropriate for every case. However, there will be a small number of cases where substantial and compelling aggravating or mitigating factors are present. When such factors are present, the judge may depart from the presumptive disposition or duration provided in the guidelines, and stay or impose a sentence that is deemed to be more appropriate, reasonable, or equitable than the presumptive sentence.

Decisions with respect to disposition and duration are logically separate. Departures with respect to disposition and duration also are logically separate decisions. A judge may depart from the presumptive disposition without departing from the presumptive duration, and vice-versa. A judge who departs from the presumptive disposition as well as the presumptive duration has made two separate departure decisions, each requiring written reasons.

The aggravating or mitigating factors and the written reasons supporting the departure must be substantial and compelling to overcome the presumption in favour of the guideline sentence. The purposes of the sentencing guidelines cannot be achieved unless the presumptive sentences are applied with a high degree of regularity. Sentencing disparity cannot be reduced if judges depart from the guidelines frequently. Certainly in sentencing cannot be attained if departure rates are high. Prison populations will exceed capacity if departures increase imprisonment rates significantly above past practice.

1. Factors that should not be used as reasons for departure. The following factors should not be used as reasons for departing from the presumptive sentences provided in the Sentencing Guidelines Grid:

    (a) Race
    (b) Sex
    (c) Employment factors, including:

      (1) occupation or impact of sentence on profession or occupation;
      (2) employment history;
      (3) employment at time of offence;
      (4) employment at time of sentencing.
  (d) Social factors, including:
      (1) educational attainment;
      (2) living arrangements at time of offence or sentencing;
      (3) length of residence;
      (4) marital status.
  (e) The exercise of constitutional rights by the defendant during the adjudication process.

Comment

The Commission believes that sentencing should be neutral with respect to offenders' race, sex, and income levels. Accordingly, the Commission has listed several factors which should not be used as reasons for departure from the presumptive sentence, because these factors are highly correlated with sex, race, or income levels. The Commission's study of Minnesota sentencing decisions indicated that, unlike many other states, these factors generally were not important in dispositional decisions. Therefore, their exclusion as reasons for departure should not result in a change from current judicial sentencing practices. The only excluded factor which was associated with judicial dispositional decisions was employment at time of sentencing. In addition to its correlation with race and income levels, this factor was excluded because it is manipulable – offenders could lessen the severity of the sentence by obtaining employment between arrest and sentencing. While it may be desirable for offenders to obtain employment between arrest and sentencing, some groups (those with low income levels, low education levels, and racial minorities generally) find it more difficult to obtain employment than others. It is impossible to reward those employed without, in fact, penalising those not employed at time of sentencing.

In addition, the Commission determined that the severity of offenders' sanctions should not vary depending on whether or not they exercise constitutional rights during the adjudication process.

It follows from the Commission's use of the conviction offence to determine offence severity that departures from the guidelines should not be permitted for elements of alleged offender behavior not within the definition of the offence of conviction. Thus, if an offender is convicted of simple robbery, a departure from the guidelines to increase the severity of the sentence should not be permitted because the offender possessed a firearm or used another dangerous weapon.

2. Factors that may be used as reasons for departure. The following is a *non-exclusive* list of factors which may be used as reasons for departure:

   (a) *Mitigating factors:*
      (1) The victim was an aggressor in the incident.
      (2) The offender played a minor or passive role in the crime or participated under circumstances of coercion or duress.
      (3) The offender, because of physical or mental impairment, lacked substantial capacity for judgment when the offence was committed. The voluntary use of intoxicants (drugs or alcohol) does not fall within the purview of this factor.
      (4) Other substantial grounds exist which tend to excuse or mitigate the offender's culpability, although not amounting to a defence.

   (b) *Aggravating factors:*
      (1) The victim was particularly vulnerable due to age, infirmity, or reduced physical or mental capacity, which was known or should have been known to the offender.
      (2) The victim was treated with particular cruelty for which the individual offender should be held responsible.
      (3) The current conviction is for an offence in which the victim was injured and there is a prior felony conviction for an offence in which the victim was injured.
      (4) The offence was a major economic offence, identified as an illegal act or series of illegal acts committed by other than physical means and by concealment or guile to obtain money or property, to avoid payment or loss of money or property, or to obtain business or professional advantage. The presence of two or more of the circumstances listed below are aggravating factors with respect to the offence:
         (a) the offence involved multiple victims or multiple incidents per victim;
         (b) the offence involved an attempted or actual monetary loss substantially greater than the usual offence or

substantially greater than the minimum loss specified in the statutes;

(c) the offence involved a high degree of sophistication or planning or occurred over a lengthy period of time;

(d) the defendant used his or her position or status to facilitate the commission of the offence, including positions of trust, confidence, or fiduciary relationships; or

(e) the defendant has been involved in other conduct similar to the current offence as evidenced by the findings of civil or administrative law proceedings or the imposition of professional sanctions.

(5) The offence was a major controlled substance offence, identified as an offence or series of offences related to trafficking in controlled substances under circumstances more onerous than the usual offence. The presence of two or more of the circumstances listed below are aggravating factors with respect to the offence:

(a) the offence involved at least three separate transactions wherein controlled substances were sold, transferred, or possessed with intent to do so; or

(b) the offence involved an attempted or actual sale or transfer of controlled substances in quantities substantially larger than for personal use; or

(c) the offence involved the manufacture of controlled substances for use by other parties; or

(d) the offender knowingly possessed a firearm during the commission of the offence; or

(e) the circumstances of the offence reveal the offender to have occupied a high position in the drug distribution hierarchy; or

(f) the offence involved a high degree of sophistication or planning or occurred over a lengthy period of time or involved a broad geographic area of disbursement; or

(g) the offender used his or her position or status to facilitate the commission of the offence, including positions of trust, confidence or fiduciary relationships (e.g., pharmacist, physician or other medical professional).

Comment

The Commission provided a non-exclusive list of reasons which may be used as reasons for departure. The factors are intended to describe specific situations involving a small number of cases. The Commission rejected factors which were general in nature, and which could apply to large numbers of cases, such as intoxication at the time of the offence. The factors cited are illustrative and are not intended to be an exclusive or exhaustive list of factors which may be used as reasons for departure. Some of these factors may be considered in establishing conditions of stayed sentences, even though they may not be used as reasons for departure. For example, whether or not a person is employed at time of sentencing may be an important factor in deciding whether restitution should be used as a condition of probation, or in deciding on the terms of restitution payment.

Concurrent/consecutive sentences

When an offender is convicted of multiple current offences, or when there is a prior felony sentence which has not expired or been discharged, concurrent sentences shall be given in all cases not covered below. The most severe offence among multiple current offences determines the appropriate offence severity level for purposes of determining the presumptive guideline sentence. Consecutive sentences may be given only in the following cases:

1. When a prior felony sentence for a crime against a person has not expired or been discharged and one or more of the current felony convictions is for a crime against a person, and when the sentence for the most severe current conviction is executed according to the guidelines; *or*

2. When the offender is convicted of multiple current felony convictions for crimes against different persons, and when the sentence for the most severe current conviction is executed according to the guidelines; *or*

3. When the conviction is for escape from lawful custody, as defined by statute. The presumptive disposition for escapes from executed sentences shall be execution of the escape sentence. If the executed escape sentence is to be served concurrently with other sentences, the presumptive duration shall be that indicated by the appropriate cell of the Sentencing Guidelines Grid. If the executed escape sentence is to be served consecutively to other sentences, the

presumptive duration shall be that indicated by the aggregation process set forth below.

The use of consecutive sentences in any other case constitutes a departure from the guidelines and requires written reasons.

Convictions for attempts or conspiracies
For persons convicted of attempted offences or conspiracies to commit an offence, the presumptive sentence is determined by locating the Sentencing Guidelines Grid cell defined by the offender's criminal history score and the severity level of the completed offence, and dividing the duration contained therein by two, but such sentence shall not be less than one year and one day.

Related policies

Establishing conditions of stayed sentences

1. *Method of granting stayed sentences*
When the appropriate cell of the Sentencing Guidelines Grid provides a stayed sentence, and when the judge chooses to grant that stay by means of a stay of execution, the duration of prison sentence shown in the appropriate cell is pronounced, but its execution is stayed. When the judge chooses to grant the stay by means of a stay of imposition, the duration of the prison sentence in the appropriate cell is not pronounced and the imposition of the sentence is stayed. The judge would then establish conditions which are deemed appropriate for the stayed sentence, including establishing a length of probation, which may exceed the duration of the presumptive prison sentence.

The Commission recommends that stays of imposition be used as the means of granting a stayed sentence for felons convicted of lower severity offences with low criminal history scores. The Commission futher recommends that convicted felons be given one stay of imposition, although for very low severity offences, a second stay of imposition may be appropriate.

Comment
When the presumptive sentence is a stay, the judge may grant the stay by means of either a stay of imposition or a stay of execution. The use of either a stay of imposition or stay of execution is at the discretion of the judge. The Commission has provided a

non-presumptive recommendation regarding which categories of offenders should receive stays of imposition, and has recommended that convicted felons generally should receive only one stay of imposition. The Commission believes that stays of imposition are a less severe sanction, and ought to be used for those convicted of less serious offences and those with short criminal histories. Under current sentencing practices, judges use stays of imposition most frequently for these types of offenders.

2. *Conditions of stayed sentences*

The Commission has chosen not to develop specific guidelines relating to the conditions of stayed sentences. The Commission recognises that there are several penal objectives to be considered in establishing conditions of stayed sentences, including, but not limited to, retribution, rehabilitation, public protection, restitution, deterrence, and public condemnation of criminal conduct. The Commission also recognises that the relative importance of these objectives may vary with both offence and offender characteristics and that multiple objectives may be present in any given sentence. The development of principled standards for establishing conditions of stayed sentences requires that judges first consider the objectives to be served by a stayed sentence and, second, consider the resources available to achieve those objectives. When retribution is an important objective of a stayed sentence, the severity of the retributive sanction should be proportional to the severity of the offence and the prior criminal record of the offender, and judges should consider the availability and adequacy of local jail or correctional facilities in establishing such sentences. The Commission urges judges to utilise the least restrictive conditions of stayed sentences that are consistent with the objectives of the sanction. When rehabilitation is an important objective of a stayed sentence, judges are urged to make full use of local programmes and resources available to accomplish the rehabilitative objectives. The absence of a rehabilitative resource, in general, should not be a basis for enhancing the retributive objective in sentencing and, in particular, should not be the basis for more extensive use of incarceration than is justified on other grounds. The Commission urges judges to make expanded use of restitution and community work orders as conditions of a stayed sentence, especially for persons with short criminal histories who are convicted of property crimes, although the use of such conditions in other cases may be appropriate.

Supervised probation should continue as a primary condition of stayed sentences. To the extent that fines are used, the Commission urges the expanded use of day fines, which standardises the financial impact of the sanction among offenders with different income levels.

Revocation of stayed sentences
The decision to imprison an offender following a revocation of a stayed sentence should not be undertaken lightly and, in particular, should not be a reflexive reaction to technical violations of the conditions of the stay. Great restraint should be exercised in imprisoning those violating conditions of a stayed sentence who were convicted originally of low severity offences or who have short prior criminal histories.

Offence severity reference table

First Degree Murder is excluded from the guidelines by law, and continues to have a mandatory life sentence.

  X   Murder 2

  IX   Murder 2
        Murder 3

 VIII   Assault 1
        Criminal Sexual Conduct 1
        Kidnapping (w/great bodily harm)
        Manslaughter 1

  VII   Aggravated Robbery
        Arson 1
        Burglary 1
        Criminal Sexual Conduct 2
        Criminal Sexual Conduct 3
        Fleeing Peace Officer (resulting in death)
        Kidnapping (not in safe place)
        Manslaughter 1
        Manslaughter 2

Table 1 *Sentencing guidelines grid showing presumptive sentence lengths in months*

Offenders with nonimprisonment felony sentences are subject to jail time according to law.

Italicised numbers within the grid denote the range within which a judge may sentence without the sentence being deemed a departure.

Severity levels of conviction offence		Criminal history score						
		0	1	2	3	4	5	6 or more
Unauthorised Use of Motor Vehicle Possession of Marijuana	I	12*	12*	12*	13	15	17	19 *18–20*
Theft-related crimes ($250–$2,500) Aggravated Forgery ($250–$2,500)	II	12*	12*	13	15	17	19	21 *20–22*
Theft crimes ($250–$2,500)	III	12*	13	15	17	19 *18–20*	22 *21–23*	25 *24–26*
Nonresidential Burglary Theft crimes (over $2,500)	IV	12*	15	18	21	25 *24–26*	32 *30–34*	41 *37–45*
Residential Burglary Simple Robbery	V	18	23	27	30 *29–31*	38 *36–40*	46 *43–49*	54 *50–58*
Criminal Sexual Conduct. Second Degree (a) and (b)	VI	21	26	30	34 *33–35*	44 *42–46*	54 *50–58*	65 *60–70*
Aggravated Robbery	VII	24 *23–25*	32 *30–34*	41 *38–44*	49 *45–53*	65 *60–70*	81 *75–87*	97 *90–104*
Criminal Sexual Conduct First Degree Assault, First Degree	VIII	43 *41–45*	54 *50–58*	65 *60–70*	76 *71–81*	95 *89–101*	113 *106–120*	132 *124–140*
Murder, Third Degree Murder, Second Degree (felony murder)	IX	105 *102–108*	119 *116–122*	127 *124–130*	149 *143–155*	176 *168–184*	205 *195–215*	230 *218–242*
Murder, Second Degree (with intent)	X	120 *116–124*	140 *133–147*	162 *153–171*	203 *192–214*	243 *231–255*	284 *270–298*	324 *309–339*

Notes First Degree Murder is excluded from the guidelines by law and continues to have a mandatory life sentence.

Figures in bold within border: at the discretion of the judge, up to a year in jail and/or other non-jail sanctions can be imposed as conditions of probation.

Remaining figures: presumptive commitment to state imprisonment.

* One year and one day.

VI Arson 2
Assault 2
Burglary 1
Criminal Sexual Conduct 2
Criminal Sexual Conduct 4
Escape from Custody
Fleeing Peace Officer (great bodily harm)
Kidnapping
Precious Metal Dealers, Receiving Stolen Goods (over $2,500)
Precious Metal Dealers, Receiving Stolen Goods (all values)
Receiving Stolen Goods (over $2,500)
Sale of Hallucinogens or PCP
Sale of Heroin
Sale of Remaining Schedule I & II Narcotics

V Burglary 2
Criminal Vehicular Operation
Criminal Sexual Conduct 3
Manslaughter 2
Perjury
Possession of Incendiary Device
Receiving Profit Derived from Prostitution
Receiving Stolen Goods ($1000–$2500)
Simple Robbery
Solicitation of Prostitution
Tampering w/Witness

IV Assault 3
Bribery
Bring Contraband into State Prison
Bring Dangerous Weapon into County Jail
Burglary 2
Burglary 3
Criminal Sexual Conduct 4
False Imprisonment
Fleeing Peace Officer (substantial bodily harm)
Malicious Punishment of Child
Negligent Fires
Perjury
Precious Metal Dealers, Receiving Stolen Goods ($150–$2500)

IV   Precious Metal Dealers, Receiving Stolen Goods (over $2,500)
Receiving Stolen Goods ($301–$999)
Sale of Cocaine
Security Violations (over $2500)
Tax Evasion
Tax Withheld at Source; Fraud (over $2,500)
Terroristic Threats
Theft Crimes − Over $2,500
Theft from Person
Theft of Controlled Substances
Use of Drugs to Injure or Facilitate Crime

III   Aggravated Forgery (over $2,500)
Arson 3
Coercion (over $2,500)
Criminal Vehicular Operation
Damage to Property
Dangerous Trespass
Dangerous Weapons
Escape from Custody
False Imprisonment
Negligent Discharge of Explosive
Possession of Burglary Tools
Possession of Hallucinogens or PCP
Possession of Heroin
Possession of Remaining Schedule I & II Narcotics
Possession of Shoplifting Gear
Precious Metal Dealers, Receiving Stolen Goods (less than
   $150)
Precious Metal Dealers, Receiving Stolen Goods ($150–
   $2,500)
Prostitution (Patron)
Receiving Profit Derived from Prostitution
Sale of Remaining Schedule I, II, & III Non-narcotics
Security Violations (under $2500)
Solicitation of Prostitution
Tax Withheld at Source; Fraud ($301–$2,500)
Tear Gas & Tear Gas Compounds
Theft Crimes − $250–$2,500
Theft of Controlled Substances

III Theft of a Firearm
Theft of Public Records
Theft Related Crimes − Over $2,500

II Aggravated Forgery ($250–$2,500)
Aggravated Forgery (misc) (non-check)
Coercion ($300–$2,500)
Damage to Property
Negligent Fires (damage greater than $10,000)
Precious Metal Dealers, Receiving Stolen Goods (less than $150)
Precious Metal Dealers, Regulatory Provisions
Riot
Sale of Marijuana/Hashish/Tetrahydrocannabinols
Sale of a Schedule IV Substance
Terroristic Threats
Theft-Looting
Theft Related Crimes − $250–$2,500

I Assault 4
Aggravated Forgery (Less than $250)
Aiding Offender to Avoid Arrest
Depriving Another of Custodial or Parental Rights
Forgery; and Forgery Related Crimes
Fraudulent Procurement of a Controlled Substance
Leaving State to Evade Establishment of Paternity
Nonsupport of Wife or Child
Possession of Cocaine
Possession of Marijuana/Hashish/Tetrahydrocannabinols
Possession of Remaining Schedule I, II & III Non-narcotics
Possession of a Schedule IV Substance
Sale of Simulated Controlled Substance
Selling Liquor that Causes Injury
Solicitation of Prostitution
Unauthorized Use of Motor Vehicle

Index

Advisory Council on the Penal System 1, 8, 16, 77, 98
Alschuler, A. 143
appellate review 2–3, 25–6, 42–4, 48, 56–9, 62, 100
Ashworth, A. J. 2, 3, 5, 81–104, 113, 118, 128, 134, 135, 137, 159, 163, 164, 170
Australian Law Reform Commission 22

Baldwin, J. 141, 142, 144
Bean, P. 77, 169
Blalock, I. 146, 147, 157
Boerner, D. 35
Bottomley, A. K. 5, 139–62, 170
Bottoms, A. E. 73, 163, 172, 173
Bullock, W. 180
Burnham, R. W. B. 17

Carrow, D. M. 47
Carter, R. 9
Chatterton, M. 145
Children and Young Persons Act 1963 111
Cohen, J. 22, 24, 29
common law 58–9
computers 10–11
construct validation 130–1
Criminal Courts Technical Assistance Project 24
Criminal Justice Act 1982 71–2, 101, 110
criminal record 38–40, 53–5, 62, 90–2, 99–100, 105–25, 165–9
criterion-related validation 128–30
Cross, R. 89
Curnock, K. 170

Dawson, R. O. 141
day-fine 95–6
decision-making 154–60
decision theory 10
deterrence 50, 57–8
Devlin, K. 105, 112
Doing Justice 17, 117, 119

Economic and Social Research Council 4
Ericson, R. V. 145, 146
Eysenck, H. J. 130

Farrington, D. P. 105, 116
Feins, J. D. 37
first offenders 71 *and see* criminal record
Fitzmaurice, C. 108, 126, 128, 130–2, 134
Fletcher, G. P. 114, 117
Floud, J. 117
Forst, M. 140, 154
Frankel, M. 26, 47

Galligan, D. 82, 142, 155
German Penal Code 59
Glueck, E. 10
Glueck, S. 10
Gottfredson, D. 12, 44, 116
Gottfredson, S. 134
Green, E. 105
Greenwood, P. 49, 105, 117
Greer, A. 154
guidance, sentencing
    Court of Appeal 1–3, 73–4, 113–114
    'guideline' judgments 2–3, 74, 134–7
    magistrates' courts 70–80, 83–4
    statutory 1, 71–3
guidelines, cautioning 5, 106–7, 147–54
guidelines, parole 4, 9–14, 25
guidelines, prosecution 5, 147–54
guidelines, sentencing
    departure from 64–5, 193–9
    descriptive 3, 14–17
    generally 3–4, 15–19, 24–5, 46–69, 134–7, 142–7
    mathematical 7
    narrative 55–66
    non-custodial 42
    numerical 47–55
    prescriptive 3, 14–17, 27
    presumptive 184–92
    stayed sentences 199–201

guidelines, sentencing (contd.)
  voluntary 37
guidelines, particular systems
  Australia 22
  Britain 7–9
  California 47
  Canada 22
  Columbia 37
  Connecticut 22, 31
  Finland 59–61
  Florida 24, 37
  Maine 22, 30–1
  Maryland 24, 37
  Massachusetts 24
  Michigan 24
  Minnesota 4–5, 7, 22, 25–30, 37–40,
    42–4, 46, 50–1, 64–5, 81, 118–22,
    183–205
  New Jersey 24
  New York 22, 31–2
  Oregon 47
  Pennsylvania 22, 32–4, 46
  South Carolina 22, 31
  Sweden 5, 61–3
  Victoria 23
  Washington 22, 35–6, 42–4, 46
  Wisconsin 37

Hanrahan, K. 47, 97, 154
Hardiker, P. 168, 170, 173
Harraway, P. 178
Harris, B. 4, 70–80, 106, 169, 170, 176
Harris, R. 174
Hart, H. 10
Hawkinson, T. 115
Hoffman, P. B. 12, 13, 116
Hogarth, J. 105, 179
Home Affairs Committee 159
Home Office 75, 76, 106–8, 110, 115, 116,
    148–50, 160, 163, 165, 169
Hood, R. 18
Huy, Jo Shin 13

Jacoby, J. E. 156
Johnston, B. L. 105, 115
Jones, R. 178
Jones, S. 84
judges
  and compliance with guidelines 38,
    65–6
  and parole 23–4, 101
  in Crown Court 3, 70–1
  independence 15, 29
  liaison 74
  just deserts 10, 27, 48–51, 53, 93,
    117–22, 131–2, 152 *and see* Doing
    Justice
justices' clerk 71, 77–9
Justices' Clerks Society 70

Kapardis, A. 105
Keeler, B. 32
Knapp, K. 25, 26, 28, 29, 38–43, 52, 54, 64

La Fave, W. R. 141
Lancucki, L. B. 91, 114
Law Commission 100
Levi, M. 84
Lord Chief Justice 2, 3, 74, 76, 82, 113

McConville, M. 141, 142, 144
McDonald, W. F. 157
McGuire, J. 168
McLean, I. 2, 135, 137
McWilliams, W. 163, 172, 176
Magistrates' Association 75, 83
Magistrates' Courts Rules 79
Maguire, M. 84, 87
Mannheim, H. 10
Martin, S. E. 22, 32
maximum sentences 1, 26
Millard, D. 177
Miller, F. W. 141
Millichamp, D. 172
Minnesota Sentencing Guidelines
    Commission 25–30, 50–5 *and see*
    Knapp, K.
Minnesota Supreme Court 43–4
Moody, S. R. 144, 152, 153

Newman, D. J. 141
Nicholson, C. G. B. 105, 108
Nuttall, C. 116

offence gradation 26–8, 33–4, 35–6, 84–8,
    132–4, 201–5
offences
  arson 112
  burglary 84, 87–8, 99
  drinking and driving 66
  drug trafficking 2, 134–5
  handling 86–7
  perjury 57, 62
  rape 2, 110
  sexual offences 85, 98, 112
  theft 83, 85–7
  traffic offences 74, 83
  Ohlin, L. E. 141, 143
Ozanne, P. A. 141, 154

parole 23–4, 97, 101, 116 *and see* judges
    and parole
Pearce, I. 171
Pease, K. 5, 108, 116, 126–38, 176
Perry, F. 169
Phillips, H. J. 30, 114
Philpotts, G. J. O. 91
plea bargaining 38–9, 41–2
politics 40–1, 99, 101

Powers of Criminal Courts Act 1973 1,
71–3, 76, 107, 109, 110
Practice Direction 78, 80, 106, 111
predictive sentencing 49–51, 114–17
Priestley, P. 168
Powell, M. 171
prison population 29, 40, 52–3, 66, 81–2,
97–8
probation service 5, 14, 75–7, 95, 163–82
prosecution 55, 143–7 *see also* guidelines,
prosecution
psychology 126–38

Radzinowicz, L. 18
Raynor, P. 166, 167, 170
Rehabilitation of Offenders Act 1974 106,
109
Remington, F. J. 141, 143
Rothman, D. J. 23
Royal Commission on Criminal Procedure
147
Rutherford, A. 163, 169

Samuels, A. 106
Sanders, A. 152
sentences
community service 1, 77, 94–6, 100,
176–7
compensation order 95
custodial sentences 97–100 *and see*
offence gradation and guidelines,
sentencing
deferment of sentence 2, 73, 95
detention centres 75
discharge 95
fine 96–7 *and see* day-fine
hospital orders 95
partly suspended sentence 1, 2
probation order 95, 177–9
suspended sentence 1, 75, 96, 100
sentencing
aggravating factors 60, 88–9
Attorney-General's Reference 2–3
ceiling principle 90–1, 108
criminal record *see* criminal record
extenuating factors 88–9
guilty plea 94
last-chance probation 113
mitigating factors 60, 90–4
non-aggravating factors 88–9
non-custodial 94–7
non-extenuating factors 88–9
real offence sentencing 146
reasons 71–3

status factors 27, 93–4, 183–4
statutory statements of purpose 59–61
totality principle 101
Sentencing Commission 7–8, 26
Sentencing Council 82
sentencing disparity 5, 16–17, 23–4, 38,
48–9, 70, 94, 140–2
Sentencing Reform Act (U.S.) 22
Shane-DuBow, S. 22, 24, 31
Shapland, J. 107, 111, 112, 164, 175
Shaw, R. 168, 175
Singer, P. 117
Smith, D. E. 75, 170
social enquiry reports 76–7, 169–76
Steer, D. 152
Stone, N. 5, 163–82
Streatfeild Report 79, 105, 163–7
Suggestions for Traffic Offence Penalties
74, 83

Tarling, R. 5, 70, 74, 94, 116
Thomas, D. A. 2, 16, 56–7, 82, 98, 106,
108, 109, 111, 112
Thorpe, J. 75, 77, 172
Thorpe, M. G. 7, 8
Tiffany, L. P. 105
Tombs, J. 144, 152, 153
Tonry, M. 4, 7, 22–45

United States Parole Board 12–15, 47
University of Manchester 4–5
University of New York at Albany 12–14

Von Hirsch, A. 4, 5, 10, 46–69, 81, 84, 88,
91–3, 97–9, 105, 117–23, 150

Walker, N. 105, 108, 111, 121, 166
Walsh, D. P. 84
Walmsley, G. R. 85, 98
Wareham, A. 171
Warner, S. B. 9
Wasik, M. 5, 28, 37, 57, 89, 90, 105–25,
165
West, D. J. 129
Whinery, L. H. 116
White, K. 84, 98
Whitehead, P. 168
Wilkins, L. T. 4, 7–21, 44, 116, 117, 146
Wright, D. 175

young offenders 71, 93–4, 120 *and see*
guidelines, cautioning
Young, W. 117

Zimring, F. 46